PRAISE FOR ~~

"As I read through *Mail-Order Kid* it was like Jessie Teresa Martin was sitting on the couch with me telling the story of her life. It is so real. I knew Jessie Teresa personally. In fact, she stayed in our home attending one of OTHSA's reunions of Orphan Train Riders. She sat in the yard swing; her feet in the air because she was so short, and laughed as she told me about flirting with the doctors and how she loved to dance. She showed me her Star of David and told how she came to have it. Her remark was that she had all her bases covered with her Catholic upbringing and her Jewish genetics.

"Everyone who met her loved her. She was just that kind of person; and Marilyn Coffey has caught the real Jessie Teresa on the pages of this book. In 1993, Jessie Teresa's story was written by her family and submitted for publication in *Orphan Train Riders: Their Own Stories Vol. 2;* however, she always wanted her story told in more detail and called me when she knew Marilyn Coffey was writing it for her. This book fulfills her desire to have her very own life story told in a way that people can understand what it meant to her to be an 'orphan.' I wish she had lived long enough to autograph my copy of her book."

—Mary Ellen Johnson
Founder and Executive Director,
Orphan Train Heritage Society of America, Inc.

"Little Teresa was so real, I could hardly wait to call her to tell her how much I enjoyed reading about her life. Sadly I could not, but by reading *Mail-Order Kid* I can 'visit' with Teresa again and again.

"Thank you for allowing me to review an advance copy of *Mail-Order Kid: An Orphan Train Rider's Story* by Marilyn June Coffey. As a descendant of an OTR, I recommend this book to everyone interested in learning about a part of America not in the history books."

—Harold Dupre
Past President OTHSA

"Congratulations for your well-deserved best seller. The reading experience was exciting because I didn't hear the usual dry 'just the facts, M'am' tone of a journalist, but also the style of a poet using analogy, alliteration, etc. This blend of journalistic and poetic styles as well as your compassionate tone for your subject, Teresa, suggested a whole new writing genre to me. Capote tried years ago with his 'true novel' to blend structure, but he never succeeded at style in the way you did for me. Again, bravo!"

—Lenore Garside
former faculty member, Interlochen Arts Academy

"I am about halfway through *Mail-Order Kid* and love it. It was so well-written...This book is a triumph, after all of the years you spent finding your way, balancing between simply telling Teresa's story and using it as a litmus paper against which to describe the experiences of all OT riders. I see Teresa in the words on each page...You tell her story as she would, but give us the coloring, fill in the blanks, through your research and close friendship with her, that we would have lacked, had Teresa written the story herself. You got it just right. Bravo."

—Carla Barber
Executive Director at McPherson [Kansas] Museum & Arts Foundation

"Quite fascinating, a new and unusual look
at the Orphan Train experience."

—Pippa White
performer "The Orphan Train,"
One's Company Productions

"An excellent job of bringing to life
a little-known part of our country's history."

—Sandy Hill
journalist, novelist

An Orphan Train Rider's Story

MAIL-ORDER
KID

An Orphan Train Rider's Story

MAIL-ORDER
KID

MARILYN JUNE COFFEY

"OUT WEST"

Omaha, Nebraska

ISBN-10: 0-9626317-2-8
ISBN-13: 978-0-9626317-2-6
Library of Congress Control Number: 2010904120
Cataloging in Publication Data on file with publisher.

"out West" Press
13518 L St.
Omaha, NE 68137
www.Mail-OrderKid.com

Cover Photo Credits:
> Orphan train, Kansas State Historical Society
> Foundling tag #4, Harold Dupre, President,
> > Louisiana Orphan Train Society

Book Design: Gary James Withrow

Production, Distribution and Marketing: Concierge Marketing Inc.
www.ConciergeMarketing.com

Printed in the United States of America
10 9 8 7 6 5 4 3 2

"Once an orphan, always an orphan."
—Eileen Simpson

To orphan train riders and their offspring,
especially to Teresa Martin and her descendants.

CONTENTS

FOREWORD

Two years ago, I met Marilyn Coffey and her *Mail-Order Kid* at the annual Nebraska Orphan Train Reunion in Fremont, Nebraska—a celebration that I organize. It didn't take me long to recognize that Marilyn has a heart of gold. I noticed the passion with which she read an excerpt from her book about Teresa Martin, the orphan train rider featured in *Mail-Order Kid*. Marilyn is a bit of an actor as well as an author, and she made Teresa come alive for those of us in the audience.

When I read her well-written, earlier memoir, *Great Plains Patchwork,* I could see that Marilyn is not the sort of writer who sits around and dreams about being a great author, but the sort who dives into subjects that are near and dear to her heart. I also could see that Marilyn takes her time researching. She made certain that *Mail-Order Kid* is a book that an orphan train rider would be proud for you to read. So many orphan train books are fictional, fabricated to add spice to the story.

I am deeply committed to the orphan train movement. It touched a quarter million people in a seventy-five-year time span, yet many people are unaware that it began what we know today as foster care and adoption.

Over the years, I traveled some 15,000 miles to interview the last surviving riders. Their stories appear in my books, *Plains Bound: Fragile Cargo* and *By Train They Came,* a series. So the first thing I noticed about *Mail-Order Kid* was Marilyn's in-depth interviews with her orphan train rider, Teresa Martin. I could tell that Marilyn believes what I believe: no amount of invention reads better than an orphan train rider's own words.

The day of interviewing orphan train riders is drawing to a close. Marilyn's Teresa Martin died in 2001, and many orphan train riders who gave me their interviews in their last, fragile, elderly years have now gone before me. I guess that's not surprising. In October 2009, hundreds gathered in New York City to celebrate the 140th Anniversary of the New York Foundling Home. The other primary orphanage that sent children West, the Children's Aid Society, is now 155 years old. Many people are surprised to learn that these places still exist and are still helping children, just in a different capacity today.

A dear friend and orphan train rider, Lester Davis, wanted everyone to know that the children on the trains were well fed. Church groups chipped in and made sure of that. Many times disabled children weren't allowed to ride the train. Davis's older sister had to stay behind in New York City. It took seventy-five years for his siblings to find each other. The train ride wasn't a fine ride like you find at the zoo. Davis rode in a cattle car lined in cardboard from NYC to Osceola, Nebraska.

Marilyn's orphan train rider, Teresa Martin, had some tough times as a child. Unfortunately, some children did fall upon abuse. However, had they not had the good fortune of the train ride, many children most likely would have perished on NYC streets.

Marilyn Coffey's book, *Mail-Order Kid,* is in your hands for a reason. Fewer than a hundred actual orphan train riders are left nationwide to tell you their stories at www.unsungneighbors.com. Sit down a spell and let Marilyn tell you a story of a time not so long ago. Help keep this history alive, as the riders would have wanted, by sharing what you learn with a friend. Then go one step further and donate your book to a local library for others to discover.

Charlotte Endorf, author
Plains Bound: Fragile Cargo, By Train They Came series

About Charlotte Endorf: Charlotte Endorf orchestrates her professional life around the orphan train movement. Since 2004, she has traveled more than 15,000 miles seeking surviving orphan train riders. Twenty-nine stories of this last generation of riders became a book, *Plains Bound: Fragile Cargo.* Endorf followed this with thirty more orphan train stories in her series *By Train They Came.*

A popular speaker for the Nebraska Humanities Council, Endorf is on the "high-use" list of the council's Speakers Bureau, thanks to her *Fragile Excess Baggage.* This is an orphan train presentation where she appears in period attire. Endorf, a long-time member of Toastmasters International, is one of its rare "Distinguished Toastmasters."

Organizer of the annual Nebraska Orphan Train Reunion, Endorf uses her training as a travel representative and tour guide to heighten the reunion's renown.

PREFACE

"Orphan trains? What's that?"

"Oh, you know." My friend Renae sounded impatient. "When they brought orphans out on trains and gave them away. You could write about that."

Write about orphan castoffs? I thought her suggestion sounded squirrelly. Surely, folks didn't ship children to Nebraska on trains and give them away. I ignored Renae's crackpot idea.

A few weeks later, I sat in the Nebraska Humanities Council's Lincoln office, hoping NHC would hire me as a speaker. After thirty years in New York City, I had relocated to Nebraska in 1990, trusting that I could carve a modest living freelancing. Program Officer Mollie Fisher and I inched down my list of proposed projects, topic by topic. She listened, pressed her narrow lips tighter, and didn't latch on to any of my ideas.

As I stood to leave, Renae's crazy suggestion popped into my mind, so I said, "Or maybe orphan trains."

What a quirk of fate that was!

Mollie beamed like a harvest moon. "You'd do that?"

Ignorant of what lay ahead, I gulped and agreed.

❧

In the University of Nebraska's large Lincoln library, I soon learned that indeed orphanages had shipped children by rail to Nebraska and to every other state in the United States. For seventy-five years, from 1854 to 1929, big city orphanages had relocated some 100,000 to 500,000 children. Such massive figures staggered me. That would be about four to eighteen children a day, day after day, year after year, torn from an old life and plopped down in a new one not of their choosing. How had they survived losing their metropolitan culture and being grafted onto another one, usually rural?

As I read about the people who were part of the orphan train movement, I became excited. I imagined its founding by visionary Charles Loring Brace, its application by stolid Clara Comstock and other agents, and their competition from a rival orphanage started by Sister Irene.

Then I read dozens of stories of children who rode the trains, some to terrible homes, others to marvelous ones. Most children probably ended up with indifferent families who used them as free labor. I read how children struggled to live on the city streets, about New York newsboys who rose before dawn from their street beds to hawk papers and about less fortunate girls who turned to prostitution and often to suicide.

To my surprise, not all of these children were orphans—that is, children with no parents. More than half had at least one parent; about a quarter had two. But Brace's Children's Aid Society (CAS) had no compunction about relocating indigent children who had living parents. Or about splitting up families.

The most horrible story I read about children separated from parents was one I called "Henrietta's Mother." She placed her toddler in a daycare center. But her employer had other ideas; she arranged with the center to send the child on an orphan train to Exeter, Nebraska. Despite the mother's desperate search for Henrietta, she could not find her.

Henrietta's mother haunted me. I imagined impersonating her the way Chautauqua performers impersonate historical figures such as Mark Twain, Thomas Jefferson, or Louisa May Alcott. When I tried out my idea in a nearby school, it went well. Soon I put together a program called "Orphan Train Riders" and impersonated Henrietta's mother, Clara Comstock, Charles Loring Brace, Sister Irene, and many children riders. To do this, I dressed in black and switched characters by changing hats (and in the case of Brace, donning a beard).

Schools and other organizations received this program eagerly. It was the second most popular NHC program during 1991–95, the span of years that the humanities council offered it.

As I trudged from school to school, I continued to wonder about these orphans. What happened to them? Oh, I knew that some were happy in their new homes and some were not, that some were educated and others not, that many grew up to marry and have children but others not. But how had being relocated influenced their lives?

I wished I could interview an orphan train rider, but the chances of that seemed slim. Most were dead or dying, and the few I had met either lived in remote Nebraska villages or were not inclined to discuss their experiences.

❧

After I realized that performing for NHC could not support me, I accepted a teaching position at Fort Hays State University in 1992 and moved to Hays, Kansas. The local paper, *The Hays Daily News,* publicized my continuing orphan train activities. That first semester, I gave programs in sixteen Nebraska towns. I visited libraries, women's clubs, an art group, a museum, and many schools, including some colleges,

Then one day, I picked up a small square hand-addressed envelope from a Mrs. Teresa Martin, an orphan train rider, and out fell a note penned by an ancient hand: "How can you lecture on orphan trains when you've never heard my story?"

I chuckled. Mrs. Martin was right. There I was, an orphan train "expert," and I'd never interviewed an orphan train rider. But how could I find time with full-time teaching and my NHC contract, due to run until 1995? Finally, I said, "Okay. I'll go hear what she has to say. But only for twenty minutes tops."

Smiling at her Hays apartment door and standing ramrod straight was Mrs. Martin, a tiny, trim, smartly dressed woman. She seemed so young! Her curly hair was not beauty-parlor black but actual black. Sprinkled with a little salt but still mostly pepper.

Inside, books, magazines, and newspapers cluttered her small living room. Fliers, stacked high on tables and chairs, drifted down the sofa. Mrs. Martin was, I discovered, a retired librarian, having worked as children's librarian in the Hays Public Library and, later, as a medical librarian in many Denver hospitals. She led me to a closet where wobbly stacks of paper carpeted the floor and gestured. "That's my life in there."

We piled her papers on the only possible place—her floor—and looked at them. "Nearly everything's there," she said. "But I can't figure out how to put it together."

The challenge hooked me. We sorted documents by date, and three hours passed before I noticed the time.

Meeting weekly, we continued our work. We became warm friends, even though she was eighty-seven and I only in my late fifties. She became "Teresa" to me instead of "Mrs. Martin." We went to see the Hays Medical Center's medical library where she worked part-time. We visited the Ellis County Historical Society to read about Volga Germans; the Foundling orphanage had placed Teresa with a Volga German family. Intrepid researchers, she and I haunted the local and university libraries.

We drove to Schoenchen, the tiny Volga German village in Kansas where Teresa grew up. It looked like a doll's town, so isolated, its houses so small. The church, in contrast, was huge with fine lines, beautiful in an austere way. Then we visited the cemetery and stood at the graves of the two people who had taken Teresa in and treated her so poorly.

Week after week, we talked and she read what I had written. Slowly *Mail-Order Kid* took form. Once when I wrote a scene, I used my imagination as well as Teresa's memory to create it. As usual, I read the scene to Teresa. "What do you think?"

"Oh," she beamed, "it makes my life alive again!"

So I balanced her acute memory, our research, and my imagination to complete *Mail-Order Kid*.

❧

Mail-Order Kid is a story of transformation. This biography depicts how the abuse Teresa experienced as a child weakened her self-esteem. It shows how she at first accepted this self-deprecation and then fought it until, through her efforts and the love of others, she no longer needed to apologize for having ridden an orphan train.

This book is the first orphan train rider biography written for adult readers. Unlike typical juvenile biographies that focus on the train ride and the orphan's placement, *Mail-Order Kid* follows the entire arc of Teresa's experience. We see not only the train ride and the placement, but also the effect they had on Teresa as an adult.

Readers will find this biography easy to believe, since the subject of the book, Teresa Martin, read and approved every page of it, except the pages about her final illness and death.

As for me, I learned a lot writing *Mail-Order Kid,* both as an author and a human being. As an author, I learned about the necessity for trust in researching a biography. If Teresa and I didn't have confidence in one another, she never could have revealed to me some of the details of her life, especially painful ones. As a human, I learned from Teresa the value of genuine humility. In her lack of pretension, she showed me the joy of connecting with other people by not putting herself above them—or below them.

Marilyn June Coffey

❧ INTRODUCTION ❧

"We are our own self-healers."

—B. Eagerman

Did you know the orphan train movement of 1854–1929 permanently relocated more children than any other attempt in world history? That's true, even though no one knows for sure how many children rode those trains to new homes.

Early figures indicate that only 100,000 children went, even though one orphanage (the Children's Aid Society) reported it alone sent 105,000. The middle-of-the road estimate—or guess— is about 200,000 children, maybe 250,000. But recent data shows that 400,000 to 500,000 children traveled from the East Coast to every state in the Union in what some call the "Greatest American Migration."

No matter which figure, if any, is correct, the orphan train movement apparently ranks as the world's largest permanent relocation of children. It certainly lords it over two other notable movements: the Native American boarding school movement and the Children's Crusade.

In 1870, sixteen years after the Rev. Charles Loring Brace gave birth to the orphan train movement, Christian missionaries began to remove Native American children from their reservations and place them in boarding schools. Fifty-eight years later, in 1928, just a year before the orphan trains stopped running, the missionary-teachers closed down the schools. During this time, they removed some 100,000 Native American children from their homes and deposited them into 500 schools. There the teachers forced them to abandon their native identity in many ways, such as cutting their hair, dressing in European-American style, and forcing them to speak only English.

A Kansas orphan train, c. 1900,
probably similar to the train Teresa rode in 1910.
(Courtesy of Kansas State Historical Society)

Some 700 years earlier, in 1212, troops of 30,000 French and 50,000 German children supposedly marched to the Mediterranean to help adult Christians wrest the Holy Land from Muslims in what has been called the Children's Crusade.

Both the Children's Crusade and the Native American boarding school movement relocated a substantial number of children, but if recent orphan train figures are accurate, the orphan train displaced nearly three times as many children as the other two movements combined. Not for nothing is the orphan train movement called the "Greatest American Migration."

This gigantic orphan train effort caught three-year-old Teresa (Jessie Feit) Martin, my subject in *Mail-Order Kid*. It whisked her from the safety of her New York orphanage, where the worst thing the nuns did was wash her hair, to Kansas. There she entered a small and strange Volga German world whose inhabitants spoke a language she had never heard. In this odd world, she encountered whippings and sexual abuse. She was like a foot soldier thrust pell-mell into a battle he doesn't understand.

To think that tens of thousands of children, like Teresa, rode into harmful families boggles my mind. Of course, not all foster parents abused orphan train riders. Many provided adequate homes and some excellent ones.

So if these children's foster homes differ, why should we examine the life of only one of thousands of riders? The orphan train phenomenon was so vast that no individual rider's childhood story can be universally true. Yet by examining the endeavor through the awareness of one individual, such as Teresa, we can hold up a mirror to the movement as a whole.

Some of our best wartime writers knew this. Stephen Crane, for instance, in his *The Red Badge of Courage* writes about the American Civil War through the eyes of a new recruit under fire. Erich Remarque's highly popular *All Quiet on the Western Front* depicts World War I from the perspective of an infantryman himself.

Reading in *Mail-Order Kid* about Teresa Martin's experience as an orphan train rider lets us understand not just Teresa's life but also the deep impact that these arbitrary relocations had on thousands of children.

Being an orphan, like Teresa Martin, leaves permanent scars, psychologists believe. The original families of orphans, by definition, have vanished, but children who rode the train to a new world lost an entire culture as well. These deprivations left their marks: physical, intellectual, and emotional wounds. Adoption alone, psychologists say, often results in post-traumatic stress disorder.

The orphan's experience of displacement is like exhaustion from a prolonged trauma, the sort of thing Rebecca West describes in *The Return of the Soldier,* a World War I novel. Her book depicts a shell-shocked British soldier as he tries to re-integrate into British society—a necessity familiar to orphan train riders who entered new communities. Some, like Teresa Martin, had to learn a second language.

We know, from riders themselves, that "prolonged trauma" was common. Often men or women shed tears when they described their childhood lives with foster parents. What happened to them varied. How they responded to it also differed, depending in part on their personalities.

Whether riders perceived a foster home as good or bad seems to pivot on whether or not the child felt loved. Some children did. Irma Schnieders was "petted and pampered." Jean L. Sexton received a bike; William Macy, a young mare; and Ann, more bonnets than she could wear. (Last names of some orphans are not available.)

Willie Dunnaway considered his new family a blessing, and Rosa Pfeifer remembers her foster parents as wonderful. Their example caused Rosa to make up her mind "that if I couldn't have any children of my own, I'd adopt some."

Some riders valued most of the things they learned. Mary Tenopir, for instance, learned to set a pretty table, dance to a fiddle, and play cards. Mary Belle Foose received a college education, unusual for a young woman then. John Wellington Danielson's adoptive parents supported him through college with a B.A. and an M.A. degree.

Margaret Weber, who considers herself "one of the lucky ones," really sums up the essence of a good foster home when she says, "I was loved."

By contrast, Alan Bankston said of the foster home where he lived with his twin brother, "They gave us everything we needed but love." Teresa Martin's home was like that, without love. And so, to a large extent, was the Volga German community where fate had deposited her.

Bad foster homes, unfortunately, were common. In those households where an adult mistreated a child, some children ran away, but others, like Teresa, toughed it out. Sometimes agents such as "Grandpa" McFeeley removed a child and arranged an alternate placement.

Adults in the orphan train era commonly punished children by thrashing them, but in the case of some orphan train riders, those whippings went beyond the pale. Katie's foster parents lashed her until she was black and blue. McFeeley, a beloved agent, once spotted scabs on a young boy's wrists and made him, under protest, remove his shirt. Scars of previous beatings striped the boy's back.

Harry "Shorty" Morris's foster parent worked the boy over so hard his screams carried to a nearby farm. When the farmer protested, the foster father stopped blistering Shorty outdoors where the neighbors could hear. Instead, he walloped Shorty indoors.

Harold Williams was "scared to death" of his foster mother, "an old lady who was a tyrant." She even flogged him when he fell sick, on the theory that sickness means you have done something bad.

In the worse case I encountered, a young boy who was herding cattle went missing. Local Harlan County, Nebraska, officials arrested the foster father, who was known to be mean to the boy. A trial proved nothing. One night, the foster father and his family vanished. After that, local inhabitants found the boy's body buried in a field.

Sometimes foster homes were bad just because of the indignities. Margaret Driscoll had to sleep on the couch and could not use the indoor toilet. Mary Goth's foster parents kept her out of school after the third grade to cook and keep house. Her foster mother wanted one of her sons to impregnate Mary so she would stay home and work.

Many children were overworked. Claretta Brown Miller, not yet eight years old, had to wait on a family of nine. Malinda, only six, had to wash dishes, even though she was so short she had to stand on a chair and a box to reach them. Paul Forch had to scrub wooden floors daily with lye; he scrubbed until his hands bled. Larry Davis had to split a pile of wood, even though he was ill with pneumonia.

Small wonder, then, to hear that Dorothy Davidson bit her foster mother or that Viola Du Frane learned, at four, that it did no good to cry.

However, even in the best of homes, loneliness must have been common. Orphan Toni Weiler said her loneliness never entirely dissipated, not even as an adult. Her loving family might surround her, but in an instant, this loneliness would drop, and she would remember that she didn't really know who she was or where she came from. Not knowing who you are implies a question of familial identity; not knowing where you come from signals a loss from cultural displacement. Teresa Martin, like many orphan train riders, experienced both.

~

The orphanage that brought Teresa from New York to Kansas in 1910 was the New York Foundling Hospital. It had sent children out West since shortly after the Sisters of Charity of Saint Vincent de Paul started the Foundling in 1869.

The Foundling Hospital's specialty was caring for abandoned babies, a dreadful problem in New York City where infant desertion, and even infanticide, had become epidemic. Mothers tossed unwanted babies in the garbage, on the street, or in the Hudson River. More caring mothers deposited infants where someone might find them—on the doorstep of a rich family, in a tenement hallway, or at a convent's entrance.

At the Foundling, the nuns kept a bassinet in the vestibule where mothers could deposit their infants incognito. Teresa's mother probably did not use the bassinet. I suspect she gave Teresa, only a few days old, directly to the nuns, for she paid for her daughter's care for a while.

For nearly sixty years, the Foundling relocated babies and toddlers on its Baby Trains, to the tune of about 600 children a year, but it was only second in placing children. The primary mover was the Children's Aid Society, the group that initiated the orphan train movement. For every baby or toddler the Foundling sent, the CAS relocated three or four children, mostly young boys, for an average of some 2,000 children a year.

Other asylums also delivered children to new homes. These included Five Points Mission, New York Juvenile Asylum, New England Home for Little Wanderers in Boston, Illinois Children's Home Society, San Francisco's Boys and Girls Aid Society, and others of the hundreds of orphan asylums in the United States.

~

Ironically, the man who founded this vast orphan train operation, Methodist minister Charles Loring Brace, did not intend it. He just wanted to help the 10,000 to 30,000 or so children living on the streets of New York City in 1853. He couldn't stand to see scruffy looking boys, barefoot and dressed in rags, sleeping on steps, in boxes, under stairways, or in cellars. Their pinched faces and hard eyes made them resemble old men. "Street rats," Brace called them. Someone had to help them, he believed, or they would rise up and "reduce our city to ashes."

Most of these boys had ridden into New York on a tidal wave of European emigrants fleeing famine, natural disasters, persecution, or revolutions. Few of these newcomers spoke English. Expecting to be welcomed into a city so rich that it paved its streets with gold, they found only poor paying jobs and a housing shortage. Half of New York's population of 500,000 lived in 18,000 tenements. Alcohol often relieved deep disappointment and justified leaving children to fend for themselves on the streets.

After Brace founded the Children's Aid Society, he experimented with several ways to help these destitute children. He offered lodging, Sunday sermons, and industrial schools, but he believed that if children stayed in the city, their futures would be bleak. Therefore, he sent hundreds of boys to farm families in Rhode Island, Maine, Pennsylvania, Vermont, and New Hampshire.

New York City street children photographed by Jacob Riis.
(Courtesy of the Library of Congress)

After these placements seemed successful, he sent forty-seven children "out West" to Dowagiac, Michigan, in 1854. Historians say that this act marked the dawn of the orphan train movement, a phenomenon that would transform Teresa Martin's life.

Brace's Protestant group, the CAS, soon made Catholic enemies. They hated the way Brace "snatched" children off the streets and sent them out of the city. They accused him of putting Catholic children into Protestant homes in order to convert them.

Because of this jealousy, the New York Foundling Hospital sent babies and toddlers out of the city, too. The Foundling baptized Jewish infants, like Teresa, and Protestant babies, readying them for placement in Catholic homes.

When it sent Teresa Martin from New York to Kansas, the Foundling had been relocating children for forty years. The orphan train campaign was fifty-six years old when Teresa Martin boarded the train.

⟿

Even though both the CAS and the Foundling relocated children, their methods differed. Teresa Martin was fortunate that the Foundling, not the CAS, sent her.

The CAS found families for their children, mostly young boys, by sending agents to likely communities and advertising in the newspaper. Any person who wanted a child applied to a committee of townspeople.

Then agents would bring out a group of children from New York, stop in selected towns, and display the youngsters on a stage or in a big room. If no room was available, agents would line children along the railroad tracks, an experience that orphan George Beaton described as "walking the plank."

People approved by the committee would inspect the children, often pinching muscles or examining teeth. Then they made their selections, sometimes fighting over particular children.

Unlike the CAS, the Foundling arranged homes for children in advance. It relied on local priests to help find good country homes for their needy Catholic babies. In New York, the nuns matched children to their new homes, pinning a numbered tag on the child and sending the same number to the chosen family. Teresa, for instance, was number four.

Because nuns chose homes in advance, the Foundling did not line up children alongside a track, and their children did not have to undergo the indignity of being pinched.

~

By the time Teresa rode from New York City to Hays, Kansas, in 1910, the orphan train movement had peaked. The Foundling would stop its program in 1927, the CAS in 1929.

Why did this placement of children end?

Well, the world "out West" was changing. States passed laws forbidding the transportation of children across state boundaries, implying, "keep your Eastern refuse out of our world." They also passed laws prohibiting child labor or requiring farmers to pay for it. Other laws required attendance at school for six or eight months of the year, which reduced a child's usefulness as a worker. These laws slowed down placement of older boys.

About the same time, trained social workers replaced orphanage volunteers. They argued that children, if possible, should stay with their families. Transporting children great distances and leaving them seemed irresponsible. Indeed, the entire orphan train system seemed onerous. Some called it slavery.

~

Mail-Order Kid reveals the orphan train movement through a detailed examination of one rider's history. The reader of this biography will not only experience Teresa Martin's being but, through it, will understand the orphan train's power to transform lives, for good or ill.

Choosing Teresa Martin as the subject of this biography proved fortunate. Although the Foundling placed her in an abusive home, she was not without strengths; she was a spunky, bright, imaginative girl. She didn't just keel over from the abuse. She fought it. She fought it—because she was an optimist.

This is a story about a courageous woman who had the strength, finally, to face her origins. I feel privileged to have the opportunity to tell Teresa's remarkable story. It's a gripping tale and one I relish recounting.

Here is a guide as you read the book.

Part I: Bitter and Battered shows what happened to Teresa because the Foundling Hospital placed her on an orphan train. We see the Foundling nuns taking three-year-old Teresa from New York City in 1910 to meet her foster parents in Ellis County, Kansas. Over the years, the Foundling placed more than a hundred children in that county. Her new parents, the Biekers, lived in Schoenchen, a German-speaking village.

The four chapters in this part not only delineate the abuse Teresa experienced at the hands of the Biekers and the local schoolchildren, but also show the helpfulness of a priest who taught her to speak German and of nuns who were encouraging teachers. This part ends in 1920 just before the sheriff arrives to remove a bloody Teresa from her Bieker home.

Part II: "Among the Lowest of the Low" depicts Teresa's life after the sheriff removed her. These five chapters cover a wide time span, from 1920 when she was fourteen to 1962 at age fifty-six.

Teresa had good reason to consider herself "among the lowest of the low" when she worked as an Orphan Annie. She escaped that fate by marrying a handicapped man and bearing him two children. However, the desire to be educated, planted by the Schoenchen nuns, provided her with ways to earn her high school diploma and then gain a college education.

By the end of this part, Teresa was earning a good salary as a medical librarian in Denver. However, her success did not heal her trauma of being an orphan train rider, a history she concealed. Like orphan Toni Weiler, Teresa didn't really know who she was or where she came from, and that brought her down.

Part III: Agents of Change shows what happened to Teresa after she decided to stop concealing the fact that she was a "mail-order kid." The six chapters in this part cover the time from 1962 in Denver to her death in Hays, Kansas, in 2001. By then, she was ninety-five and had become a strong voice in the orphan train movement, telling her story to journalists and to public groups. In 1999, the national Orphan Train Heritage Society of America gave her its Sister Irene Award for her role in preserving orphan train history.

What had happened to Teresa in these four decades to let her proudly embrace her heritage instead of trying to hide it? Two forces changed her: support from other orphan train riders and from blood relatives. Finally, she knew who she was and where she was from. That made all the difference.

PART I:

BITTER AND BATTERED

❧ 1 ❧
OUT OF THE FOUNDLING,
INTO THE FIRE

"Wh at's the matter with you!" Bappa, her foster father, said. "You don't even dress like a girl." He reached across the table, grabbed the bread, tore off a hunk, and pointed it at Teresa. "And what kind of hairdo is that? You look like a rat with your hair slicked back that way."

Teresa, who had lived in this cracker-box house with Bappa and Grandma Bieker for ten years, knew better than to answer. She touched her hair, carefully combed and secured at the nape of her neck with a bright yellow bow. Leaving her lunch on her plate, she rose, hoping to retreat to the security of her room, but Bappa stood up, too.

At fourteen, Teresa stood as high as she ever would, four feet, eleven inches. Bappa towered over her. "Here, let me show you how a real girl wears her hair."

He moved toward Teresa, but she knew he just wanted to grab her breasts. She tried to keep the table between them, but for an old man, he was agile. Soon his rough hand was heavy on her upper arm. Before she could cover her breasts, he'd grabbed a nipple and twisted it sharply. She cried out, wrenched out of his grasp, and ran for the front door, but he stood before her, panting, his beer breath hot on her face.

Teresa, center, with her caretakers, Conrad "Bappa"
and Elizabeth "Grandma" Bieker.
(Courtesy of Teresa Martin)

"Not so fast, young lady." He swung at her. She sidestepped him, crossing her arms to protect her breasts. The two seemed caught in a strange dance, she lithe and agile, he long-limbed and lumbering, stumbling, catching himself, his face crimson. He missed her again, brayed like a donkey, and cried for her to stand still. She ignored him.

Grandma watched, saying, as usual, nothing.

Then Bappa twisted and grabbed Teresa's hair where she'd tied it at the nape of her neck. Roaring in triumph, he yanked it up so hard that he ripped the skin off the bottom of her head. Teresa heard someone howl in anguish before she recognized her voice. Bappa let loose. She grabbed her hair with both hands. She felt the yellow grosgrain ribbon still tied, she felt her clump of hair, but her skin, still attached, rose in the air like a clamshell opening.

"You've scalped me!" she screamed as she saw her hands, red with blood, felt her hair a damp weight flopping against the back of her head.

⤳

She screamed again when she saw the wrinkled face of their next-door neighbor, Aldo Finster, at a window. He looked like a huge owl, staring.

"Now you've done it." Grandma walked to the window and pulled the curtains shut.

Bappa stood looking at Teresa, his body limp. "It'll be all right." He reached toward her.

She struck his hand.

What was that flat slapping noise? She looked down.

Her blood, dripping. Already a cranberry pool.

"Do something!" she cried.

"Here, it's not so bad." Bappa lumbered across the room and returned with an old gray enameled wash basin, big enough to bathe a baby. He held it toward her. She jerked away.

"Here. You do it." Bappa thrust the pan toward Grandma, but she ignored it. "She's scared. Take it! Take it!" Grandma didn't move. "She won't let me do it." He thrust the pan at Grandma again. "What? You want to let her bleed all over your floor?"

Grandma took the pan and held it below the nape of Teresa's neck to catch the blood.

Teresa felt weak. She could hear ping, ping, ping as her blood hit the pan's bottom. Then she heard splash, splash as blood hit the blood pooled in the big basin. Eventually the noises stopped.

Grandma set the basin in the kitchen and returned with a cold, wet towel.

Teresa pressed the towel against the back of her head. She looked around for Bappa. He sat at the table, his fingers full of food. She watched him pour another glass of beer.

Grandma walked Teresa to her room. As soon as she left, Teresa collapsed on her Russian feather mattress, her hair and the bow bunched beneath the towel. Gingerly, she untied the bow. It uncurled in her hand, no longer yellow but covered with orange splotches. It had been so beautiful. She whimpered.

Through her bedroom window, she saw the garden, its brown stalks and leaves blowing. She folded the towel, no longer cold, and pressed it against her neck. She heard the front door slam, then saw Bappa in the garden, basin in hand. *What's he going to do? Give it to the cow?* But no, at the garden's edge, he poured the blood out.

She nestled in a corner of the bed until she heard voices, Bappa's and someone else. She turned to the window. There stood funny Mr. Finster, his overalls hanging in the crotch, his wiry hair standing like a sentinel. He spoke loudly, but not loud enough for her to hear, and pumped his arm up and down like the handle of a water pump. Bappa scowled. Then Mr. Finster shook his fist at Bappa—whatever could they be talking about?— and Bappa wagged his head and shouted, *"Nein! Nein! Nein!"*

Mr. Finster shrugged and cut across the yard, heading toward Saint Anthony's church. Before he disappeared, he turned again and called out, punching the air to accent his words. Bappa made a dirty gesture.

She returned to her bed, her back against the wall, determined to sit tall and ready to defend herself against Bappa should he dare to come into her room, but before long, sleep pressed her head against her shoulder. Then her body slumped and she stretched out on the bed, her bloody towel falling to the floor.

Teresa woke like a shot when she heard her door creak, but it was only Grandma. The day had turned dark. Grandma carried a kerosene lamp.

"Hold this."

Teresa held the lamp.

Grandma picked up Teresa's few clothes and stuffed them in an old cloth sack.

"What are you doing?" Teresa put down the lamp and tried to retrieve her clothes. "Sending me back to New York?"

"Stop!" Grandma slapped Teresa's hand. "Mr. Finster called the law."

After Grandma packed Teresa's clothes, they went into the main room. Teresa put the lamp on the table. Bappa sat, his back to them.

Then Teresa noticed Sheriff Loreditch standing awkwardly at the door.

"Hello, Teresa," the sheriff said. "You're coming with me now."

Grandma handed him Teresa's bundle of clothes.

"No! I'm not going with you! I'm not going anywhere." Teresa tried to wrestle her clothes out of his hand.

"Stop!" Grandma slapped her. "Do what he says."

The sheriff grabbed Teresa's arm and pulled her, crying, out of the Bieker's house.

Ten years earlier in New York City, little Teresa Feit had roused when a rough hand had clamped on her shoulder and shook it. "Rise and shine!" The Foundling nun's shoes clattered to the next bed. Teresa snuggled into her warm blanket and opened her eyes. Kerosene lamps bobbed around the large New

York Foundling Hospital dormitory, illuminating dozens of small iron beds. But why were they rising so early? Uncertain, Teresa closed her eyes.

"Come, Missy." Another Sister of Charity nun whipped the blanket off Teresa's body. Cool air struck her legs, a smarting sort of pleasure. She lifted her arms, but the nun moved to the next orphan.

Awake, Teresa scooted to the edge of her narrow bed and waited for the next nun. Her feet dangled above the floor. Less than a month shy of being four years old, she was small for her age. Around her, girls edging out of bed made creaks, their bare feet plopped on the floor, but Teresa sat still. Someone would come for her. Someone always did.

This time a nurse nun came; her white habit glowed in the dim light. Teresa raised her arms high and smiled as Sister Agnes enveloped her. Teresa dipped inside the nun's ruffled bonnet to kiss her ample cheek, and then snuggled into her neck as they hurried away.

When Teresa saw the washroom, she struggled to get down, but Sister Agnes laughed and pressed the girl into her cushiony body.

"No, you don't, Missy! The last time I let you go, you ran down eight flights of stairs, before anyone could catch you. Sister Ursula! Hurry up! I can't hold her much longer!"

When warm water cascaded over her curly black locks, Teresa screamed.

"God forbid!" Sister Ursula said. "You'd think I was torturing her, not just washing her hair."

She gently massaged suds into the girl's mop, but Teresa's ringlets managed to coil themselves around the nun's fingers like grasping tendrils. Each scrub of the girl's head—and each twist and turn of her agile body—yanked her hair, uprooting her black curls follicle by follicle.

Sobbing when Sister Ursula released her, Teresa plucked at the wet nightie stuck to her chest.

～

So far this spring day, April 30, 1910, seemed like many days Teresa spent at the Foundling since she arrived nearly four years ago. Then the day turned topsy-turvy. Nuns shepherded her with about fifty other girls into a dressing room. There Sister Ursula removed Teresa's nightie and held out a pair of new white bloomers. New bloomers! Teresa had worn only bloomers well bleached by multiple washings. She stepped into them and pressed the smooth cotton cloth against her thighs.

"Teresa! Pay attention!" Sister Ursula's pinched face swam into view. The nun held a scrunched piece of white cloth.

Another new garment! Teresa's arms shot into the air. What was this? A slip cascading around her body, pure white, and—amazingly—a perfect fit.

Around her, dozens of other girls stood dressed in equally fine undergarments. Some already wore radiant white dresses. Then Sister Ursula turned back to her, bearing a gorgeous white dress, all pleated and puckered. The Sister turned over the dress's hem to show her where nuns had stitched her name and birth date. What curious dark marks! Teresa held her breath as sheer fabric swirled around her tiny torso. Then she patted it in place.

Then here came Sister Ursula bearing a white hat trimmed in narrow ribbons. The nun set the remarkable creation on Teresa's head, fluffed up her curls, and said, "Don't you look sweet."

Little girls dressed in brand-new frocks and hats filled the room. Teresa hardly recognized them, although she'd played dolls with some on the Foundling's sun porch. They seemed transformed, from orphans into real children, as splendid as the children she'd seen on the street when Sister Ursula took her for a walk. Satisfied, Teresa patted her hair. She, too, must look radiant, her black curls glistening beneath the fine white hat.

A clatter of horses drove Teresa to the sooty window pane. Below her on the sunny street stood five large wagons. Why were they here? Perhaps she'd go for a ride in her splendid new clothes instead of being pushed up the street to the post office lobby, which Sister Ursula liked to do.

"Teresa! Hurry!" Sister Agnes beckoned, and they joined orphans streaming from the ornate building and down the double set of stairs to the sidewalk. The boys, in sailor suits or Buster Brown outfits, looked as resplendent as the girls did. Nuns pulled their charges aside so younger nuns could load boxes into the wagons.

Then Teresa noticed Sister Teresa, head of the New York Foundling Hospital. The administrator stood at the crowd's edge, her ruffled bonnet neatly tied, her shoulders stooped from long hours at her desk. She smiled and patted nearby boys and girls, but her eyes roved over the crowd.

"Oh, there you are!" she said as she strode toward Teresa, her long legs rippling her habit. When she reached the girl, Teresa held up her arms.

"Aren't you sweet!" The Sister picked her up; Teresa planted a moist kiss on the nun's cheek.

"You be a good girl, my little namesake." The nun brushed the corner of her eye. "Don't forget me."

As the crowd moved forward to the wagons, Sister Teresa put little Teresa down.

"Good bye," she called.

Teresa turned and waved.

"Where's she going?" Teresa asked Sister Agnes who held her hand. But the nun didn't answer. Instead, she said, "You were her favorite."

Sister Teresa Vincent, co-founder of the Foundling Hospital.
(Courtesy of New York Foundling Hospital)

Then the drivers helped the Sisters into the wooden wagons and handed children up to them, first blanketed infants, then squirming toddlers. A gnarled driver plucked Teresa from the sidewalk with two strong, heavily veined hands. Sister Ursula pulled her into the wagon and set her on a long wooden row that ran along the side.

A breeze tilted Teresa's hat. She straightened it and swung her legs. What an outing this is! Then Sister Ursula placed a skinny older girl right beside her.

"Mary Childs, this is Teresa Feit. Teresa, Mary. You two will ride together." The nun patted the older girl's knobby knee, and then turned to help some other child.

Teresa knew Mary. At meals, she sat farther down the table, and sometimes Sister Ursula took them on walks together. Teresa didn't much like Mary; she had a long face and she looked mean, but Teresa smiled anyway. Mary stuck out her tongue, so Teresa kicked a big burlap sack beside her.

"Don't do that."

Startled, Teresa stopped.

"Thems apples in that bag. We gotta eat 'em. We don't want your feets in them apples."

Then both girls grabbed the seat as the wagon lurched forward and the horses' hooves began a steady clop, clop, clopping.

Teresa turned and looked back at Sister Teresa alone on the sidewalk, a black figure waving a white handkerchief. Teresa waved vigorously, but the Sister, now far away, turned and walked toward the main building. It looked tiny from this distance. So did the four nearly identical buildings that created an inner courtyard where Teresa played. The whole complex covered a city block, but as the buildings diminished from view, they glowed like sand castles in the morning sun.

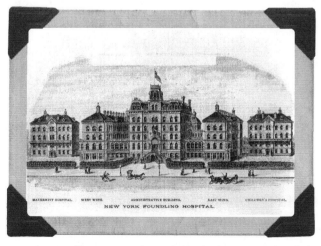

New York Foundling Hospital as it looked when Teresa lived there.
(Courtesy of New York Foundling Hospital)

❧

After the children rode some twenty blocks south, much farther than Teresa had ever gone, the wagons stopped before a huge structure, even bigger than the Foundling's main building.

"Grand Central Station." Mary's voice sounded singsong.

"Is this where we're going?"

"No, silly. Here's where we catch the train. Now sit still. Don't get down 'til I tell you." Mary pushed Teresa back in her seat. The little girl brushed her dress where Mary's hand had touched it.

Soon the wagon driver lifted her and Mary out of the wagon. "Careful," he said. "Watch your step." The place was a mess. Pieces of wood, slabs of stone, and construction workers stood scattered all over the lot.

"Don't be afraid." Sister Agnes, the hem of her white habit already dusty from dragging along the ground, took Teresa's hand. "They're tearing down the old building, so they can build an even bigger one."

"Biggest in the world," Mary said.

Sister Agnes smiled, "That's right."

The nun helped the girls step around the debris. Holding hands, the children wound their way into the temporary structure. Inside, grownups rushed this way and that. Such activity electrified Teresa. So many travelers staring at her, even though she was only one child in a parade of little girls in smart white dresses and lively boys in sailor suits, all herded by the Sisters of Charity.

Her elation swung to fear as she hastened through the havoc caused by the construction. The Sisters swooped down on her and swept her beneath the protective wings of their raven-black habits as they hustled her between flimsy board fences that shielded pedestrians from the rubble.

Finally, Teresa walked down a long narrow platform. The air smelled metallic. Then she saw the train. It was huge, as big as a house, its wheels higher than her head. She and the other children walked alongside it for a while. Then the nuns separated the children, putting some in one railroad car, some in another. Teresa had to stretch to climb up the train steps. Inside, two long rows of seats nearly filled the car. She'd never seen anything like it. She delighted in it, it was so different, but at the same time she couldn't help wondering why she was on this train and where the nuns were taking her.

Teresa sat where Sister Ursula pointed, on the stiff seat beneath the smeared window. She held up her hands so the sister would pick her up, but the nun walked away. Around her sat many other children, some a few years older, some younger, some just babies. Up and down the aisles scurried the Sisters, two nurses dressed in white habits, the other nuns in their floor-length black habits with their big ruffled bonnets tied neatly under their chins. They loaded boxes of milk, of bread and fruit, of cloths for diapers on the overhead shelves.

Then Mary sat next to her. "Mary will be your big sister for the trip," Sister Ursula said. "Both of you are going to Hays, Kansas. Won't that be nice?"

Unsure how nice it would be, Teresa peeked at Mary. The girl sat staring straight ahead, her face frozen into a frown, but when she noticed Teresa staring, she smiled a bit. Just then the train jolted forward. The girls fell against one another. When they sat up again, they were holding hands.

Teresa watched the nuns coming down the aisle, stopping to undress each child and redress her in everyday clothes. When they reached Teresa, she clung to her hat with both hands.

"Come now." Sister Ursula pried Teresa's fingers apart. "In a few days, you can wear your new clothes again."

The girl let the nun change her clothes, but she was not consoled. In her new clothes, she was someone special, but this everyday wear transformed her. The other children became common, too. They looked as they did sitting around the long dining room tables or playing with used and often broken toys on the orphanage sun porch.

The train picked up speed. Scenery whipped by faster and faster, until the train flew down the tracks. Children cried until Teresa's stomach curdled. Should she cry, too? She felt lost as the train sped on and on and on. For hours, it seemed, the coach rolled past brick walls and ugly tenement buildings with the morning sun occasionally glancing off windows.

A Sister gave Teresa and Mary an apple and a slice of bread. Mary broke the bread and took the bigger piece for herself, but Teresa didn't care. Her appetite had fled. She chewed tiny bites of bread until they melted; even then, she found swallowing difficult. They shared the apple as the train whistled. Instead of houses, brick walls sped by on either side. All turned dark. Teresa dropped the apple and clutched Mary as children screamed. Then as suddenly as darkness had fallen, the train burst into light. They rushed by the backyards of wooden houses in another city, the train's long whistle sounding.

"Look what you done." Mary pointed to the apple, covered with dirt and rolling under the seat ahead of them. Teresa jumped down to get it, but Mary stopped her. "Don't. It ain't fit to eat now."

After supper, Sister Agnes brought milk for the girls. When she handed them bottles, Mary refused. "I ain't no baby." But Teresa grasped hers, sucking even after the milk was gone. The empty nipple made a fine spluttering noise, but Mary said, "Stop that," and grabbed the bottle.

"When will we go back home?" Teresa asked Mary.

"We're not going back. We're going to a place where they give out mothers and fathers, and each of us will get some."

A mother and a father? Could it be true? Teresa didn't remember her actual mother or father; her earliest memories were set in the Foundling, but the orphanage seemed distant as the train jerked forward, gathered speed, and rumbled down the track.

When Teresa heard the car door clang, she saw a handsome woman enter their car. Her tailored gray outfit matched a gray bonnet edged with white lace. *Oh, look at her, dressed so fine.* Teresa pulled her faded dress over her knees.

Sister Ursula clapped. "Children, this is Mrs. Spallen, the Foundling agent. She'll speak to each of you."

When Sister Ursula stopped talking, the children's cries welled, and Teresa plugged her ears. She turned to the window. The train swept through a hilly land, sometimes empty of houses, sometimes with little houses scattered along the ridges.

Then Mrs. Spallen appeared next to their seats.

"Here, Teresa, let the lady sit." Mary scooted over, squashing Teresa to give Mrs. Spallen room. Teresa noticed the agent's smooth face, without a pockmark or pore as so many nuns had. And the woman smelled so clean. Teresa smiled and raised both arms. Mrs. Spallen leaned across Mary to pick Teresa up and place her on her lap; Teresa threw both arms around the agent's neck and kissed her fragrant cheek.

"Aren't you sweet!"

"She always does that," Mary said. "It don't mean nothing."

"Does she?" Mrs. Spallen rumpled Teresa's curls as Teresa snuggled into Mrs. Spallen's lap.

"Do you girls know where you're going?"

"Hays, Kansas," Mary's voice sounded hoarse.

"Both of you?"

Mary nodded.

"Now do you know your new family's name?"

"Mine's Schumacher," Mary said.

"And you, Teresa?"

But Teresa hid her face. The agent groped in her tapestry purse.

"Here it is," she said. "Bieker. Beeeeeeeeee like a honey bee. Beeeeeeeeker. Can you remember that, Teresa?"

"Beeeeeeeeeeeker."

"Good. You'll help her remember it, won't you, Mary?"

"Yes, Ma'am."

By morning, the train stopped in a city, then sped through vacant country, stopped in another city, and again left. At each stop, Teresa expected to meet her parents, these Beeeekers, but each time the children remained on the train, sometimes watching nuns bring fresh milk and clean diapers aboard. Finally, after five days and four nights, Teresa arrived in Kansas City where they all changed trains, boarding a small local to cross the wide prairie state of Kansas. Teresa happily climbed on board. She was almost home!

Still in everyday clothes, she envied the orphans being dressed in their finery, getting ready to join their families at towns along the Kansas route. At the first stop, Teresa smashed her nose against the sooty window to see the nuns give children to their parents, but she noticed that the children seemed reluctant to leave the nuns. One boy clung to Sister Ursula's arms. Were the Sisters giving children to strangers? At the next stop, she listened to the calling of numbers and the matching of tags until truth claimed her. *I won't see my mother and father but strangers pretending to be my parents. Why are the Sisters doing this?* She trembled.

Finally, the nuns changed the clothes of the few remaining children. Teresa and Mary dressed up, and the nuns pinned a numbered tag to each bodice. Teresa's tag read "4," Mary's read "3."

"Your new parents have a tag that reads 'four' also," Sister Ursula told Teresa. "That's how we'll know which person to give you to. See. Your name's on it, too." She watched the nun point out some dark marks on the tag. "And your new parents' name is Bieker. Do you think you can remember that? Bieker."

Bieker. That's what Sister Edna called her nose, "Here. Blow your beak."

When the train pulled into Hays, Kansas, that Wednesday, May 4, 1910, Teresa saw the town was bigger than the villages where the train stopped earlier. She quivered as the train stopped alongside an attractive brick building with a roof that drooped oddly—the Hays railroad depot. *What would these Biekers be like?* She so hoped they'd be as kind as the nuns and wear nice clothes.

When the Sisters ushered the children inside the depot, a huge crowd surged forward. Teresa's heart leaped. The depot seemed as full as Grand Central Station. No sooner did she step inside than hands reached to pick her up. Perfect strangers lifted her and fussed over her.

Frightened, she glanced at Sister Ursula who nodded her head and smiled. Teresa then promptly kissed the cheek of the stranger who held her. *Maybe this is my mother.* She kissed the woman again. Soon this person and that one held her, cuddled her, and carried her around the crowded waiting room.

One man told her he was Mr. Funk.

"Wouldn't you like to come home with me?" he said. She noticed that Mr. Funk's clean cheek smelled almost like perfume when she kissed him. *Maybe he will be my father.* When she saw Mr. Funk's handsome wife, her hopes rose.

Then a big man with bushy eyebrows claimed her. "Oh, aren't you cute," he said when she kissed his cheek. She liked the way his strong arms secured her. *I want this one for my father.* She snuggled closer; he was her favorite among all those who carried her.

"Attention please! Attention please!" She heard Sister Ursula call and clap. "Will those receiving children come forward please?"

The crowd quieted. About a dozen adults moved toward the nuns; the others held back. The man with bushy eyebrows stood at the front of the crowd, still holding Teresa. "Let's see your number." He looked at her bodice. "Four."

"As we call out your number," Sister Ursula said, "please step forward to claim your child. Examine the child we selected for you. If it's satisfactory, take it to your home and treat it as you would your own flesh and blood."

The Sister called number one. A couple broke out of the crowd to take a boy about Teresa's age, Albert. Then a woman swept up two-year-old Gertrude. Next, Mary stepped forward to leave with the Schumachers. Afraid she'd never see Mary again, Teresa held out her arms, but Mary walked away. Finally, the nun called, "Four." The bushy eyed man set Teresa on the floor, and she walked to meet Conrad and Elizabeth Bieker, her new caretakers.

They appeared ancient, all shriveled and old and coarser than the Funks or the man with bushy eyebrows. How could they be her parents? They weren't even good looking. Mr. Bieker, a tall, skinny man with a mustache, was mostly bald and his few hairs were gray. Heavyset Mrs. Bieker had thin wisps of black hair pulled tightly away from her face. How drab she looked! Both Biekers stooped, especially Mrs. Bieker, whose long black dress dragged on the ground. Teresa didn't hold up her arms to them, and neither of the Biekers touched her.

"Pardon me," said the man with bushy eyebrows. "I'm Mr. Tillison, a barber here in Hays with two young boys, and I'm wondering if I could buy this little girl from you. My wife's not here with me, but I'm sure she'd agree."

Mr. Bieker shrugged and held up his hands, but Mrs. Bieker tugged sharply on the elbow of his jacket and spoke to him in a foreign language. Teresa watched Mr. Bieker lumber to the nun. The little girl grasped Mr. Tillison's hand. How happy she'd be if he bought her! She watched eagerly as Mr. Bieker and Sister Ursula returned.

"You wish to buy this child," the nun said.

"Yes. She'll make an excellent sister to my two young boys."

"But are you Catholic?"

"No, Presbyterian."

The nun shook her head. "I'm afraid it's out of the question. If you were Catholic, we could perhaps consider it."

Teresa's hope flickered like a flame doused in water.

As the Biekers and Teresa started to leave, Mr. and Mrs. Funk intercepted them, offering cash in exchange for the girl.

"Catholic?" Mr. Bieker said.

Mr. Funk shook his head.

Mr. Bieker shrugged and moved, with Mrs. Bieker and Teresa, toward the exit. He held her hand lightly. Once, when they passed a middle-aged couple, Mrs. Bieker hissed, *"Jude,"* and twitched her long black skirt away.

Outside, Teresa saw the other children leaving with new parents. She wanted to run to Sister Ursula, but the nun was gone. The Biekers took Teresa to their horse and buggy. Mr. Bieker lifted her up front to sit between his and Mrs. Bieker's shoes. The overcast sky, which drizzled off and on, turned the spring day unseasonably cool. Mrs. Bieker covered the girl's lap with a dark Russian shawl.

The horse and buggy moved rapidly out of town, over a bridge and up a gently sloped hill that seemed endless. As the buggy crested the hill, Teresa saw the western Kansas prairie over the horse's head. Her stomach dipped as though she were a bird flying. The prairie loomed much larger than it had through the train window—as large and flat as a fallen sky.

The three traveled quietly to Schoenchen, twelve miles south of Hays. Teresa tried to chatter, but her new parents couldn't understand her. The Biekers spoke seldom, but when they did, they used harsh words she'd never heard. The language sounded like dogs barking.

Teresa's heart sank. *Who are these people? Where are they going? How can I possibly live with them? Oh, how awful to have no mother!* For there was no one to turn to, not for miles and miles. Surrounded by silence except for the sharp clop of the horse's hooves and the ominous whir of buggy wheels, Teresa chewed her nails.

2

BECOMING A BIEKER

A fter the buggy crested the high land that divides Big Creek and Smoky Hill river valleys, the road dropped off and the prairie turned hilly. Down they went. At the bend of the swift-flowing Smoky Hill River they turned, crossed the bridge, and entered Schoenchen. Teresa gazed in dismay at the dilapidated village, its streets cluttered with simple cracker-box houses, some little more than shacks. To her relief, they drove past a fine stone cathedral. Then they stopped by a T-shaped wood-and-stone house. Although tiny, it looked substantial.

"Yours?" she said, but no one answered.

Mr. Bieker lurched out of the buggy, then helped Teresa and Mrs. Bieker down. Mrs. Bieker grasped the girl's hand and picked up her bundle of clothing. As they walked to the house, a small black-and-white barking animal and a gray, fuzzy animal rushed toward them. Teresa jumped. She'd never seen such creatures. When the black-and-white animal licked her hand, she squealed.

"Fanny." Mrs. Bieker pointed to the barking animal. "Kitty." She pointed to the other one. Then she opened a tall door, and they entered the house, stepping directly into the main room.

Inside, Teresa could barely see her hand until Mrs. Bieker lit a lamp. Then the room swelled with golden light, which illuminated a kitchen along one wall, a table and chairs, and a big bed in the far corner.

When Mrs. Bieker sat down, sighed, and removed her shoes, Teresa took her shoes off, too. When the girl resisted the removal of her good clothes, Mrs. Bieker slapped her. Blood drained from her face. She'd never been slapped.

Next Mrs. Bieker carried the girl's good garments, with Teresa at her heels, into a small bedroom, empty except for a mattress lying on the floor and a wooden crate. Teresa plopped on the soft mattress, squishy like a pillow but thicker. She talked while she watched Mrs. Bieker fold her good clothes and place them in the wooden crate. Her fine new hat rested on top.

When they returned to the main room, Mr. Bieker sat at the table drinking a yellow liquid with white bubbles on top. He beckoned, so she went to him and let him lift her on his lap. As he drank, he rubbed her legs. She leaned uneasily against his chest.

A bit later, Teresa glanced out her bedroom window to see an enormous brown four-legged creature staring at her. She screamed. When both Biekers ran into her room, she pointed at the strange animal.

Mr. Bieker laughed and shrugged, *"Kuh."* He led her outdoors to the pen where the *Kuh* stood, staring and slowly chewing. They walked right up to the creature, big as a horse.

"Kuh." Mr. Bieker stroked the animal and placed Teresa's hand on the short stiff fawn-colored fur—*"Kuh"*—the fur warm, the muscle beneath stout. She smiled and stroked.

At bedtime, Mrs. Bieker removed Teresa's dress but not her petticoat, then left. The girl waited for the woman to bring her a nightgown, as the nuns did, but she didn't return. *She's not my mother.*

Teresa's bedroom was so dark she could barely see the shape of the window, but she didn't mind. The strange darkness was an adventure. So was being alone. She'd never been alone. She stretched out on the plush feather mattress. She touched her hair, her hands, her belly, and her ears to make sure that the blackness took nothing away from her. It didn't. She preferred isolation to being in the main room, afraid of what the Biekers might do next. She rolled on her side and drifted to sleep imagining that her mother floated on a cloud holding out a filmy nightgown.

Teresa woke early the next morning and for a moment couldn't remember where she was. Dawn's thin light crept through her window, so she walked over and peered out. Her bedroom overlooked a big yard but no houses, for the Bieker house stood on the edge of town. Beyond the yard, fields stretched so far she thought she could see the world's edge. No way to escape. No one to befriend her. She would just have to make-do.

When the Biekers stirred in the main room, she picked up her clothes to go ask for help dressing. Soon after she dressed, Saint Anthony's bell rang. Mrs. Bieker put her finger to her lips, so Teresa stopped talking as the Biekers bowed their heads, fingered their beads, and whispered strange words.

Later, still barefoot and wearing her everyday dress, she entered the cathedral with the Biekers. The sanctuary was enormous; she clung to Mr. Bieker's hand as he chose a pew near the altar. Hardly anyone was there, just the Biekers and one other man and some old women.

As soon as the service began, Teresa relaxed for the priest spoke the familiar Latin she knew from the Foundling. After the service, the priest, Father Wenzel, smiled at Teresa and said, in English, "Well, what have we here?" When she reached up her arms to be picked up, he smiled and shook her hand instead. She squirmed with pleasure.

Before the noon meal, Saint Anthony's bells rang out, and again the Biekers stopped to finger their beads and murmur. After the meal, Teresa, talking all the way, walked with Mr. Bieker two and a half blocks to the post office on the far side of town. Both walked barefooted. She enjoyed dust swirling around her toes, the warmth of his hand around hers.

The houses they passed seemed oddly quiet. No children played in the yards, no dogs barked. The only people she saw that day were at church.

Afterward Mr. Bieker took Teresa to his store, a rectangular wooden building on the lot next to his house. She scrutinized the groceries he stocked and watched him wind a handle on a wooden box and talk into its funnel.

"What's that?" She pointed, but he didn't reply.

Then Mr. Bieker sat on a chair, put the little girl on his lap and lifted her dress. He touched her all over her body, even her private parts, and then rubbed her rump hard against his own body. *How strange! Is this what fathers do?*

After Mr. Bieker finished, he gave her a lemon drop. She sucked it eagerly, releasing its sweetness into her mouth. The sweetness lasted a long time.

〜

A few days later, young Father Wenzel greeted Teresa and Mr. Bieker in the parish priest's tidy rectory. When Mr. Bieker dropped her hand, the little girl held up her arms to the priest. Mr. Bieker swatted them, *"Nein! Nein!"*

Nein, nein, everything's always *nein, nein* with Mr. Bieker! *Nein, nein,* shhhh, shhhh, don't tell. She ran to Father Wenzel and flung herself against his legs. Mr. Bieker scampered forward, grabbed her shoulder, and pulled her away.

The priest gestured toward his sitting room. "Won't you come in?" How his refined English enunciation caressed the girl's ears! At last, someone who spoke proper English as she did, not like Mr. Bieker's broken English when he told her, "You wait here."

Teresa could hear the men's voices at the front door, speaking polite German goodbyes to one another. The language sounded like a cascade of thick harsh tones. How she hated it! Her mother never spoke German!

Teresa peered around the priest's sitting room admiring its wingback chairs and serpentine-back sofa, its tea table and whatnot shelves, its Oriental carpet in Indian reds and buffs—so pretty, not a hovel like the Biekers' shanty with its single drab main room used for cooking, eating, and sleeping. Oh, if only she could live with the Wenzels! She would feel so safe. She stroked the shiny dark wood of an armed chair, and then started at a noise in the next room. *Probably his wife in the kitchen.*

"*Hallo!*" The priest strode briskly into the room. "Hello."

"Hello!" Teresa ran to him, remembering to hold her hands behind her waist.

"*Hallo!*" he repeated. "*Hallo!*"

She hesitated, and then tried it: "*Hallo!*"

"*Gut!*" The priest clapped. "*Gut,* good, good!"

She puzzled a moment, and then clapped, too. "*Gut, gut, gut!*"

When the priest's housekeeper came out of the kitchen, Father Wenzel introduced her as his sister, Miss Wenzel. Teresa stared at the tall, good-looking woman, dressed in a smart ankle-length dress and wearing no shawl on her head. *She could be my mother.* The priest settled down on his plush, brocaded settee, his sister beside him. Teresa looked at them, smiled. and said, "*Kuh.*"

The priest smiled back. "You saw a *Kuh?*"

She nodded.

"Cow," he said.

"Cow?"

"Big." Father Wenzel held his hand above his head. "Probably brown."

"Looks like this." Miss Wenzel lowered her head, stared and slowly chewed.

Teresa clapped. "Yes, yes!"

The priest nodded. "Cow. *Kuh*."

Teresa's German lessons with the Wenzels had begun.

Friday afternoon the silent village leaped into life. Adults and children, horses and dogs streamed to their village homes from farms where they worked all week. Next door, Mr. Bieker's son, Fred, and his family opened doors and windows to air out the house. Fred, only twenty, and his daughter, Regina, visited. Regina, a year older than Teresa, spoke no English, but the girls played with Teresa's doll, a wooden stick with rope hair. They marched it up and down the floor and hid it beneath the bedclothes. Teresa remembered playing in a closed-in porch with English-speaking children. The nun gave her a doll, prettier than this one, but Teresa didn't mind. She liked to swing the stick, whipping the rope hair in circles.

Saturday morning, Mrs. Bieker set a pan of warm water on the table. Then she sat Teresa with her back to the pan, pulled her head back, and covered her hair with water. Teresa screamed and jerked away, shaking her head and scattering water. Mrs. Bieker yanked her back and scrubbed her head with a bar of soap. When Teresa screamed and jerked away again, Mrs. Bieker grabbed her hair, yanked it, and slapped her. Hard. Furious, Teresa spit on the woman. Slapped again, Teresa tried to squirm away, but Mrs. Bieker lifted her by her hair and pushed her back on the chair. Finally, Teresa shuddered and settled into bitter resignation.

Mrs. Bieker sent Teresa to the store so Mr. Bieker could watch her. Teresa expected Mr. Bieker to be alone but he wasn't. A well-dressed young man stood barefoot at the counter, turning some liquid-filled bottles, examining their crudely written labels, and arguing with Mr. Bieker. By the time the young man paid for two bottles, some women stepped inside, dropping their shawls from their heads. They stood by a table piled with bolts of fabric, fingering cloth and talking in the same harsh language the Biekers used.

"Psssst," Mr. Bieker beckoned. She watched him open a box of cigars, select one, and run it below his nose. He held it for her to smell. She inhaled the pungent earthy odor. Then Mr. Bieker eased the ornate paper circle off the cigar and slipped it on her finger, like a ring. Delighted, she raised her arms. He lifted her, she kissed his cheek. When he sat her down, he patted her rump and pushed her out of the way of a woman bustling to the counter, a bolt of cloth in her arms.

That night when they went to Fred's house for a party, Teresa played peek-a-boo with Regina. Around them adults laughed, drank, chattered incomprehensibly, and played cards, their coins jingling. Most men sported flowery mustaches that dangled on both sides of their chins. The women, like Mrs. Bieker, dressed in black with shawls covering their heads.

Later some grownups sang strange plaintive songs. Then a man with a fiddle joined them, and grownups danced barefoot on the earthen floor. The men's long hair cascaded around them. The women's skirts were so long Teresa could barely see their toes. Two women, wearing elaborately embroidered black shawls with fringed hems, opened their shawls as they spun. The air ripened with the odor of moving bodies. As the fiddler's tunes leaped and soared, a strange energy entered Teresa's body. She stamped her feet and whirled like a small cyclone, matching the adults' movements. Once, when she looked up, she saw Regina's mother clapping and smiling as she looked at Teresa.

After Sunday breakfast, Mrs. Bieker unpacked Teresa's good clothes and dressed her in her finery, including her shoes and her hat. What a pleasure! Teresa chattered like a squirrel as she watched the Biekers push their resistant feet into unaccustomed shoes. Mrs. Bieker threw a finely embroidered black shawl over her head; its long fringe quivered with every turn. At ten, they walked to Saint Anthony's with other villagers, all wearing shoes. She could see leather toes peeking out from under the women's long skirts.

The ten o'clock service packed the sanctuary. The organ played and a choir sang exquisite songs. Father Wenzel stepped up to a podium, looked over everyone's heads, and talked and talked and talked in German. Teresa couldn't understand him. She squirmed and chattered, even after Mrs. Bieker pinched her. At last, Father Wenzel walked to the altar and spoke Latin. Teresa relaxed. In this odd new world, Father Wenzel's Mass was the only activity that remotely resembled the Foundling. She drank in the priest's familiar gesture as he lifted the ornate chalice.

After Mass, Teresa and the Biekers joined the villagers for a chicken dinner with green beans and dumplings. Shocked, the girl watched as adults ate with their fingers, then she did, too. When children played, Mrs. Bieker kept Teresa beside her. Teresa watched children who rode with her on the train. Little Gertrude played contentedly with a stuffed sock, but Albert didn't stand still. He turned and twisted and fell down and got up so swiftly that Teresa expected him to turn inside out.

When the Biekers finally got home, they immediately removed their shoes, and so did Teresa. She still wore her beautiful white dress when the door pushed open and in walked a friend of the family. Teresa, who'd never seen the man before, rushed to him, arms held high. Before the bemused man could lift the headstrong little girl, Mrs. Bieker jerked her away, marched her into her bedroom, and stripped off her clothes. Teresa, in her undergarments, followed Mrs. Bieker into the main room, but the woman pushed her back into the bedroom and closed the door.

Teresa pounded on the door but no one came for her. She paced around her room, faster and faster, until she burst into dance, twisting and twirling as she had at Fred's house. She danced until she collapsed. Then, she pulled a feather out of her mattress, took it to the window, and dusted each pane. Outside, the cow stood and chewed its cud.

~

By Monday, the town was deserted and would be until Friday afternoon. Teresa had little to do except for her daily German lessons. The Wenzels taught her to speak High German, the language that scholars and refined people preferred. She loved these lessons. Their praises pushed her concentration to a peak; before long, she could converse with them. The Biekers spoke a Volga German dialect, but so many Volga German words matched High German words that Teresa could talk with the Biekers, too.

By the end of two months, she had everyday fluency in both tongues, but the language she cherished was High German. Speaking it made her feel superior, perhaps because only Father Wenzel, his fashionable sister, and a scattered few in Schoenchen could speak it.

At home, Teresa proved too clumsy to help with household chores and taciturn Mrs. Bieker didn't care to chat, so Teresa occupied herself. As she played, she spoke English so Mrs. Bieker couldn't understand. Sometimes she played with her rope hair stick; sometimes she draped a towel over her head and pretended to be a nun. Now and then she danced, crazy little dances in tight circles, dances she invented. Her imagination entertained her for hours. Sometimes she dreamt about the gorgeous clothes she would wear instead of the ill-fitting old-fashioned dress Mrs. Bieker sewed for her. Sometimes she imagined her real mother walked by the Bieker house, looked through the window, and recognized her daughter. Teresa's heart tightened when she saw her beautiful mother, dressed as finely as Mrs. Spallen or Miss Wenzel. She thrust both arms in the air and ran to the window.

"*Halt!*" Mrs. Bieker's harsh voice crackled.

Teresa stopped and dropped her arms. Mrs. Bieker waved her away from the window. When the girl looked out again, her mother was gone, so she played another favorite game: she pretended her shoulders sprouted wings, like an angel, so she could fly away.

On nice days, Teresa sat outside with Fanny and Kitty, unexpected treasures. Her initial fear had dissolved into love, especially for Fanny. Teresa adored him; she petted him whenever she could. She tried to teach him to dance, but he was awkward on his two hind legs and didn't last long. All summer Fanny and Kitty sat side by side in the yard. If a strange dog appeared, Fanny and Teresa watched Kitty skitter up a tree. When the animals tired, Fanny stretched out on his side, and Kitty used his soft belly as her pillow. Occasionally a buggy would stop by the yard, and the occupants would point at the unusual pair. Sometimes a villager walked across town to see what the dog and cat were doing. Then Teresa, forgetting Mrs. Bieker's lessons, would fly across the yard, arms outstretched, lips pursed. Every strange woman had begun to look like her mother.

The Biekers named their little male dog Franz but called him Fanny, so Teresa thought he was female. Every day she crawled under Mr. Bieker's store porch, her private place, to pray for puppies, but Fanny never became pregnant. Still he listened well. Teresa could confide in him, and he never told a soul, but she continued to pray for pups so she'd have more playmates, maybe one that would love her as much as Fanny loved Mrs. Bieker.

Teresa noticed that she petted Fanny whenever she could and Mr. Bieker petted the dog every so often, but Mrs. Bieker never did. Of course, she never caressed anyone, but Fanny didn't mind. He followed only Mrs. Bieker, obviously his favorite. *Because she feeds him,* Teresa thought. As she watched the two, she understood that Fanny loved Mrs. Bieker because she loved him and he knew it. She envied Fanny.

So the weeks passed until the end of June. Then someone knocked on the Biekers' door, an odd occurrence; villagers just walked in. Mrs. Bieker opened the door to an outsider: Ann Spallen, the Foundling agent who rode from New York to Hays on Teresa's train. The girl fled to her, arms held high. Mrs. Spallen set down her satchel and squatted to embrace the girl. *She's come to take me home!* Teresa clung to Mrs. Spallen's neck. *I knew it, I knew it, I knew this was a mistake, I knew this couldn't be my home.* Then she realized in surprise that neither Bieker had jerked her away from Mrs. Spallen. Instead, both watched with expressionless faces.

Soon Teresa, Mrs. Spallen, and Mrs. Bieker sat around the table waiting for Mr. Bieker to return with Father Wenzel to help in translation. While they waited, Mrs. Spallen sorted papers on the table, then asked Teresa, "Are you happy here?"

The girl knit her eyebrows.

"Do you have plenty to eat?" Mrs. Spallen said.

Teresa nodded.

"And a nice room of your own?"

She nodded again.

"And new clothes that Mrs. Bieker made for you?"

"Yes."

"So you're happy here." Mrs. Spallen made that sound like a statement, not a question.

If I say "yes," nothing bad will happen, but if I say "no," what will she do? Maybe tell Mrs. Bieker, who will slap me later.

"Yes."

"Good."

The door opened, and Mr. Bieker entered with the priest. How Teresa wanted to run to Father Wenzel with her hands up! Sometimes during lessons, he let her kiss him, but never in front of Mr. Bieker, so she pinned her arms to her sides.

After everyone sat, Mrs. Spallen showed the priest her papers, and he translated them for the Biekers. Since she heard her name, Teresa struggled to understand Father Wenzel, but the flip-flop of Mrs. Bieker's curtains distracted her. Tacked top and bottom, they snapped and buckled like the sails of a ship. Still, even with the curtains flapping, Teresa understood that the Biekers were agreeing to house her, clothe her, and feed her until she grew up, to treat her like their own child. In turn, she would work for them. But other parts she didn't understand, something about indenture, about "ordinary branches" of learning and about inheritance.

She watched Mrs. Spallen and Mr. and Mrs. Bieker each sign the document, Mrs. Bieker with an "X." Then Mrs. Spallen folded the document and placed it in her satchel; the Biekers' copy lay on the table.

Mrs. Spallen patted Teresa on the cheek as she and Father Wenzel rose to leave, but when the Foundling agent left, Mr. Bieker spoke privately to the priest. Father Wenzel turned to Teresa and smiled. "He says to tell you that from now on your last name will no longer be Feit, it will be Bieker."

"I'm Teresa Bieker?"

The priest nodded.

Teresa shook her head. "No. No. I won't be Teresa Bieker, I won't, I won't." She stamped her feet on the floor. "No! No!

No!" she screamed. Even the Biekers understood the girl's "No." The adults stared wide-eyed at the tantrum Teresa threw. When it ran its course, Mr. Bieker grabbed the contract, shook it in Teresa's face and shouted at her in German. Too shaken to follow his words, she turned to Father Wenzel.

"He says you agreed to be his daughter."

Then the priest sat Teresa on his lap and said, "You're lucky, you know. Not every orphan gets to be somebody's child. Most of them become chore boys who get up every morning at dawn to work on the farm. Or kitchen helpers, scrubbing floors and baking bread and taking care of babies. But you get to be the Biekers' daughter."

Teresa squirmed off his lap. She knelt beside the Biekers' bed, fished out her stick doll, went into her room and closed the door. As she sat on her bed, combing the doll's thick hair with her fingers, she talked to it. How could she be a Bieker? She wasn't coarse and dumb like them. She was a Feit, who spoke English and High German and knew how to eat with a fork and spoon. Besides, if everyone called her Teresa Bieker, how could her real mother find her?

She dropped her doll and chewed her stubby nails.

3

TEACHER'S PET

I n the fall of 1912, Teresa entered first grade. Hand in hand with Bappa, as she now called Mr. Bieker, she walked not to the schoolhouse but to Saint Anthony's. The buzz of children's voices enveloped her as she entered the sanctuary. Down the aisle she and Bappa walked, row by row, past children in pews according to their ages. When they reached the front row, Bappa gave her to the nuns, owl nuns whose pleated white wimples circled their faces.

Teresa clambered onto the pew, swiveled, and stood to look at the children. She knew most by sight and some by name. She spotted other orphans, pretty Mary Ruder, near the back, and John Graf with his shock of red hair. A tug on Teresa's dress made her turn. A stern-faced nun stood face to face with her and pointed to the pew. Teresa, afraid of the nun's long, overlapping front teeth, sat.

Too excited to remain still, Teresa discovered that nuns quieted children who whisper or squirm. After Father Wenzel's mass, the

Sisters escorted the children to Schoenchen's tiny schoolhouse adjacent to the church. Only nuns taught in this public school. There Teresa entered a classroom for first-, second-, and third-grade students. She was among the youngest and certainly the tiniest of those students.

School confused Teresa. She spoke three languages: elitist High German the Wenzels taught her, Volga German dialect with its smattering of Russian that the villagers spoke, and English she used personally and when the men who wanted to buy her at the train depot came to visit. Mr. Funk from LaCrosse or Mr. Tillison from Hays visited her regularly, especially Mr. Tillison.

At school, her teacher, Sister Gertrude, spoke only English or High German while the students spoke nothing but Volga German. Teresa was the only child in the first three grades who could speak three languages; it marked her as the teacher's pet. What should she do? Speak High German and English to impress the teacher? Or speak only Volga German and align herself with her classmates? Who would befriend her?

She soon found out, for the schoolchildren's taunts began immediately. Their words rang in her ears. At recess, children called her *"das verrucktee"* or "the crazy one." This brought her to tears. She knew she was different, tiny and dark-haired and excitable, not stocky and stolid like them, but that didn't make her crazy. On the way home from school, other children called her ugly. No wonder. Grandma, her name for Mrs. Bieker, braided Teresa's naturally curly hair so tightly that she looked homely, even to herself.

A few days later, children called Teresa *"ein yud,"* meaning a Jew. Was she? The Biekers sometimes called her *"Jude,"* which meant Jew in German, but Teresa thought they were guessing. What was a Jew anyway? Something bad? She tightened her stomach against them all.

But when children start to sing, "Nobody wants you! Your own mother didn't want you," Teresa's stomach twisted into a knot. *How dare they say such a thing!* She knew her mother wanted her. She knew it! Then she wondered, did her mother really want her? A warm flush of shame drenched her when she thought her mother might not.

One day some schoolchildren cried, *"Da komt ya das geschickte"* or "Here comes the sent-for one," as though she were a mail-order kid requested from a catalog. Teresa considered that. In a sense, the Biekers had sent for her. Still, the children's ridicule made her feel small, especially when one said: "You were shipped like a package of Arbuckle's coffee." Teresa knew Arbuckle's coffee. Grandma used it when she had no time to roast green coffee beans in the oven. Bappa didn't sell the popular coffee in his shop, because people could buy it only from a catalog, as Teresa's tormentors well knew.

Fortunately, Teresa found a champion in Sister Gertrude, her first-grade teacher. Like all the Saint Joseph teachers, Sister Gertrude wore black robes topped with a white yoke, a pleated white wimple encircling her face, and a white boxlike hat. When the nun heard the schoolchildren's taunts, she said, "Teresa, you stay in for recess today. I want to talk to you." The children cheered.

After they left, Sister Gertrude sat Teresa on her lap, "Don't let those dumb Roosians bother you."

The nun's words poured over Teresa like cool water on a hot day.

"Pay no attention to them. You're better than they are. You are smart."

That soothed Teresa, even though her teacher—like the schoolchildren and the Biekers—called her Jewish.

"It's your Jewishness that makes you so bright."

That made being a Jew sound attractive, if, indeed, she was one.

"Don't tell the other children what I said to you," the Sister cautioned as she released Teresa to the playground, but when children yelled, "Goodie, goodie, you had to stay in," Teresa yelled back, "I am smarter than you." Then she remembered the nun's caution and fell silent.

Sister Gertrude's words healed some of Teresa's anguish, but they also made her smug. When children called her names, Teresa called back, "I'm not dumb like you are." Her pride swelled. In class when a student stood to read and stumbled over words, Teresa, who could read so much better, plugged her ears.

None of this increased her popularity.

But Sister Gertrude ameliorated the stings. The nun often held the girl on her lap during recess or gave her a holy card featuring a picture of Mary, Christ, or the Sacred Heart. However, not even Sister Gertrude could keep the boys from throwing snowballs at her as she ran home from school that winter.

When Mr. Funk or Mr. Tillison visited, Teresa no longer held up her arms. Grandma had divested her of that evil. Still the girl missed Mr. Funk's sweet smell, the roughness of Mr. Tillison's cheek. Sometimes she imagined that one of the men would say, "It's all arranged. You're coming to live with me." After all, the nuns gave her away to the Biekers; why couldn't the Biekers give her away just as easily? However, her visitors always left without her.

When they asked Teresa about school, she told them how she wrote many words, both German and English, and how well she could read. Once she astonished Mr. Tillison when she read from his English-language newspaper. Sometimes she would recite a prayer or sing a song she had learned, but Teresa never mentioned the children's taunts. That embarrassed her, as though being an outcast was her fault.

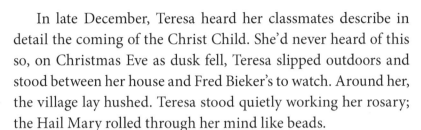

In late December, Teresa heard her classmates describe in detail the coming of the Christ Child. She'd never heard of this so, on Christmas Eve as dusk fell, Teresa slipped outdoors and stood between her house and Fred Bieker's to watch. Around her, the village lay hushed. Teresa stood quietly working her rosary; the Hail Mary rolled through her mind like beads.

Then down the street flowed a heavenly apparition—the Christ Child's herald, she knew—wearing a white gown. Behind the herald walked Mr. and Mrs. Mentsch from the south end of town, each carrying a big bag stuffed full. When the apparition drew closer, Teresa saw a veil over its face and a switch in its hand. *It's coming here, it's coming to see me!* But no, the specter turned.

From where she stood, she saw the shiny faces of Regina and her younger brother at the door as they watched the herald ring a tinkling bell.

"Praised be Jesus Christ," it said, its voice low, mysterious. A chill ran down Teresa's spine.

Teresa watched through Fred's window as the herald scattered nuts on the floor. While the children grabbed them, Mr. and Mrs. Mentsch reached in the bags and laid cookies, candy, and presents on Fred's table. *Oh, how I wish I were Fred's daughter, not Bappa's!*

Teresa slipped back into the shadows as Christ's heralds left. She didn't want them to see her; that apparition might whip her with that switch. Still, better a switch than a visit from *der Belznickel,* that stout old man who came in the night to strike bad children with a chain. Teresa hoped never to hear his warning, a rattle of his chain at your window.

That night a strange sound woke Teresa: chains rattling outside her bedroom window! *Der Belznickel,* coming for her!

Terrified, she cocooned herself in her blanket. *It's my temper, my bad temper that brought him!* She didn't mean to lash out at the Biekers, her schoolmates, at nearly everyone. Her tantrums never lasted long, but oh! until they stopped, they blazed!

The next morning when Teresa dared to crawl out of bed, she received—to her relief —a present from the Biekers of two pretty, little dolls instead of a whipping. *So I must not be all bad.* Grandma sat the dolls high on a shelf for Teresa to see but not touch. That was all right. Teresa pretended they came alive and danced with her. Oh, how they danced!

One spring day as Teresa sat at her desk inscribing letters, she heard Father Wenzel cry out. Her habit slapping, Sister Gertrude ran to the window, then turned, "Quick! We must go outdoors. He's calling for us." They all bustled into the yard where Father Wenzel stood staring at the sky. Teresa looked up to see a huge silver object.

"An airplane," Sister Gertrude said.

Teresa clapped. She'd wanted to see a plane ever since she found Grandma in the backyard, whispering, "The world is coming to an end! The world is coming to an end!" and craning her neck to look at one. Teresa had looked up to see only a trail of smoke. But she could see this airplane; it resembled a fish with wings. How curious!

Back in the classroom, Teresa raised her hand. "Is it true what Grandma's friends say that someday they'll fasten wings on their arms and fly?"

Sister Gertrude smiled. "Would you like to do that, Teresa?"

"Oh, yes!" *Then I'd fly out of this village and far, far away.*

"Maybe it will happen, who knows? Nobody thought those Wright brothers could fly either. We'll have to wait and see."

Teresa's heart skipped. With wings, she could fly to her mother.

❧

Teresa wept as the villagers left town that May for the summer. Even Sister Gertrude and the other teachers returned to their Motherhouse in Concordia, Kansas. Who would console her? Oddly, Teresa also cried when her tormentors, the schoolchildren, returned to their farm homes. She knew that if the children stayed, they'd torture her, but Schoenchen would be so quiet without them. Everyone would be gone. She'd be the only child in the village with nobody but the little dog, Fanny, for company.

Soon Teresa invented a game, school, which she played for hours. Her ten fingers became schoolchildren. All her "pupils" were girls, each with a name and a distinct personality. Teacher Teresa talked to each girl personally, as Sister Gertrude spoke to her. Quick to punish her poor students, Teresa vigorously shook any bad finger. If a finger didn't behave well, she lost her temper. Sometimes she whipped it. Once she imagined that her real mother visited this school. Teresa made her fingers promise to be on their best behavior then, so her mother would nod her head and smile approval.

All that laid-back summer, Teresa tended the nuns' petunias, marigolds, and phlox, sometimes touching delicate petals, imagining each blossom a nun. The flowers reminded her of Sister Gertrude's kindness. Teresa missed the nun, but not so much that she couldn't find time to dance in the street. She loved the warm street dirt, the way it pushed between her toes and swirled into the air.

Teresa also helped the Biekers farm. In addition to his store, Bappa had land near Schoenchen that his son, Fred, farmed. Grandma owned a nearby eighty-acre farm, which she rented out, receiving a third of the produce.

Plus they owned an acre plot behind their house. Here Teresa, still too clumsy to aid with household chores, could help garden. Grandma raised potatoes, watermelons, and cucumbers as well as her prized pumpkins and tobacco from seeds that Bappa's parents had brought from Russia.

Teresa loved tending the tobacco plants. When tiny green shoots enlarged into leaflets on stately stalks tall as corn, she was amazed. She plucked the large leaves, a simple chore, as easy as pulling leaves off lettuce. When they dried, Teresa pressed them together, and Grandma sliced them like noodles. Then Teresa laid the strips in the sun. Later she packed the strong dried tobacco in boxes, some for Bappa, some for sale.

Not only did Teresa delight in tending the tobacco, but also she loved the pigs that lived in a sty between the tobacco plot and the house. She liked to pet their short tight hairs and watch dust fly, but she particularly liked their oink. However, that summer, Grandma showed Teresa how to feed them pigweed, an awful chore.

Finding pigweed was easy; it grew all over town. Since everyone was gone, Teresa could find pigweed in any yard. Then Teresa had to pick it. Unlike tobacco, pigweed didn't snap off readily; she had to grab the bottom of the thick stem and break it.

Grandma demonstrated how to fill the bucket. She punched weeds deep and she punched vigorously. *"Arbeit macht das Leben suess,"* she said, or "Work makes life sweet," but Teresa saw nothing sweet about punching pigweed. As soon as Grandma stopped supervising her, Teresa stopped punching. Instead, she packed the weed loosely so the bucket looked full. Then she danced to pass the time when she should be punching pigweed. Finally, limbs tense, Teresa showed Grandma the bucket. Grandma nodded and shooed Teresa away. She ran to the pig pen smiling for she knew she'd get a licking if Grandma punched that bucket and saw how lazy she was. Grandma whipped her whenever she made a mistake.

Bappa believed in physical punishment, too. Both Biekers hit or whipped Teresa at the least annoyance, and particularly at her frequent loss of temper. Bappa struck her head and said, "I'll slap you on this ear until the other one rattles." She learned to dodge her caretakers whenever she passed them. Now seven, she hated them far more than she did when she first arrived.

Sometimes the Biekers didn't hit but made Teresa kneel on her bedroom floor for an hour. She didn't mind that. Used to kneeling in church, she entertained herself with her ten fingers. Sometimes her tall, slender mother, who became more real with each visit, came to see her. Thanks to her vivid imagination, Teresa's punitive hour evaporated.

When Bappa sent Teresa to the post office, she walked down dusty streets imagining that her real mother walked alongside her. Her tall beautiful mother wore a handsome ankle-length dress with a smart hat. As refined as Father Wenzel's sister, Teresa's mother looked totally unlike any Volga German woman. Teresa, walking beside her striking mother, turned into a tall beautiful woman, too. Together these two remarkable ladies strolled down Schoenchen's streets. Teresa knew that anyone who saw them couldn't help but be impressed.

To her delight, her mother talked to her.

"Why did you give me up?" Teresa said.

"Because I had to," her mother said. "I didn't want to. Oh, God, no! But I had to."

These conversations comforted Teresa so much she often talked to her mother. Soon every time she walked alone, her mother joined her.

So the long slow summer days slid past until August 15, Assumption Day, when Catholics celebrate the ascent of the Blessed Virgin Mary into Heaven. Even more exciting, on that day the Sisters, including tall stately Sister Gertrude, returned to Schoenchen. When Teresa saw them in the front pew during Mass, she had to restrain herself from dashing across the sanctuary and throwing herself in their laps.

During their first week, the nuns let Teresa help them clean, sweep, and scrub the convent house and the school. She worked much harder for them than she did for Grandma, but she couldn't keep up with tiny Sister Borgia, who worked like a draft horse. When the house and school were clean, Sister Gertrude thanked Teresa and gave her two holy cards. She hid them under her mattress so she could find them when she had to kneel for an hour. That night, whenever she glanced at the Biekers, she smiled and thought, *The Sisters are back! The Sisters are back!*

That fall Teresa expected school to begin with Mass as it had last year, but no. Students went directly to school. Nor was Sister Gertrude teaching first, second, and third graders, as she had last year. Instead, behind her desk stood Claud Urban, a trained secular school teacher who replaced the sister when Kansas forbade Saint Joseph nuns to teach in Schoenchen's public school.

Mr. Urban seemed nice. Every day he sported a red necktie and smelled as fragrant as a flower. Still, Teresa felt queasy as she watched him rip students from their desks and beat them.

Would he whip her? But why? She came on time to school with her lessons prepared and never made a fuss.

During one study period, her lessons already prepared, Teresa flipped page after page in her reader. Absorbed in the book's illustrations, she didn't notice Mr. Urban until he grabbed her and flung her across her desk. His wooden stick bit the backs of her thighs.

Teresa told no one. She knew the Biekers, like most adults, would side with Mr. Urban. After that, her chest tightened whenever Mr. Urban walked near her. *Is it my turn?* In self-defense, she studied her teacher's whippings. She expected him to whip most frequently students who ignored their lessons, but he didn't. In fact, he just nodded when some children said they couldn't finish Monday's assignment because of their parents' Sunday night beer party. He didn't even protest when mothers pulled their daughters from class to help with the washing. Maybe he knew, as Teresa did, that Volga Germans respected teachers but had scant use for education. Eventually she determined that while Mr. Urban whipped everyone, he whipped noisy students more often than quiet ones. *Look at that,* she told her mother. *He'd rather have students silent than learning.*

∼

On Saturday, August 1, 1914, a rumor whipped through Schoenchen like a train whistle on the night plains: the Germans had declared war on Russia. Adults, frightened for relatives living along the Volga River, talked of little else. Their insistent talk scared Teresa. What if Germans came to Schoenchen?

Then that autumn by God's good grace, Hattie Weigle—not Mr. Urban—taught third grade.

Mrs. Weigle, a lovely woman, favored white blouses and long form-fitting black skirts. She encouraged students and never threatened to whip, so Teresa hoped for another Sister Gertrude. However, Mrs. Weigle failed to challenge Teresa's mind like the Sister. Nor did her teacher consider Teresa special. At last, Mrs. Weigle became a bore, hammering the same simple ideas day after day until Teresa longed for Sister Gertrude's active classes, full of guessing games, cheerfulness, and learning. She dreaded Mrs. Weigle's favorite subject, Helen Keller.

"Just think," the teacher would say, "here was a woman born blind and deaf and yet learned to read, write, and speak. Now if she could do that, just think what you could do if you tried."

By this time, Teresa had advanced so rapidly in reading and writing that she read and wrote letters for several illiterate Volga Germans, including the Biekers. That season these villagers kept her busy writing to relatives living in Russia. From reading letters, Teresa learned that the Germans had attacked France and that Britain had attacked Germany.

"Don't worry," wrote one relative. "It can't last long."

Despite Mrs. Weigle, Teresa preferred school to home. The Biekers, however, forbade her to leave early for school after lunch.

"You'll wear out your shoes," Bappa said, "running around on the playground."

"No, I won't. I won't run at all," Teresa said, although she knew she might skip or dance.

Nevertheless, the Biekers persisted unless they drank too much.

Bappa used to drink only on Sundays and holidays, but now every day was a holiday and frequently Grandma drank with him. Whenever Teresa came home for lunch and saw beer mugs already on the table, her spirits soared for she knew they'd send her to school early. This delighted her, even though those "dumb Roosians," her classmates, continued to taunt her.

Then Grandma's father, Johannes Werth, died.

When Teresa arrived at the wake, a lively affair that featured plenty of eating, beer drinking, and reciting the rosary, she intended to see what a dead person looked like.

"Bappa," she said, "lift me so I can see in the casket."

He did.

There lay Grandfather Werth, suited out in his Sunday best, his eyes closed and his hands folded. Oddly, he wore a cloth tied around his head and under his chin.

"Why is he wearing that bandana?" Teresa asked.

"Keeps his jaw shut."

From this she learned that when you die, you can't keep your mouth closed, a curious fact.

Then amazingly, the next day she found herself a celebrity among her classmates for having dared to look at a corpse.

Teresa's celebrity was short-lived, but she thought of another way to win friends. One day when she heard Bertha, a classmate, talking about Johanna, she told Johanna what Bertha said.

Johanna's reaction—"What else did she say?"—startled Teresa, as did the stares of Johanna's friends.

"Nothing much," Teresa said. "I didn't listen long."

Johanna convinced Teresa to go back and listen for them. She did this enthusiastically; her reports brought her a lot of attention. *At last,* she thought, *these girls are my friends.*

Then Bertha, ringleader of the other clique, noticed that Teresa was spying.

"They found out," Teresa told Johanna. "They're mad at me."

She dared not eavesdrop again, so Johanna promptly shut Teresa out. Once more, her classmates ignored her or taunted her.

This failing lay heavy on her mind.

Soon after, Teresa spotted Mary Childs, her big sister on the train. Mary often visited from Victoria where she lived with the

Schumachers. *She never calls me names. Maybe she can help.* Teresa raced to catch up with her.

After she caught her breath, Teresa asked Mary, "Why do they hate me so?"

She expected Mary to say, "Because they envy you."

Teresa knew her position was enviable. Bappa was rich. She had her own room while most of her classmates slept five or six in a room, maybe five or six in a bed. And she slept on a plush Russian feather mattress while most Schoenchen residents slept on straw.

But to her amazement, Mary answered, "Because you're stuck up."

Teresa considered that. She did believe herself better than her classmates, but she was! Brighter. Quicker to learn. Sister Gertrude told her so. Besides, she knew she was superior to the Biekers: already she could read and write, which Grandma couldn't do at all and Bappa couldn't do well. And certainly she held herself above the villagers who ate with their fingers, hardly ever washed their hair, and liked their liquor almost as much as Bappa did. Did that make her stuck up? Or just better?

As she considered this, Teresa noticed she differed not only from her Volga German classmates but also from the local orphans. They managed to blend right in. Teresa didn't understand how. The other orphans spoke only Volga German, stumbling over English when they read aloud in class. She spoke every language used in Schoenchen, even bits of Latin, but she remained isolated.

Were the other orphans as unhappy as she was? Mary Childs was not. Teresa knew, because Mary told her so: "No point in being miserable." Gertrude Deoger, only six, who came on Teresa's train, sat contentedly in Saint Anthony's with the Rupp family.

Mary Ruder, John Graf, and Joe Wagner, older orphans who came to Kansas years ago, seemed satisfied. Beautiful Mary said her life with the Paul Ruders was "wonderful." John Graf, only two when he came, had a good home with Ferdinand and Pauline Graf. With his bright red hair and lively, often loud, manner, John didn't look a bit like a Volga German, but he fit in.

Joe Wagner refused to discuss being an orphan. "My parents didn't want me, so I don't want them, either." Was he unhappy? She wasn't sure.

Teresa's favorite orphan, Pete, was content. Dark enough to be Italian, Pete rode the train ten years before she had. He was so sweet that everybody loved him. After Sunday's High Mass, he led the Windholtz's team to Bappa's water pump. How those horses adored him! They nudged him, nuzzled him, and rubbed their heads on his body.

In all of Schoenchen, only orphan Jody Gassman seemed as unhappy as Teresa, although she wasn't sure, for Jody didn't talk much. She lived catty-corner from the Biekers, but she kept distant and looked dissatisfied. *If Jody is as unhappy as she looks, then she is like me.*

Teresa became convinced that Mrs. Gassman treated Jody unfairly and paid more attention to her own children than to Jody.

Teresa understood that indignity, for Grandma kept candy in an upper kitchen cupboard for Bappa's numerous grandchildren. Fred and Theresia were producing children at the rate of about one a year; Fred's older sister, Dorothy Hepp, already had a brood of ten. When the grandchildren visited, Grandma gave each one a sweet, but none to Teresa. Her protest resulted in a well-placed slap, so she stopped protesting. Instead, she began to steal.

First, she considered stealing pennies for pennies definitely tempted her, but in the end, she only stole candy. Again and again and again. Her real mother didn't mind. Teresa knew because she could see her mother smiling when she climbed to the upper kitchen cupboard and grasped, oh, maybe two or three pieces of candy that melted in her mouth with a sweetness that lasted for hours.

Then one day Bappa said, "The Gassman's little orphan's run away."

"Jody?"

"Whatever they call her, nobody's seen her. Looks like they won't find her."

That night in her room, Teresa wondered: *How did she do it? How did she get away? Where did she go?*

~

On the day of Mrs. Spallen's spring visit, Teresa kept bouncing outdoors, hoping to spot the Foundling agent's hired buggy.

"Sit down," Bappa said. "The watched kettle never boils, you know."

But Teresa couldn't sit. As she waited outdoors, safe from Bappa, she practiced a little dance step she'd invented.

Finally Mrs. Spallen came, right on time. She greeted Teresa with a kiss that left a moist spot on her cheek. As the agent rustled into the house with her satchel, the Biekers' main room seemed warmer. Grandma poured Arbuckle's coffee for the grownups and put a glass of milk in front of Teresa.

"Well," Mrs. Spallen said, "how are you? How are things working out?"

She addressed Teresa, but Bappa answered, "I don't think we'll have to send her back to New York this year."

He laughed, but his joke chilled Teresa. For some time, whenever she became too energetic or lost her temper, Bappa threatened to send her to the Foundling, which he described as a reform school. Or Grandma mentioned Albert, alarming Teresa. Grandma knew Albert; she was a Werth before she married, and the Werths took Albert. He rode out on the same train as Teresa, but they soon sent him back.

"Albert looks just like you," Grandma would say. "He's your brother."

Teresa hated it when the Biekers compared her to Albert; how could she possibly be as horrible as he was. The Werths had sent him back. She knew Grandma meant she and Albert were related because they both were so contrary and high-spirited. The thought that Mrs. Spallen might take her, like the notorious Albert, back to New York made her shrink.

But Mrs. Spallen spoke again, asking routine questions: "Are you getting enough to eat? Does Mrs. Bieker make you new clothes? Are you happy here?"

Teresa answered affirmatively. What else could she do? Say that living with the Biekers left her feeling unwanted, a feeling that haunted her like a ghost. Mention the slaps and the whippings? The strange way Bappa touched her? But the Biekers sat right there listening!

Besides, if she said she was unhappy, what would Mrs. Spallen do? Take her to New York as she'd taken Albert? Would living in that reformatory be better than living in Schoenchen? So Teresa smiled, nodded, and tried not to choke on her milk.

Bappa's drinking often resulted in his touching Teresa. Sometimes he looked at her and she saw desire flush his face. Since Bappa was the only father she knew, she supposed all fathers acted this way, even though Bappa warned her to tell no one about it. She never said anything. No! Oh, God!

Teresa feared Bappa's fondling, insistent even when she tried to wiggle off his lap, but her fear of Grandma weighed like a block of ice in her stomach. What if Grandma found out? Or even suspected?

One day, as he sometimes did, Bappa gave Teresa a penny after he finished. She laid the coin down in the kitchen, but later, when she returned to pick it up, it was gone. *It has to be here somewhere.* She searched and searched.

Then the door opened, and Teresa saw Grandma staring. "What are you looking for?"

"A penny."

"Where'd you get a penny?"

"Bappa gave it to me."

"What for?"

Teresa considered saying, "For running an errand." She often ran errands for Bappa, whose store doubled as a central office for the telephone company. His were the only phones in town except the priest's, but many villagers had telephones at their farms. Sometimes a farmer called Bappa to bring a person to the store phone, and Bappa often sent Teresa to fetch the person. Usually she received a nickel or a dime in return, sometimes only a penny.

When Teresa looked up, Grandma's eyes seemed to bore into her. The girl could almost hear her say, as she often did, *"Wer einmal luegt, dem glaubt man nicht, selbst wenn er auch die Wahrheit spricht"* or "He who tells one lie will not be believed even though he tells the truth." Teresa shivered. She dared not lie to Grandma, but she dare not break her promise to Bappa either. Whose anger should she risk? She chose a small lie to Grandma to avoid both Biekers' wrath.

"No reason."

4

"OH, SWEET JESUS!"

I n the fall of 1915, when Teresa entered fourth grade, her
teacher's homeliness, his buggy eyes and full lips, surprised
her. She was even more astonished to learn that this same
Carl Engel was engaged to marry snobbish Alicia Werth, a
beautiful young woman.

"How can that be?" Teresa asked Grandma, formerly a
Werth.

"The Engels carry weight," Grandma said. "Carl teaches and
his brother is a priest. People will look up to Alicia."

In the classroom, Teresa stared at ugly Mr. Engel and shook
her head. *How dare Alicia marry a man she can't possibly love?
When I marry, I'll marry a good-looking man.* She barely heard
Mr. Engel call her name.

"Do you know what 'veracity' means?" he said.

"No." She knew the answer, but better to wait and let a boy
reply. In fourth grade, the world seemed disparate for male and
female students. Mr. Engel told the boys, "You can grow up to

be president," but such an idea seemed absurd for girls. Not only were Kansas girls denied the presidency, as adults, they could not even vote for president. Somehow these differences made Teresa feel horrible to be a girl, but she didn't want to be mistaken for a boy either.

Often she squeezed her fingers to prevent her hand from shooting into the air in response to Mr. Engel's questions. Secretly she hoped that not answering might make her seem less of a teacher's pet, which in turn might make her classmates like her, but they didn't. She remained isolated, except for her imaginary mother and for the Biekers' little dog.

Teresa was surprised to discover that Mr. Engel didn't teach German. No High German? But she loved the language, ever since she'd studied it with the Wenzels. She lingered after school, stood beside her teacher's squat wooden desk, watched him grade papers so rapidly the sheets fanned by. Then she said, "Why aren't we studying German?"

"Nobody's teaching it." Mr. Engel looked at her briefly. "The war, you know. Teaching German's no longer prudent."

She knew what he meant. The Great War seemed an obsession in Ellis County. Teresa watched the adults seek military news from each other, make phone calls in Bappa's store, and send letters to relatives still living along the Volga River. At home, Teresa translated war stories from the *Ellis County News* for the Biekers and listened to the grownups argue about European hostilities.

Of more immediate concern was the news that German-Americans had become targets of hostility. In Nebraska, the paper reported, a German-American was jailed for four months for not buying war bonds, even though he couldn't afford them. Closer to home, the familiar "dumb Roosian" jeer seemed mild compared to "dirty Kraut" and more odious names Schoenchen villagers heard. Hays residents long considered Volga Germans "benighted foreigners, bowed down with superstition" and inclined to vote in blocks when they couldn't even read. However, this name-calling was worse. Bappa refused to take Teresa or Grandma into Hays.

Despite their unease, Schoenchen villagers continued to celebrate New Year's, Teresa's favorite day. They celebrated with a custom, *Wünsching* or wishing, that Teresa loved. On *Wünsching* day, she rarely had reason to lose her temper.

Wünsching started at four or five in the morning. Lights flickered on in houses all over the village as people prepared to receive guests. As soon as Teresa dared, she ran next door to Fred's house.

"Regina," she called. "Hurry, let's get started."

The girls ignored their freezing hands as they went from house to house wishing a Lucky New Year, often with other children. When they came to a door, they pushed it open slightly, squeezed in, and recited their piece: *Ich wünsch Euch ein/glückseliges Neues Jahr,/langes Leben, Gesundheit,/ Friedeneinigkeit und nach/euren Tot das Himmelreich* or "I wish you a lucky New Year, long life, health, peace and after your death, eternal happiness."

For this recitation, each child received a gift, often a penny and sometimes two cents or a nickel. The amount of money received usually depended on the child's importance to the adult who gave the money, but Teresa often received generous contributions from Volga Germans who barely knew her. She wondered what they thought as she squeezed through the door, a strange little creature with bushy hair and an excitable manner among such stoic, stolid Germanic people.

In one house, a big man with a huge mustache stared at Teresa.

"Who is that?" he said. "I doubt if she'll ever do a day's work. She looks so English."

Volga Germans called people "English" if they looked as though they couldn't stand at a wash tub all day—that is, if they didn't look German.

Then the big man grunted and said, "Give her two cents."

Lucky Teresa, to receive two pennies so often, even from frugal Volga Germans with large families. No matter how the villagers regarded her, her difference turned, on New Year's Day, from a blemish to an ornament. Her pride swelled. Here she was, nothing but an orphan, the lowest of the low, yet able to participate in the great day.

That year, even though most children only *wünsched* twenty-five or thirty cents, Teresa wünsched $2.88. Was she rich and happy, even though she knew Grandma would just tuck her money away. When other children asked, "Why do you get two cents?" she bragged, "Because I am an orphan."

Wünsching day was the only day when she didn't feel like an outsider.

⌁

Early in April 1917, Teresa sat at the Bieker table watching Bappa light the kerosene lamp. He never lit the lamp until it was so dark she could hardly see. He was stingy that way, but Teresa didn't mind. Watching dusk fall inside the house pleased her.

When the lamp glowed, Teresa pulled the *Ellis County News* close and translated. Congress was debating whether to draft citizens, a horrible prospect to Volga Germans who had left Russia to avoid a draft there. Before the villagers could decide whether to honor a draft, their sons settled the issue for them: they volunteered.

Their parents threw a big party for the boys; everyone attended to drink, laugh, dance, and gamble. On Sunday before the young men left, Teresa shook their hands after Mass, as did the rest of the congregation. *Where would they go? What would they have to do? Face tanks? Machine guns? That awful yellow gas?*

A few days later, Bappa stormed into the house.

"Those sons of bitches! A man can't even shop in peace." Bappa laid his rifle on the table and poured a beer. He told them how the fathers of a couple of boys that enlisted "went shopping in Hays, and those SOBs grabbed them right off the street and took them to some Veterans of War lodge and made them kneel in front of the American flag and say the Pledge of Allegiance. Just to prove they weren't slackers. Slackers! Not likely, when they let their sons go."

Bappa gulped some beer, then loaded his rifle. "Well, those bastards aren't going to grab me." After that, he carried his loaded rifle everywhere.

The war brought many changes. "Uncle Sam wants you" recruiting posters decorated the Schoenchen post office wall. The government had rationed flour, so the Biekers ate corn bread so often that Teresa grew to despise it. Fanny liked it though.

However, deprivation didn't color all life. The Volga Germans partied each weekend, so Teresa danced to the fiddle and the pipe. How she loved it! The music's energy seemed to slip inside her body, pressuring her until she had to move. At eleven, she danced as well as some of the women, but she'd learned never to dance in front of Bappa; that seemed to set him off.

One day Mr. Funk from LaCrosse arrived driving a Model T, a rare sight in Schoenchen. Americans had driven Ford's Model T for nearly a decade, but Schoenchen residents still considered horseless carriages a novelty. The Funks took Teresa for a ride. The sensations awed her: the movement, the breeze blowing through the car, the curtains, tacked at top and bottom, flip, flop, flopping.

Before long, nearly every family in town owned a car, and each driver considered his superior. Even Fred Bieker bought a car, not a practical mass-produced Ford but a much more expensive Maxwell. With its white-walled tires, electric horn, folding mohair top, and sporty lines, Fred's extravagant car seemed elegant to Teresa. She envied Regina, even when she heard Bappa worry about how deeply into debt his son had gone to buy it. Soon, over Grandma's protests, he loaned Fred money to make the payments.

❧

That summer, Teresa heard that the nuns might return to teach. She could hardly believe it: Sister Gertrude back in the classroom? To Teresa's delight, the rumor proved true; that fall of 1917 the Saint Joseph nuns returned. The state certified the new school, built on church land, and the nuns, trained as public school teachers in the interim, now qualified to teach school.

Here Teresa entered sixth grade, dismayed to be too old to have Sister Gertrude teach her. Instead Sister Rosina, an erudite nun whose flaming red hair sometimes peeked out beneath her wimple, taught Teresa's class along with seventh and eighth grades. Despite her disappointment, Teresa reveled in memorizing religious prayers and songs again and in hearing a nun call the class to order.

Sister Rosina, like Sister Gertrude, led a variety of classroom activities. She sometimes held a spelling contest or played "Questions and Answers." Sister Rosina might ask, "Who wrote 'The Children's Hour'?" Students, when they knew, replied, "Longfellow." Teresa no longer pretended to be ignorant. Her hand often shot up first. Having a bright female teacher role model made participation easy.

Sister Rosina also read to her students, often choosing biographies about women. Teresa particularly enjoyed hearing about Ann Rutledge, the young woman Abraham Lincoln loved.

"One day," the nun told Teresa, "you'll see a building filled with books. That is a library."

A building filled with books didn't sound too plausible. Teresa had never seen a library, not even the Carnegie Library in Hays, despite the Biekers' frequent trips to town.

As time passed, Teresa grew to love gentle Sister Rosina. The nun, unlike Sister Gertrude, never held Teresa on her lap, but she was tender in the attention she paid to the girl. She often called her "smart." In particular, Sister Rosina praised Teresa's writing, as day after day, she handed in stories written at home.

"Maybe someday you'll be published," Sister Rosina said.

Encouraging Teresa to write, Sister Rosina assigned her to translate, each Monday, the priest's hour-long Sunday sermon at Saint Anthony. This Teresa did. First, she translated the German sermon in her mind; then she wrote it in English. She loved this chore for she loved everything about Saint Anthony. Its High Mass's pageantry soothed her. When choral voices surrounded her, Teresa sensed her mother's presence beside her in the pew.

❦

That spring, a nasty strain of influenza struck Schoenchen. People panicked. Some, covered with blankets, soaked their feet in hot water. Others swallowed small balls of French tallow and then drank piping hot four-flower tea to melt it. The melted tallow oiled lungs and was supposed to cure the disease, but nothing cured Bappa's mother, Maria. Teresa missed her. An old-fashioned roly-poly lady, Maria once wrapped Teresa in a shawl to keep her warm in the cold church. Her death made the girl so anxious that every morning she checked to see if Bappa or Grandma's skin had turned blue, a harbinger of death. As days passed and the Biekers remained healthy, Teresa hoped that the awful Spanish flu might pass by them.

In November, the flu vanished as unexpectedly as it had arrived. Thirteen had died in Schoenchen, including Pete, the beloved orphan who watered horses at Bappa's tank. "Pete's gone," Teresa told Fanny. She did not cry, but Pete's death left her with the odd sensation of a rock stuck in her throat.

~

Meanwhile, Russian news became steadily worse. Communists seized a Volga German village; they kidnapped the leading citizens of another village; they plundered a third village during church services. Similar news came about village after village on both sides of the Volga: food, clothing, wealth, livestock seized; citizens terrorized and often killed. Volga Germans fought back with pitchforks, scythes, axes, farm tools but lost. "We farmers are afraid to work in the fields," Teresa read. "No house, no horse, no land, and no one's life is safe."

After Maria's death, Bappa's father, Joseph, in his eighties, came to live with the Biekers. A spindly man never without his tall fur boots, he talked a lot. "He can talk the hind leg off a mule," Bappa said, and Joseph did rattle on about the good old days in Russia. Everything grew bigger and better there, he claimed.

"Why, Russian wild plums must grow larger than oranges," Teresa told Fanny. "But why did he come to America if he liked Russia so much?"

To go to his room, the guest room, Joseph walked through Teresa's room. His room contained a mattress, his kerosene lantern, and Bappa's large Victrola box. When grandchildren visited, Bappa brought the Victrola out, attached the big horn, replaced a needle, wound the machine up, and played his few records. Teresa liked "Silent Night" best. The Victrola wound down as it played, slowing the music's beat and warping the sound until Bappa wound it up again.

Joseph was filthy and full of lice. Grandma hated lice. She had so little hair that lice never bred on her head, but they loved Teresa's curly mop. She attracted them as though she were as foul as Joseph. Grandma scrubbed Teresa's hair daily to keep the tiny insects at bay. Teresa gritted her teeth and tried not to struggle. Bad as her lice were, they didn't cling as tenaciously to her hair as Joseph's lice clung to his clothes. Grandma could hardly persuade the vermin to leave. Teresa watched her boil Joseph's clothes outdoors in a big black kettle used to render fat into soap at butchering time until, at last, the lice disappeared.

That summer the bumper watermelon crop allowed Bappa to stack melons beside the road where Teresa sold them. Bappa no longer owned his store. Generous about letting customers charge, he had had difficulty collecting. Teresa knew, because when he got drunk, he called his lawyer to complain about his debts.

Teresa enjoyed selling watermelons. It brought her into pleasant contact with villagers who chatted as they searched their pouches for coins. Day after day the pile dwindled. When Teresa sold the last melon, she gave Grandma $30. How pleased Grandma and Bappa were with her—a rare occurrence!

⁓

In the middle of the night, Saint Anthony's church bell rang like crazy. *Fire!* Teresa sat up in her dark room, then groped her way into the main room where Grandma stood at the telephone. Bappa lay in bed, a heavy comforter pulled over his shoulder. Then Grandma hung up, turned, and said, "The war is over."

Teresa couldn't believe her. The war over? Just like that?

The good news swept through Schoenchen like an untamed river. When Teresa heard horns honk and bells ring, she ran into her room, pulled her dress over her head, and dashed outdoors. Villagers filled the street. Their lanterns created pools of light in the 4 a.m. darkness.

A kind of frenzy filled the air. Men slapped each other on the back and brandished liquor. Women waved their shawls and danced. Children marched ringing cow bells and crying, "The war is over! The war is over!" When Teresa joined the women's dance, no one seemed to mind. She swirled and spun, dipped and leaped until the rising sun sent everyone home.

In school that day, Teresa listened to Sister Rosina say, "At eleven in the morning on the eleventh day of the eleventh month of 1918, the Great War ended." That was eleven o'clock French time, six hours later than ours, she explained. She told the class how men met in two railroad coaches in a French forest to sign the treaty. The Germans didn't come. They sent their acceptance on a machine called a radio, which sends voices over the air.

"Like a telephone?" Teresa said.

"Not quite. When you speak on a telephone, only the people on that line can hear you. But if we had a radio in this room, and someone spoke over it, everyone in the class could hear him."

Now in seventh grade, Teresa rejoiced that the Allies had won, but she suspected that wars are rarely won, not even by its victors, and especially not the Great War, which caused so much suffering. Sister Rosina said eight to nine million solders were dead, more than had ever been killed in a single war. Teresa could not imagine that many dead men; she couldn't even imagine a million. Then when Sister Rosina told the class that the Spanish flu killed twice as many people as died in the Great War, Teresa gripped the corners of her desk. How many people were in the world, anyway?

⌒

When the Schoenchen soldiers returned, Teresa saw that fighting had changed them. After Mass, she and the rest of the congregation shook hands with each returning man. One winked at her, which startled her so she looked at him again. He was humming, "How you gonna keep 'em down on the farm after they've seen Paree."

She laughed, but Grandma jerked her elbow, "Come along, Trasia."

At home later, Bappa and Grandma discussed her nephew, Wilhelm, who refused to marry the Schoenchen girl his parents picked out for him. Teresa pricked up her ears. She never heard of a Volga German marrying someone that his parents didn't choose for him. It just wasn't done. Everyone knew the rules. However, in the following months, soldier boy after soldier boy refused to marry "his own." These young men didn't just refuse to marry Volga German girls from the correct village, some of them refused to marry Volga German girls at all.

Such independence thrilled Teresa. Maybe she could marry whomever she wanted, but when she declared her intent, Grandma said, "No, no. We'll pick out a fine man for you." Teresa tried to argue, but Grandma shook her head. "No, you listen to us. The old ways are best."

But the old ways continued to change. Young local women mimicked America's Roaring Twenties styles. Hair was bobbed. Skirts no longer swept the streets; they rose daringly to the ankle. Women exchanged shawls worn over the head for fashionable hats. Necklines crept downward.

"Grandma, why don't you shorten your skirts a little?" Teresa said. "You'd look so stylish."

"Stylish?" Grandma snorted. "Those hussies!"

When the fashionable young women wore hats, bobbed hair, shortened skirts, and drooping necklines to church, Father Wenzel branded their new styles dangerous to health and morals; he scolded the women for wearing them: "They are the hallmarks of loose women."

Grandma nudged Teresa.

But Teresa envied those women. She so wanted to be daring and stylish.

❧

The next afternoon, Teresa saw Grandma slide her pint of moonshine whiskey from behind her sugar sack and pour herself a drink. She didn't bother to hide the pint again. Seeing Grandma drink so openly annoyed Teresa. Grandma didn't used to drink as much or as often as Bappa, but now the two seemed to race to see who could drink the most.

Teresa wished they'd both stop. She hated when they drank, especially Bappa. When she saw his lopsided grin, she knew he was about to come after her. Sometimes she slipped outdoors and eluded him by fleeing to a safe spot along the Smoky Hill River.

By the time Teresa turned thirteen, she could no longer endure Bappa's hands on her body. His long flat fingers tickled worse than spider legs, and his curious smile caused bile to rise in her throat. At fifty-eight, Bappa was a repulsive old man.

Teresa supposed that all fathers did to their daughters what Bappa did to her until one day, out of the blue, she asked Regina if Fred did that to her. She expected Regina to say, "Yes," and then they could talk about it, but Regina surprised Teresa by saying, "No, ugh, he would never do anything like that." Regina shuddered. The two regarded each other strangely.

Later Teresa wondered if she were the only child whose father did that or if Regina was the only child whose father didn't. She decided to ask Mary Childs; she was honest, blunt even. So when her family visited Schoenchen, Teresa asked Mary if her foster father did that. To her amazement, Mary's father didn't either. This made Teresa wonder about Bappa's activities.

"What do you think?" she asked Fanny. Fanny said nothing, but Teresa knew what she thought: Bappa was doing something he shouldn't be doing. The real question was how to make him stop.

What if Bappa's touching her was a sin? Perhaps she should tell Father Wenzel. She'd gone to Saturday confession since she was seven. Why not mention it there? What if she did, then what would Father do if he knew the things Bappa did to her? A strange thought occurred: What if Father believed the sin was hers, that she let Bappa do it? What if Father made her say hundreds of thousands of Hail Marys as penance?

Several Saturdays passed before Teresa found the courage to speak to Father Wenzel. Even so, waiting in line, she continued to question whether to tell him. If her confession made Father mad at Bappa, then Bappa would be really angry with her. But what if it made Father angry at her? At the last minute, as Teresa slipped inside the dark confessional, she decided to take the risk.

"Sometimes I let Bappa touch me all over," she said. Father Wenzel was silent. "I mean, I let him lift up my dress and touch me all over." Still, Father said nothing. "I mean even between my legs."

There! That was as far as she could speak about this indignity she'd suffered so many times. She let herself cry and waited for Father's comment. None came. Teresa smoothed her dress. When Father Wenzel remained silent, Teresa changed the subject: "And I lost my temper again this week and I wished I were grown up so I could wear my neckline low."

Then Father told Teresa how many Hail Marys to say. Not many. Just about what he usually said. She left the confessional uncertain. Did Father not believe her? Did he believe her but thought it didn't matter? She didn't know what to think.

"How dare Father ignore me?" Teresa asked Fanny. "Bappa shouldn't be doing that to me, I don't care what Father thinks, Bappa shouldn't make me sit on his lap like that."

She understood that Father Wenzel would not help her, that she would have to help herself. So she decided not to let Bappa touch her anymore, even though Bappa couldn't seem to keep his hands off her now visible breasts. He reached and crunched one even if Grandma was in the room. Teresa hated that. Wasn't anything hers alone?

One day that summer, Teresa wandered into the Bieker guest room, vacant since Joseph died. When she heard Bappa—*"Unfruchtbar! Unfruchtbar!"* —she knew that he called Grandma "unfruitful" because a surgery, after a miscarriage, left her with no uterus. Bappa hated that.

Teresa walked to the open window and looked at the Biekers arguing. Bappa held his rifle over his shoulder, as usual.

"Why the hell don't you give me that farm of yours?" Bappa's face was red. "It should have been part of your dowry."

"Be glad I have income." Grandma seemed wobbly on her feet.

Then Bappa saw Teresa in the window.

"What are you looking at?"

But before she could answer, Bappa ranted about her hair. Teresa never wore her hair to suit him. He wanted her to wear it "like a girl," full and loose, curling around her cheeks and bouncing down her forehead. But when she wore it that way, Bappa laced his fingers through her curls and embraced her breast. So Teresa never wore her hair full and curly. Today she had combed her curls high above her forehead and pinned them in place.

"Why do you wear your hair that way?" He gestured at her. "It's ugly. All those curls lifted straight up from your forehead. You look like George Washington."

Teresa felt anger flush her face as red as Bappa's.

Then Bappa lifted his rifle and pointed it right at her. *What's he doing?* The bark of his rifle shocked her but not nearly as much as the whistle of the bullet tearing through the open window right past her head. *Oh sweet Jesus! He shot at me!* She trembled so she could hardly run, her legs awkward as stumps. *He shot at me! He shot at me!* One part of her mind was insistent, but deeper down, she couldn't believe what Bappa had done.

Outside, she ran from house to house, until she remembered that of course no one was home. It was summer, the houses all stood empty. She could find no one to help her. Even Father Wenzel didn't answer his door. She'd have to deal with this alone.

Teresa sat by the riverbank a long time, rubbing both arms and thinking. She knew why Bappa shot at her. Not because of her hair, but because she avoided him, attaching herself like a leech to Grandma's side, leaving the house the instant Grandma did, not ever wanting to find him alone. He hadn't touched her for days. *He'll probably give me away now, like the Foundling gave me to him.*

Suddenly Teresa imagined creeping back to the house, finding that gun, and turning it on Bappa, shooting him in the back, the belly, the chest, the head. Between his legs. Her desire frightened her. She struggled to calm herself. At least, luckily, the bullet hadn't hit her. This could be worse. What if the next time he didn't miss?

After a while, Teresa returned to the house, still furious at Bappa. She vowed to keep her distance, although how she could avoid him in the main room they shared for meals she didn't know.

Teresa skulked around the edges of the house for days, even though Grandma called the shot an accident. "He didn't mean to shoot."

But Teresa wasn't sure. Had he pointed it at her by accident?

She stayed out of the house by day, helping Grandma or reading in the outhouse. The *"Nuschik,"* the Biekers called it. A Russian word. She stayed inside for hours, reading and rereading the catalogs: Sears and Montgomery Ward. In the evenings, she stayed in her room. She didn't mind the solitude and the darkness, but she missed reading and writing in the main room under the kerosene lamp's golden glow.

September brought relief. In her eighth grade classroom, hours passed without a thought of Bappa. Instead, she dreamed about Heinrich Dreher, a cute classmate whose cowlick, which fell over one eye, made her quiver. She never spoke to him. Oh, no! Watching him struggle to translate English in class or standing beside him for a moment at recess was sufficient.

One day as Teresa explained her failure to translate the Saint Anthony sermon again, Sister Rosina said, "You're sure it isn't your fondness for Heinrich that keeps you from your studies?"

Teresa quivered like a trapped rabbit. *How does Sister Rosina know? Can she see right inside me?*

After school, troubles escalated. Bappa seemed obsessed with pinching Teresa's breasts. He lay in wait for her, springing, grabbing a nipple, twisting it so hard she shrieked. How he infuriated her! When she refused to let him touch her, he beat her. His heavy blows felt worse than Mr. Urban's did because she could not change her behavior to protect herself.

Worse yet, Grandma could be right in the room and say nothing. She was no shield.

So Teresa holed up in her dark bedroom and continued to neglect her studies.

"Do you think they'll get rid of me?" she asked Fanny. "I don't know what to do."

Sometimes dancing by the river helped; sometimes it didn't.

Riddled by uncertainty, Teresa couldn't concentrate. As she became increasingly inattentive in school, Sister Rosina grew concerned but her support didn't flag. "You'll amount to something someday," she said. "I know you will."

Teresa dared to turn to no one, not even Sister Rosina who seemed to understand the girl's anguish, both physical and mental. She kept cautioning, "Teresa, be careful."

❧

Then Fanny died. He died instantly when Prince, one of the Bieker horses, kicked him, and Bappa laid the little dog's corpse at the river's edge. When Teresa heard, her legs wobbled, her heart pounded faster than her feet as she raced to the river. When she saw Fanny, as dull and heavy as a human corpse at a wake, she broke into a sweat.

"No! No!" She picked up his body and cradled him in her lap, blind to his caked blood smearing her good school dress.

After that, Teresa walked to the river every day to visit Fanny. She went because she couldn't imagine life without him. She sat by his still body, stroked his stiff hair, and talked. She didn't mind the stench of his decomposing body. Besides, if she sat upwind, fresh river air blew the odor away.

Day after day, as she always had, Teresa told Fanny everything: how she sidestepped Grandma's fast hand, what Sister Rosina told her, how Bappa beat her again, how her desire to dance had collapsed. Week after week, she talked to him. She talked to him until his bones crumbled, and she could no longer see what he had been.

~

In the spring of 1920, Teresa passed her final exams to complete her grade-school education, but no one came to see her graduate, not Bappa or Grandma, not Mr. Funk or Mr. Tillison. Angry, she moved in a vacuum, although she did experience a flush of happiness sitting on the platform with her classmates and Sister Rosina. She knew that Schoenchen residents considered finishing grammar school a major educational feat, one that few adults accomplished, so graduating proved her superior intelligence.

Eight students, four boys and four girls, graduated. Except for Teresa, all were Volga Germans: five Werths, one a Zimmerman, and one a Dreher but not Heinrich. He'd been held back again. The girls wore white dresses, but Teresa alone wore white stockings and shoes. The other girls wore more fashionable black stockings and shoes. *As usual, I'm an outsider.* Teresa's face tightened. A scowl pinched her brows.

At home, Teresa discovered that the Biekers didn't come to her graduation because Bappa's black rabbit escaped. Bappa caught it, but the incident kindled his temper, so Grandma felt reluctant to leave him alone. He was drunk, of course.

In her room, Teresa peeled off the ugly white stockings.

Later that week, her graduation photograph arrived showing the eighth-grade class in all its finery. The girls sat in the front row, their black and her white stockings and shoes in full view. How she hated the photo! Just looking at it reminded her of her inferiority. One day she tore it to bits.

⌒

Summer turned into a miserable time. All desire to dance left Teresa; reading became a chore. Few people, as usual, remained in town. At night, Teresa winced as she listened to the Biekers discuss what to do with her. They planned to find her a job, perhaps at Saint Anthony's Hospital in Hays, so she could bring them her salary. Teresa, however, wanted to continue her education, but she could not make them understand.

That fall Teresa did attend a brand-new high school in Schoenchen, but only for a short while. There she learned that United States women could now vote in the upcoming presidential election. That pleased her. She knew Volga Germans were dead set against women voting. She'd heard Bappa say, "Mark my word, they'll vote in strict Sunday laws and outlaw beer gardens."

However, high school soon palled. Teresa was so bright in grade school, but in high school, her mind blanked, probably from her concern about Bappa and her rising fear that the Biekers would give her away.

Finally, Grandma and Bappa agreed on a goal for Teresa: she would learn to cook and marry. As soon as possible. Grandma never taught Teresa to cook because she was so clumsy, but at fourteen, perhaps she could learn the fundamentals.

"They want to get rid of me, they do, or they wouldn't want to marry me off," Teresa whispered into her featherbed that night, talking to her imaginary mother.

Try not to be too discouraged, her mother counseled. Then matters suddenly deteriorated.

PART II:
"AMONG THE LOWEST OF THE LOW"

5

A WARD OF THE COURT

Teresa struggled to repress tears. Shame replaced the fear she felt when Sheriff Loreditch removed her from her home, when he put her on this train with these other dislocated Ellis County children—all five strangers. *We didn't work out.* A chill etched her bones. *We're going back to New York, like Albert.* She traced her fingertip along the back of her head where her hair had been shorn and her scalp stitched.

After the train pulled out, Teresa asked her freckled seatmate and the fair-haired boy in front of her where they were going, but neither knew. The farther the train traveled the more convinced Teresa became that she'd suffered Albert's fate. She slipped from her seat and walked down the aisle toward stout Kate Bissing, their escort. Teresa knew Mrs. Bissing had to work for the county because, gossip said, her filthy rich husband, old Judge Justus Bissing, had found greener pastures.

"You there!" Mrs. Bissing said. "Sit down."

But Teresa continued to grab seat backs and edge toward the plain-faced woman. "Please." Tears trickled down her cheeks. "Where are we going?"

"Go back to your seat."

"Just tell me the worst. Are we going to New York City? Please. I have to know."

"The only thing you have to know, Missy, is what I'm going to do if you don't sit down."

Mrs. Bissing's hand rose, so Teresa trudged back down the aisle, sat down, and covered her face, her shoulders shaking.

When the train stopped, Teresa looked out the window, expecting to see New York City's busy streets. Instead, a sign read "Abilene." They were still in Kansas, only about a hundred miles from Schoenchen, stopping to take on new passengers, Teresa supposed, but no. Mrs. Bissing marched up the aisle, sweeping the Hays children before her. When Teresa saw some Saint Joseph's nuns greet Mrs. Bissing, she nearly fainted with relief.

The nuns took Teresa and the other children to Saint Joseph's Orphanage. They toured the entire building, but the only thing Teresa noticed was a tall blond boy. Seeing him made her feel as weak as Heinrich Dreher had. When the nuns assigned her to the same dining room table as the boy, Gilbert, she saw he had a crooked smile and was about her age. Everyone else looked older or younger, mostly younger. Sitting across from Gilbert, watching him push his hair out of his eye ignited a strain of music in Teresa's mind, music good for dancing. Dancing! How long since she wanted to dance? She moved her feet in a box shape under the table and glanced at Gilbert, pretending to dance with him.

That night, the nuns took Teresa and the other new children to their second-floor sleeping quarters, a big open dormitory with the boys on one end, the girls on the other. To her surprise, the nuns gave her a nightgown. She hadn't slept in a nightgown since she was three. Grandma made fun of people so stuck up they slept in nightgowns. Since the dormitory had no private place to change, a nun showed Teresa how to put on her nightgown over her dress, and then take off her dress.

At 5 a.m., a nun clanged the wake-up bell. Teresa shivered as she dressed under the privacy of her nightgown. She looked for Gilbert, but the boys had gone. By six, everyone filed into the chapel for Mass, but the boys sat behind the girls, so Teresa couldn't see Gilbert. Resigned, she settled into her hard pew. Soon the customary Latin words of Mass enfolded her. Hearing those words nine times a week in Schoenchen had rendered them indelible. Even her memory of saying Hail Marys alongside the Biekers comforted her.

After Mass, Teresa walked down long narrow wooden stairs to a humid basement where she helped other girls hang damp clothes. The sheets, heavy with moisture and hanging like huge rectangles, reminded her of the Foundling laundry room. No wonder she loved to smell freshly washed clothes. She surreptitiously picked up a boy's shirt, pretended it was Gilbert's and buried her face in it.

After a blissful breakfast at the table with Gilbert, Teresa returned to the basement and ironed. Back and forth, back and forth, she pushed the heavy flat iron across the pillowcase, creating more wrinkles than she flattened. Maybe the heat from the iron, which seemed hotter than a wood-burning stove, or perhaps the strain of the past few days made her feel dizzy. Then the pillowcase turned black as she crumpled to the floor.

When Teresa woke, she lay in a small square room with two high windows opposite her bed. Late afternoon sun drifted through the panes. Beside her sat Sister Agneta, her face wrinkled as a prune. "Feeling better?" She stroked Teresa's forehead with a damp cloth. Teresa nodded, but she seemed to be floating.

"I'll come see you later." Sister Agneta placed a thin pamphlet on Teresa's chest. As Teresa dozed, the pamphlet slipped down by her ribs. When she woke, she grabbed the pamphlet just as it was about to slide off the bed.

The cover featured a nun who was dressed more somberly than the Saint Joseph nuns. She wore black except for a pointed white collar and some white stripes on her black bonnet. Her serene face gazed right at Teresa. *Why she could be my mother!* Teresa opened the pamphlet, entitled "Sister Irene," and read.

Sister Irene, co-founder of the New York Foundling Hospital.
(Courtesy of New York Foundling Hospital)

"Sister Irene, born into a prosperous New York family, was christened Catherine Fitzgibbon. By her late teens, Catherine had become quite a beauty."

"Quite a beauty?" Teresa looked at the photograph. She noticed the high round cheeks, the slender lips, the half smile, and the dark eyes. A deep blue, Teresa imagined. She dreamed

that she was Catherine, born into unimaginable wealth. How gorgeous she would look in a teal blue satin dress that brought out her blue eyes as she rode around New York City attending high teas. Still smiling, she dozed again.

Sister Agneta woke Teresa with supper. She tried to eat but finally pushed the soup, which she could barely swallow, aside and turned to the pamphlet. To her dismay, she read that an epidemic of cholera, a disease that had killed millions worldwide, swept through the city. The epidemic reminded her of the Spanish flu, of Pete and his horses. She shuddered, then continued:

"All Catherine's beauty and the riches of her family could not shield her from this awful disease. The cholera pulled Catherine into a coma, a coma so deep she could not move a muscle, not even to blink. When her breathing apparently stopped, her parents believed Catherine was dead, but she was not. She could still hear, and she listened to her parents and the undertaker plan her burial."

Teresa froze, pretending to be unable to move a muscle as she heard the Sisters plan to bury her. She lay so deep into her imagined trance that she jumped when Sister Agneta came in to remove her tray.

"Did I startle you? Sorry." The nun laid her tiny dry hand on Teresa's forehead. "Still quite cool," she said, "and damp." When she left with the tray, Teresa picked up the pamphlet again.

"Catherine lay helpless as hands removed her clothes, washed her skin, and dressed her body for burial. Desperate, she prayed for a divine act of mercy. The answer to her prayer came in the form of a vision of dozens of infants, pleading for her help. In response, Catherine dedicated her life to God and vowed to help the babies. As she did, her coma broke. The undertaker, about to close the coffin lid, saw her eyelid flutter and spared Catherine a terrible death."

Teresa froze again. Then she fluttered her eyelids and squinted until the window panes stared at her like square black eyes. Next to her, a lamp shed a pool of light on her bed. Then she shifted to her side and read.

"After she recovered, Catherine joined the Sisters of Charity of Saint Vincent de Paul and became Sister Mary Irene, to her family's dismay."

How upset her parents must have been when such a lovely daughter became a nun instead of the beautiful wife of some fine man and the mother of their grandchildren.

"After she became a nun, Sister Irene begged her superior, Mother Jerome, to let her care for abandoned infants, but Mother Jerome objected: 'What can we give them, poor as we are?' Finally, in November 1869, she relented and gave Sister Irene and three other nuns five dollars to open a home."

Five dollars to open a home! So little money. What could Sister Irene do?

"Someone donated a brownstone at 17 East Twelfth Street in Greenwich Village."

Ah, she had helpers.

"Sister Irene and the other nuns scrubbed the building, furnished it with barrels for tables and boxes for chairs, and spread straw on the floor for mattresses."

The same as in Schoenchen.

"On January 1, 1870, the nuns opened The Foundling Asylum of the Sisters of Charity of the City of New York, later called the New York Foundling Hospital, and finally, simply New York Foundling."

Startled, Teresa sat right up. The New York Foundling. Her orphanage. She was reading a history of how the Foundling began. She lay down and eagerly read:

"The rusty doorbell of the old brownstone rang as soon as the Foundling opened. An abandoned baby, the Foundling's first, lay on the stone stoop. 'Infants were left faster than cribs, clothing and nurses could be obtained for them,' the Foundling physician reported. That first year, the nuns rescued more than a thousand babies.

"Within months of opening, the Sisters moved to a larger building at 3 Washington Square. By 1873, backed by state money, the Sisters moved into new quarters at Sixty-eighth and Lexington, into five connected buildings."

Teresa turned the pamphlet sideways and examined a black-and-white sketch of the five buildings. Tiny people walked up and down the sidewalk in front of the buildings and little horses pulled carriages. High above the top turret of the tallest building waved an American flag. Teresa had few conscious memories of the Foundling, but she knew these buildings as well as she knew the Biekers' house. She saw the color of the brick, the green of the fenced hedge around the block. She could even smell the acrid odor that overwhelmed her whenever she entered the building. "Home. My first home." Unexpectedly she remembered Sister Teresa waving goodbye.

Weakened by her exertion, Teresa lay down and pretended to slip into a coma. Soon she slept and didn't hear the footsteps of nuns who dropped by her room during the night. When she woke, she reached for the pamphlet and devoured it as she waited for breakfast. Slowly she realized that, in an odd way, Sister Irene really was her mother, that she had been one of Sister Irene's babies, that her fate had been determined in Sister Irene's coma. Tears, seeping from the corners of Teresa's eyes, refused to stop. When she finally dried her eyes and opened them, the beauty of the quiet room rushed upon her and, for a moment, she felt loved.

As Teresa healed, she worked in the kitchen, whistling as she peeled potatoes or set the tables. A small, industrious nun, Sister Sebastian, who worked in the kitchen, cheered Teresa. From Germany, the nun called forks "fogs." As Teresa set the tables, Sister Sebastian would yell, "How about the fogs?"

One day the head nun asked to see Teresa. The girl sat in Sister Regis's office wondering what she had done. Late autumn sun poured like butter through the windows and onto Sister Regis's desk, brightening the papers she shuffled. At last, she pulled one to the top.

"Here we are," she said. "The Foundling has decided that you will no longer be known as Teresa Bieker."

What does she mean? Am I to become a nun?

"From now on, you will use your real father's name. You will be Teresa Feit."

The news rang in Teresa's heart like Saint Anthony's Easter bells. How she hated being a Bieker! She could scarcely grasp that this prize, which she believed never to win, was hers.

"Oh, thank you, thank you, thank you." She wanted to rush around the desk and hug Sister Regis, but the nun's flowing habit looked a bit too starched. "How can I ever repay you?"

"You don't owe us anything, Teresa." The nun rose. "Now go along. Aren't you supposed to be working in the kitchen?"

All the way to the kitchen, Teresa danced a little jig. Maybe she would bump into Gilbert so she could tell him her real name, but she didn't.

~

When Teresa healed enough to leave Saint Joseph's Orphanage, Sister Regis offered her two alternatives: to become a nun or a housekeeper. If Teresa chose "nun," she would go to the

Motherhouse for the Saint Joseph's nuns in Concordia, Kansas, where Sister Gertrude and Sister Rosina went every summer. If Teresa chose "housekeeper," she would go to nearby Salina, take care of the Geist children in their handsome home, and attend Sacred Heart High School.

Neither choice appealed to Teresa; she'd prayed every night to go back to Schoenchen, not to the Bieker home but on a big farm with lots of children. Strangely, she longed for her childhood home. Even that awful last day at the Biekers seemed vague. However, she wasn't being offered Schoenchen; she had to choose "nun" or "housekeeper."

Ever since Sister Gertrude held Teresa on her lap and placed a picture of the Virgin Mary in her hand, the girl had dreamed of becoming a nun. She developed an immense love for nuns, feeling secure in their presence. As a child, she'd spent hours wearing a towel over her head, pretending to be a Sister, but faced with the opportunity, Teresa hesitated. *These Abilene nuns don't really know me. They don't know what Bappa made me do. I'm not good enough to be a nun. Besides, if I become a nun, then Gilbert will never know that I love him.*

As matters now stood, Gilbert had no way of knowing. Although they ate at the same table, they never spoke, but twice he had smiled at her. Mostly Teresa just looked at him. If she became a nun, he would fade away until he was only a photograph she held in her heart.

If she went to Salina? Then she and Gilbert would somehow, magically, manage to get together, she felt certain. Besides, living in a handsome house appealed to her, as did the idea of returning to school. So Teresa chose Salina.

After she had chosen, she wondered if she'd made the right decision. She waited after a meal to confide in Sister Nolaska, a tall, good-looking nun, head cook in the orphanage kitchen.

"I probably shouldn't feel this way," Teresa said as the cook prepared some beans to soak. "I know it isn't proper, and certainly not for a nun." She quietly revealed a tiny fragment of her passion for Gilbert.

"Let me show you something." Sister Nolaska strode out of the building with Teresa behind her. Fresh air slapped Teresa's face; she could feel winter looming. The nun led Teresa to a barn behind the main building and slid open the door. In a corner sat a dozen dust-covered trunks, some quite old.

"We keep our things here," she said. "Each of us has a trunk."

Sister Nolaska wrestled her trunk out, used a tiny key on a chain to open its lock, and flung open the lid.

"I keep a few civilian clothes down here."

She pulled up the top tray to reveal neatly folded clothes, some flowered.

"But what I want to show you is up here."

She lifted a pile of photographs, some in paper folders, and sifted through them.

"Family, you know." She showed Teresa a group of people waiting stiffly for the photographer to shoot.

"Oh, here, here he is!" She handed Teresa a picture of a nicely groomed young man, well dressed. "Do you know who this is?"

"Your brother?"

"No, Teresa. This is the man I almost married before I became a nun. My Gilbert."

Teresa gasped. "How old were you?"

"Fourteen."

"Just my age." She watched Sister Nolaska dust off the photo with the sleeve of her habit and place it in the trunk.

So I'm not the only one who likes the boys. If she could be a nun, then so could I.

The idea of living in the Concordia Motherhouse where Sister Rosina and Sister Gertrude spent their summers seemed more appealing than before, but now she couldn't go. The nuns had already promised her to Mrs. Geist in Salina.

❧

The Geist house resembled a palace. Brand-new modern furniture on loan from the Geist Furniture Store, nothing nicked or marred, filled the rooms. Such luxury made Teresa feel small.

Mrs. Geist, an energetic woman, swept Teresa through the rooms, explaining her duties. They rushed from the master bedroom with its huge canopied bed into a small dark adjacent room. Mrs. Geist touched the wall and light filled the room. Teresa gasped. *How did she do that?*

"I want these fixtures spotless, especially the commode." Mrs. Geist touched the wall again and plunged the room into darkness. She wheeled out before Teresa knew which fixture was the commode, whatever that was. The girl reached out and touched the wall, but nothing happened. *It must be magic.* She shivered.

The two barreled down the curving staircase.

"Here's the kitchen—obviously!" Mrs. Geist laughed. "You must watch out for that stove." She pointed to a square metal box totally unlike any stove Teresa knew. "Be sure to shut it off properly. If you don't, the fumes could kill us all."

Later, alone, Teresa returned to the shiny kitchen and examined the ogre stove. She opened the big door in the front, but found no wood or ashes inside. She looked outdoors, but wood was stacked nowhere. She might never have figured out how to light the stove if she hadn't seen a friend of Mrs. Geist turn it on with a match. When the fire started with a whoosh, she jumped and stared at the flames.

What made the fire burn? Mrs. Geist had said, "Gas," but Teresa didn't see any gas. *More magic.*

Later, Teresa tried lighting the burner but nothing happened. When she tried again, fire flared and frightened her, so she dropped the match and fled. When she returned, flames burned merrily in a circle. Was that right? The stove hadn't boomed when Mrs. Geist's friend lit it. Teresa agonized. What if she killed somebody? Her anxiety escalated.

The next day, she entered Salina High School, an activity she anticipated, but the school was huge—five times bigger than Schoenchen High was.

Inside, Teresa stood uneasily by the door until a teacher led her to the school office. Then she trudged to her classes. Each new class meant a new teacher and new bunch of student faces. How would she ever remember where to go?

In her last class, the teacher discussed rivals, defining the word, and reading examples of usage. Unexpectedly the boy in front of her turned, grinned, and said: "You have rivals."

What does he mean, I have rivals? For his favors? He doesn't even know me.

At the end of class, she waited until the boy moved away in a cluster of students. Then she picked up her books, only to watch them cascade to the floor. She wiped her clammy hands on her skirt and longed to be back in Schoenchen High, where she knew everyone, where life wasn't so complicated.

The Geist children, aged three and five, were so cute Teresa expected to like them, but she didn't. They had more toys than she had ever seen, but each wanted the toy that the other one held. The children fought like little animals, leaving scratch marks on Teresa's arm when she broke them up. And she found washing diapers repugnant. She longed for the familiarity of the Bieker home, a place she'd once scorned, but at least there she knew how to behave.

Two days later, Teresa stood at the stove again. She had to light it to heat water to warm the baby's milk, but after she turned on the gas, she took too long to light the match, and the stove lit with a frightening whooooom. Her heart was still pounding when she sensed that someone was watching her. She turned. There in the kitchen doorway stood Bappa, his shoulders stooped, his Sunday-go-to-church jacket sleeves long on his wrists.

"Goodness!" She felt more relieved than frightened at seeing him. "What are you doing here?"

"I've come to take you back to Schoenchen," he said. "The young people in your class want you back."

Teresa had to laugh at the idea that her classmates wanted her back, but she didn't hesitate at this opportunity to leave Salina. Quickly she gathered her few belongings. *Bappa won't hurt me again. Ripping my hair off was an accident, like his shooting at me. He didn't mean it.* Shortly, without goodbyes, she walked out of the Geist home, leaving the children alone and gas burning on the stove.

To Teresa's surprise, Sheriff Loreditch met her and Bappa on the train platform in Hays and took her away again. In his office, the sheriff barked, "Why did you come back after we took all that trouble to take you to Abilene and after others found you a good home in Salina?"

Teresa cringed. She knew the sheriff must think her behavior deplorable. How could she have come back indeed? She had no ready reply. When she glanced up, the sheriff seemed menacingly large, and she didn't think he'd understand how frightened she was of Mrs. Geist's modern house or how relieved she'd been to see Bappa and know she could go home. No matter what Bappa had done to her, she had never known any home but the Biekers'.

The sheriff brought Teresa before Judge John B. Gross, probate judge in Hays, who declared her a ward of the court. As a ward of the court, Teresa had to report to Judge Gross, Sheriff Loreditch, and Father Bernadine. Until she turned eighteen, she had to report to the Foundling. When she attended Girls' Catholic High, she also would report to Sister Remigia there, but primarily she reported to Judge Gross. Unfortunately.

Mrs. Spallen of the Foundling arranged for Teresa to live at Judge Gross's home until she could find a domestic job that paid room and board. Mrs. Gross showed Teresa to the second-floor guest room, and, after his wife left the house, the judge, his stern face softened, led Teresa to his bedroom. She watched him turn back the patchwork quilt, revealing clean white sheets.

"Here, you don't need so many clothes on."

After the judge disrobed Teresa, he took her to bed, fondling her and kissing her all over. She lay petrified. *Here I am in his care, and he's doing worse to me than was done before. At least Bappa never undressed me and took me to his bed.*

So frightened that she scarcely breathed, Teresa found herself high in the corner of the bedroom, caught like a spider clinging to a gossamer web, gazing down on what the judge was doing to her, and to himself, as though she were a spectator in the top row of a large stadium looking at a strange game.

When the judge finished, Teresa grabbed her clothes and scampered down the hall to the guest room. *Thank God his wife didn't come back! If she had, he'd say it's all my fault.*

Who could she tell? No one. Not even Mrs. Spallen would believe her. Teresa could scarcely believe it herself, but what could she do? She didn't dare cry out, not knowing who might hear her. She couldn't protest to the judge. He wasn't cruel like Bappa; he hadn't struck her, but he didn't have to. One word from him would send her to reform school.

Judge Gross's caresses coupled with Teresa's fear propelled the girl to find a domestic job that paid room and board so she could leave. Every day after school, she visited prospective homes, but her diminutive size worked against her. Although full grown, Teresa stood only four feet, eleven inches tall and weighed just ninety pounds. Many potential employers didn't believe she could handle domestic work. She looked too "English."

As days passed and the judge's passion persisted, Teresa feared she'd never find work. *Why didn't I stay in Salina? The work was okay, and I would have learned how to light the stove by now. Why oh why did I let Bappa bring me to Hays?*

Then Dr. A.D. Herman's family hired her as a part-time housekeeper, leaving her mornings free to attend Girls' Catholic High. She tossed her clothes into a bundle and raced to the doctor's house, determined to work diligently for Mrs. Herman, even though Teresa knew that she was clumsy.

"Remember," brusque Mrs. Herman said, "this is the home of a doctor. It must be more than clean; it must be immaculate."

During that first week, Mrs. Herman repeatedly explained what she wanted, especially how to clean the bathroom, and particularly the commode. By now, Teresa knew what a commode was, but no matter how she scoured, she never got it "immaculate." She marveled when Mrs. Herman inspected the bathroom and found dirty spots on white porcelain that Teresa had just cleaned.

By the end of ten days, Teresa hated getting on her hands and knees to clean the floors or standing on a stool to polish the tops of furniture that no one would see, but she especially hated cleaning the commode. On Saturday, the day before her first day off, she hurried through her hateful tasks, hoping her efforts would be good enough.

What a relief it was on Sunday to leave the Herman's house! Just stepping outdoors made her giddy. The autumn day was glorious, a crisp pungent sunny day.

After she strolled around downtown, Teresa attended morning services at St. Joseph's, an enormous cathedral. There she met Euphersine Staab, a new friend from school. Euphersine, a tall gangling girl, seemed spinsterish except for her sharp sense of humor. Her intense devotion to Catholicism made her kind-hearted; a senior, she didn't mind that Teresa was only a freshman.

That afternoon, they walked the streets, kicking brown leaves heaped in gutters. Then they sat side-by-side on Euphersine's front steps and laughed a lot, until Teresa finally tore herself away to return to the Hermans' house.

As she climbed the front steps, she noticed her cloth satchel sitting next to the front door. *That's strange.* Inside her clothes lay neatly folded. *What does this mean?* Gingerly she opened the front door.

Mrs. Herman seemed to be waiting for her. "I don't want you." She waved Teresa away. "I want someone who can wash and shine the bathroom until it's immaculate."

Shattered, Teresa sat on Mrs. Herman's front steps. She had expected to eat supper with the Hermans, but she could skip a meal. She wished she didn't have to return to Judge Gross's house, but she had nowhere else to go. Eventually she picked up her satchel and started down the street, walking randomly. When the evening turned chilly, she pulled a shawl from her bag and wrapped it around her shoulders. She wished she could stay out all night, but she dared not arrive at the judge's house too late.

The Grosses' petulance at Teresa's return matched her reluctance at being there. How she wished that she'd gone to Concordia and become a nun! No one would touch her there. How foolish of her not to go, even if it meant losing her curly locks. And Gilbert. Where was Gilbert now?

The next day Teresa searched out Euphersine and described her bad luck.

"I know just the person," Euphersine said. "She has seven kids; she'll need help."

When classes ended, Euphersine took Teresa to visit Mrs. Denning. As they approached the Denning house, they heard spirited singing. Soon Teresa saw a corpulent woman dancing on the Dennings' front porch with a broom. As she danced, she sang, with a good deal of verve, "If only I'd died in my cradle."

Dancing in broad daylight instead of scrubbing floors? Teresa didn't know what to think of such behavior, so unlike Volga German ways, but her hopes skyrocketed. Wouldn't she love to work for a woman who sang and danced?

Mrs. Denning listened to Euphersine's plea, but she hesitated to hire Teresa. "I'll have to think about it," she said.

After the girls left, Teresa said, "That's what they all say. She won't hire me. I'm too English."

However, the next day, Mrs. Denning offered Teresa a part-time job in exchange for room and board. "You can wash socks, diapers, and dishes," she said, "help with meals, and go to Girls' Catholic High in the mornings." So Teresa moved in with the Dennings, their seven children and their big black dog.

Mrs. Denning's home seemed like utopia after Mrs. Herman's immaculate commode. Her new employer did not keep a spotless house. Teresa expected she'd have to clean the children's dirty hand prints that smeared the Dennings' walls, but Mrs. Denning never asked her to scrub walls or polish furniture or do any house cleaning chores. Even the dishes didn't have to be washed immaculately. The worst chore was cleaning dozens of odious diapers.

Mrs. Denning amused Teresa with tales of pranks she'd pulled and sometimes they danced. However, the two Denning boys near Teresa's age were ornery. They bullied her into standing on a chair so the smaller boy could stand on her shoulders and snitch their father's tobacco hidden high on a pantry shelf.

Sometimes Judge Gross telephoned for Teresa to visit. Usually she grit her teeth and went, but once she didn't.

"You'd better go," Mrs. Denning said. "You could get into trouble if you don't do what he says."

However, Teresa knew that going to the judge's house would result in trouble of another kind.

The next day, Teresa told Euphersine that going to Judge Gross's house scared her.

"Tell me the next time he calls," Euphersine said. "I'll go with you."

So when Judge Gross called in late November, Teresa stopped by Euphersine's house and the two picked their way through freshly fallen snow to the judge's porch. The judge seemed surprised to see Euphersine, but he invited the two girls inside. They diligently wiped their shoes. As Teresa expected, Mrs. Gross was nowhere to be seen.

"So who is this?" the judge said.

"My friend, Euphersine Staab. We're on our way to a movie." That was a lie, but only a white one.

The judge asked a few routine questions, and then dismissed them.

"That didn't seem so scary," Euphersine said as they left.

"He's not so polite when we're alone." Teresa slid on a sheet of ice, her arms wobbling to keep her balance.

"Oh." Euphersine slid, too.

Judge Gross didn't call again until January, when she went to his office and answered a few questions for his annual Foundling report. Euphersine went with her. The judge commended Teresa on her excellent first-semester high school grades. Then his calls ceased.

6

"LITTLE ORPHAN ANNIE"

When school ended that spring, Mrs. Denning said, "The kids can help me during the summer," and she let Teresa go. But she told her Volga German friends, the Dreilings, about Teresa, and that June she moved to the Dreiling farm north of Hays. There she milked seven Holstein cows, mornings and nights, helped Mrs. Dreiling with housework and cared for their seven children. Constantly busy, Teresa didn't mind the work except for the mountains of nasty diapers.

The Dreilings loved to party. "You don't mind watching the children, do you?" Mrs. Dreiling said. "You'll be staying home anyway." Teresa agreed, and night after night, especially on weekends, she watched Mr. and Mrs. Dreiling gulp their supper and leave, often returning after midnight.

On one of these nights, Teresa heard two older boys playing with the Victrola in the gloomy parlor. Before she could go keep the boys from scratching a record, she heard an awful crash. She ran to the parlor door to see Richie and Bill picking records up off the carpeted floor and piling them on a table. The boys were too busy to notice Teresa.

"Oh, no, we broke one." Bill held two shiny black pieces.

"Here, put it in the middle. Maybe they won't notice it."

Bill laid the pieces together so they looked like a single record. "But what if they find it?"

Richie laughed, "We'll tell them Teresa broke it."

Teresa slipped away from the door. She had to nip this, but how? She was folding diapers when she decided what to do.

After Richie and Bill went to bed, Teresa grabbed a sheet and sneaked out of the house. The night was cool and a three-quarters moon illuminated the road that ran near the boys' bedroom. *Perfect.* She draped the sheet over her body and danced, moving so the sheet seemed alive.

"Oooooh, ooooooh," she called louder and louder, until the boys' screams burst through the window. Then she ran, still calling, to the back door where she threw the sheet under the porch. She rushed into the boys' bedroom, pretending to be irritated, and said, "What's wrong with you?"

The boys stood squished together in a corner by their bed. "We saw a ghost," Richie said.

"Oh posh and bother," Teresa said. "You saw no such thing."

"No, really," Bill said. "It ran down the road and disappeared."

"Come, now, get back in bed." Teresa pulled the blanket over the boys. "Maybe that ghost came looking for you because of the lie you plan to tell."

"What lie?" Richie sat upright, his tousled hair a crown of fur.

"That I broke those records."

"Are you going to tell?"

"No." Teresa smoothed the covers. "But if you tell your folks I broke that record, I'm sure the ghost will come back to haunt you."

To Teresa's relief, her ruse worked.

The weather turned unseasonably cool that August. Teresa nearly froze as she sat on the Dreilings' front stoop, shivering and wondering if she would ever return to Girls' Catholic High in Hays. She used to believe her eighth-grade education made her "learned," but reading newspapers and listening to her high-school teachers revealed her ignorance. Much as she wanted to return to high school, Teresa didn't know how to part company with the Dreilings. She had never quit a job.

Day after depressing day passed until finally, after working there six months, she woke one November morning, packed her clothes in a bundle, and slipped out a side door. Only four miles north of Hays, she could walk to town if the Dreilings didn't catch her. She rubbed her chilly hands, grateful when a neighbor stopped and drove her into town.

School had started several months ago, so she couldn't attend, but she expected to find an employer who would let her go to school next semester. This proved difficult. Although quite a few people wanted to hire her for room and board, no one promised her time off for school. At last, she turned to Father Julius, head of the local Capuchin order, who sent her to Mrs. Rupp, a widow suffering from ill health. However, Mrs. Rupp, like the others, offered only room and board.

Teresa gave up. She moved into Mrs. Rupp's house.

From the beginning, this job lay on her heart like a block of ice. She spent her days sweeping, mopping, scrubbing, polishing—all activities she hated. When Mrs. Rupp inspected her work, she'd sniff and say, "Tibbie could do it better." Tibbie was her nickname for her slightly retarded son, Tibalt, who cleaned houses professionally. Still, Mrs. Rupp didn't make her repeat her work the way Mrs. Herman had.

One benefit was Mrs. Rupp's radio—or wireless telephone, as some called it. Radios were a novelty in Hays in 1922; Mrs. Rupp's radio was the first Teresa heard. She loved it. When it poured out dance music, she had to shake a leg until Mrs. Rupp forbade dancing. Sometimes they listened to Dr. John R. Brinkley, who made millions implanting goat testes into men to increase their sexual vigor. He spoke twice a day. Mrs. Rupp, who hated him, dubbed him "goat man." Whenever she heard his voice, she hit the radio, which amused Teresa.

The radio's pleasures didn't offset Teresa's discomfort around Mrs. Rupp's slow son, Tibbie, who sometimes looked at her the way Bappa did. Tibbie kept asking Teresa to marry him and, worse yet, Mrs. Rupp kept saying she should.

When the weather warmed, Teresa went out in the afternoons to meet a new friend, Irene. One day she complained about her lack of dates to Irene. They decided that Teresa needed to look more popular, so Irene fetched two men, youngsters, really, and the four paraded in front of Mrs. Rupp's house, talking and laughing. Once Teresa saw a curtain twitch in the front window and knew Mrs. Rupp must be spying on them. *What must she think? Such a straight old woman, set in her ways. She'd never do something like this.*

A week later, Teresa met Mrs. Howard Brown, a pretty little woman who struggled to keep her three young children in line while she pushed her baby in a buggy. Teresa helped her. Soon they sat on a park bench talking and taking turns bouncing the baby. When Mrs. Brown learned that Teresa had minded seven Dreiling children, she said, "Oh, I wish you'd work for me. I do so need help with the children. If you do, I'd pay you $4 a week plus room and board."

Four dollars! Such largesse astounded Teresa, who had yet to earn a penny. Besides, she liked this tiny brunette with the high thin voice, so she agreed. She didn't tell Mrs. Brown about Mrs. Rupp, and she didn't tell Mrs. Rupp that she was leaving. Abandoning her clothes, she worked for Mrs. Brown.

Mrs. Brown complained a lot about her "worthless" husband. Often out of town, Howard, a sales agent, provided so poorly for his wife and four children that Mrs. Brown couldn't pay Teresa.

"I'm so sorry." She twisted her hair. "If only he would apply himself … "

Teresa didn't care. She liked working for Mrs. Brown who treated her like family, at least when Howard was away, which was most of the time. Teresa enjoyed minding the children, and she saw that Mrs. Brown did need help. Taking care of four lively children left Teresa little time for housework, which suited her fine. She did have to wash loathsome diapers, but that seemed better than working for Mrs. Rupp, so Teresa stayed. She knew she should return to Mrs. Rupp, inform her of the change, and pick up her belongings, but fearing trouble, she didn't go.

Then one bright June day trouble found her.

As Teresa and Mrs. Brown chatted and sorted clothes, someone knocked. Teresa ignored the dirty clothes strewn around the living room and opened the door. There stood her agent, Mrs. Spallen, on her annual visit from the Foundling.

Mrs. Spallen stepped into the living room, but she didn't smile and hug Teresa. "I stopped at Mrs. Rupp's, looking for you," she said.

Teresa cringed.

"Mrs. Rupp said someone told her you've been going to the Methodist church."

Teresa froze. Unless a dire emergency, such as a funeral, justified it, attending a Protestant church was a Catholic sin.

Maybe Mrs. Rupp told Mrs. Spallen that the Browns weren't Catholic, but why would her agent think Teresa went to the Browns' church?

"Oh, my!" she cried. "I would never, ever go to a Protestant church. I've never been to a Protestant church in my life, and I'll never go to one." She winced as she glanced at Mrs. Brown. What must she think to hear Teresa speak so heatedly against Protestant churches? But she dared not have Mrs. Spallen turn against her.

Next Mrs. Spallen, still solemn, removed a bungalow apron from her satchel. "Mrs. Rupp told me this was yours. She said you took it off for someone so you could give him sexual favors."

"Let me see it." Teresa took the bungalow apron, a tent-like cotton garment similar to a housecoat with scooped neck, sleeves, and belt. When she unfurled it, it spread out as big as a blanket, so Mrs. Spallen saw it was much too large to fit her. Teresa believed she knew why Mrs. Rupp accused her. She remembered when she, Irene, and their presumed boyfriends paraded in front of the Rupp house. She knew Mrs. Rupp had watched them and no doubt surmised that Teresa was a "loose" woman.

After Mrs. Spallen heard how Mrs. Rupp wanted Teresa to marry her retarded son, she relaxed and arranged to move the girl's few possessions to Mrs. Brown's home.

Before she left, the agent stepped outside with Teresa and said, "I think you should know that when you were an infant, someone paid your keep at the Foundling for fourteen months."

Paid her keep! For more than a year! A chill careened down her spine. Then she hadn't been discarded like a piece of bad luck. Someone—surely her mother—actually cared for her.

"Did she come every month to see me?" Teresa said. "Where did she get her money? Was she working somewhere like me?"

"I don't know. All I know is that someone paid your keep. Sister Teresa told me. You were one of her favorites, you know."

Teresa tucked Mrs. Spallen's words away as a bride preserves a piece of wedding cake. She always felt her mother loved her, but the agent's words solidified that belief. Precious, they illuminated her past. This was all Teresa knew about her family except, of course, that her mother had given her to the Foundling.

~

Near the end of August, someone inside Byers upscale clothing store rapped on the window as Teresa walked past. She looked up to see a woman in an up-to-date suit motioning her inside. Surprised, Teresa entered the store where the smartly dressed woman, Mrs. Combs, called Teresa by name and took her to the bathroom.

"Why would a cute girl like you use all this makeup?" She washed Teresa's face. "You don't need it. It only distorts you. There." She patted Teresa's cheeks with a towel. "See how pretty you look?"

Teresa glanced at the mirror. It confirmed that she didn't look a bit pretty—her nose was too big and her forehead too high—but she smiled as though she agreed.

"You do housework for Mrs. Brown, don't you?" Mrs. Combs plucked the rats out of Teresa's hair.

Teresa nodded.

"How would you like to work for my husband and me instead?" Mrs. Combs combed Teresa's curls lock by lock, turning each one around her finger and gently disentangling snarls. "Our housework isn't difficult, and we need someone to keep our daughter, Ruth, company in the evenings while Jack and I work in the store. We don't like to leave her alone at night. You'd like Ruth. She's about your age."

Mrs. Combs flounced Teresa's curls on either side of her face.

"There. Don't you look much nicer? You don't need those rats, you have such beautiful hair. So black and curly. I wish I had your curls." Mrs. Combs styled her straight hair in a bob. "But what do you think? Would you like to work for us? We could pay you room and board, and I'll buy you some new clothes."

New clothes! Teresa had long wished to dress in style, and Mrs. Combs certainly seemed to be the woman who could help her. Then, too, chumming with someone her age appealed to her. It was bound to be more fun than washing diapers for the Brown children. So she agreed.

She returned to the Browns unnerved about telling her employer. Upstairs, she packed her clothes in her satchel as she had when she slipped out on the Dreilings. For a moment, she considered slipping out on Mrs. Brown, but she liked Mrs. Brown; she couldn't just ditch her.

Teresa found her employer in the kitchen peeling potatoes. "Oh good, you're back," she said. Then her eyes fell on Teresa's bundle.

"Actually, I'm just leaving."

A long brown potato skin spiraled to the floor. Davey, the youngest, picked it up and played with it. Mrs. Brown didn't stop him.

"I'm going to work for the Combses."

Mrs. Brown twisted her hair. "It's money, isn't it. They're paying you, and Howard makes so little, I don't have anything to give you. If only he had more ambition! I keep telling him … "

"No, it isn't the money." Teresa decided not to mention the clothes. "But the job will be easier. The Combses have only one child, a daughter." No need to say how old.

"So it's the children." Mrs. Brown looked down. "Oh, Davey, don't eat that dirty old potato skin." She yanked it out of his mouth, and then looked up. "Well, go, if you have to go. Go!"

So Teresa moved in with the Combses, an "upper crust" family whose manner of living fascinated her. The Combses not only ate with knives and forks, but they also placed them just so on either side of the dinner plate. They spoke politely, saying "Please" and "Thank you" to each other. They even owned a player piano where Ruth and Teresa pedaled favorites like "Barney Google" and "I Want to Be Happy." And they wore nightclothes to bed, even Mr. Combs. Teresa could imagine what Bappa would say about that.

Being a companion to Ruth satisfied Teresa. Ruth was shy, but Teresa's tales of life as an "Orphan Annie" drew her out until they laughed and fell against each other on the sofa like any two teenagers. When she wasn't entertaining Ruth, Teresa struggled with the dreadful housework. Mrs. Combs, to Teresa's relief, found her work good enough. In return, she received a smart-looking frock—from Byers, of course. As she had hoped, Mrs. Combs chose an up-to-date style that flattered Teresa. Best of all, the Combses encouraged her to return to school.

In January, at Mrs. Combs's insistence, Teresa enrolled in a Hays public high school, not her beloved private Girls' Catholic High. Studying with boys seemed strange, but she reveled in resuming her education. Teresa was older than Ruth, but they attended some of the same classes since Teresa's education had been interrupted. At night, after supper, around the dining room table, the two girls compared their homework.

Then late in February, someone knocked on Teresa's door as she got ready for bed.

"May I come in?" Ruth called.

Teresa, dressed in her nightgown, ran to the door. Ruth stood there, her face ashen.

"Ruth! What is it?" Teresa pulled her into the bedroom. "You look like you've seen a ghost."

"Worse than that." Ruth collapsed on the bed. "Oh, Teresa, Mums and Pop lost their jobs."

Teresa tried hard to occupy Ruth so she wouldn't dwell on her parents' plight. Before a week passed, Mr. Combs announced at the dinner table that they had decided to move to Wichita where jobs were plentiful.

"Won't you come with us?" Mrs. Combs laid her hand on top of Teresa's. "You and Ruth get along so well. And who knows, we might even be able to place you in a nursing school."

But Teresa, afraid of moving hundreds of miles away to a town even bigger than Salina, turned the Combses down.

Before they left, Mrs. Combs arranged with a friend, Twyla Brown, to hire Teresa. This Mrs. Brown, the second one to employ her, was as upper crust as the Combses. These Browns, a middle-aged couple, had been married only a few months. The wife reminded Teresa of Mrs. Rupp; she was fussy about housekeeping but not a stickler. Unfortunately, she didn't allow Teresa to go to school, not even half days. Without school or children to tend, Teresa had nothing to do but housework.

Teresa disliked Mrs. Brown. She was a snob, maybe because her mother taught at the local college, or maybe because Mrs. Brown herself had earned a master's degree in domestic science from the University of Kansas. She was so proud of that degree! When the family ate, she lectured about the food's scientific part, describing how food changes when cooked.

Once Mrs. Brown found Teresa in the basement talking to a man who came to repair the furnace. "Teresa," Mrs. Brown called. "Come upstairs." When Teresa did, her employer said, in a hushed voice, "We do not talk with people who fix furnaces."

Another time, after Teresa cut her finger, Mrs. Brown opened the wound and washed it each morning. Eventually, the wound healed, but Teresa couldn't understand why Mrs. Brown had to work on that finger so diligently. Perhaps she believed that the wound, like food, could be transformed by an external force.

One Sunday that spring, Irene, Teresa's friend, introduced Teresa to an odd-looking fellow, Jess Binder. He held his head to one side, the result of diving into some mud at a swimming hole. His friends, trying to pull him out, twisted his spine and broke his neck, nearly paralyzing him.

Jess seemed to like Teresa, and afterwards Irene teased, "Ooooo, I saw you making eyes at him. You better watch out for him. He jazzes."

"Jazzes!" Teresa's ears perked at the word; she knew it meant sexual intercourse. *Just as well I don't have a crush on him.*

Teresa didn't know what to make of Jess. He did look strange, but he couldn't help that. He seemed friendly, despite his dirty mouth. She'd never heard a person use so much profanity, but he was a Binder, and the Binders had such a reputation for being hot heads. But Jess had a steady job; he drove a truck. And jazzed. Teresa decided to write him off.

A few days later, Jess grabbed her arm as she walked up Chestnut Street and said, "Hey, why the devil did you tell Ida I got the clap?" Ida Binder was a sister-in-law.

Teresa froze. "I told Ida no such thing." She didn't know what clap meant, but from Jess's tone, something bad. She shook off his hand and kept walking.

"Bullshit! That's not what she says." He grabbed Teresa's arm again and stopped her. "That bitch says you told her I got a dose."

Dose? That made no sense either, but Teresa didn't want to look green. "Oh that Ida! She must have a screw loose. I never said anything like that." She shook free again.

Jess's face looked like a thundercloud. "You frigging expect me to believe you?"

"Why not? I'm telling the truth." Teresa, a bit frightened, cried.

"Oh, Christ, don't do that." Jess pushed his hands in and out of his pockets. "I don't have a frigging handkerchief."

"That's all right," Teresa said as she used the back of her hand to wipe her tears away.

"Come on. I'll walk you home."

That seemed safe enough, so they walked down the street, Teresa a respectable distance from Jess's side.

To her disgust, a few days later Jess told her that Ida was joking about Teresa saying Jess had a dose. *Just like that Binder bunch.*

By that time Irene, now a senior in high school, explained what clap and dose meant.

Early that October, F.P. Mandeville, the popular football coach at Kansas State Teachers College in Hays, asked Teresa to live with him and his wife and care for their little daughter. When he told Teresa she could go to high school, she left the snobbish Browns. The Mandevilles proved to be as upper crust as the Browns and the Combses combined.

Mrs. Mandeville, who called most people "commoners," came from "high society." A commoner was anyone she deemed beneath her, including her husband. When Mr. Mandeville, an Oklahoma boy, attended Kansas University, he washed dishes and played football to earn his way. He was a KU football hero when the two met, and Mrs. Mandeville was the beautiful daughter of a wealthy Kansas City family.

When she was not in school, Teresa spent most of her time minding little Peggy Jane, only a year-and-a-half. Both

Mandevilles doted on their daughter, a picture-perfect blonde who took after her gorgeous mother. Teresa also helped cook, washed dishes, and fired up the furnace every morning before the family rose. Mrs. Mandeville rarely asked her to help with housework, so the only part of the job Teresa disliked was washing the revolting diapers.

Teresa (right) with her little blonde charge, Peggy Jane Mandeville.
(Courtesy of Teresa Martin)

Many people dropped by the Mandevilles. They liked and trusted Coach Mandeville, or "Mandy," as his fans called him, and he clearly loved and spoiled his wife. Mrs. Mandeville fascinated Teresa, especially the way the woman went to the beauty parlor to prepare for faculty wives' meetings. Afterward, Teresa lingered to hear Mrs. Mandeville describe the meeting, certain that belonging to the faculty wives' club must be heaven.

One night when Mrs. Mandeville was out of town, Teresa slipped into the living room where Mr. Mandeville sprawled in his favorite chair, the only one in the house big enough to hold him comfortably. She wanted to call Jess and see if he'd like to go to the band concert with her and Irene. She and Jess were friends. They didn't exactly date, but he was often at her side when she and Irene hung out with his crowd.

She cleared her throat, "May I use the phone to call Jess?"

Mr. Mandeville looked up from his newspaper, a toothpick hanging from his lips. Removing it, he rolled his eyes and asked her, in the slang of the day, if Jess was her boy friend: "This Jess, is he your sweet green onion top?"

Teresa froze. She knew what rolling eyes meant. *Here it comes. He will want to grab me.* But Mr. Mandeville didn't. Instead, he looked at Teresa strangely for a moment and nodded at the telephone, "Go ahead." Then he plopped his toothpick back in his mouth, a habit Mrs. Mandeville couldn't break, shook out the newspaper, and resumed reading.

Teresa studied Mr. Mandeville for days, but he never bothered her. Weeks went by, but still he didn't pursue her. Gradually she learned to trust him, although she didn't trust many men.

Now a sophomore, Teresa attended Hays High half days and performed well in all her classes except geometry. She simply couldn't figure out those triangles. "When it comes to angles," she told Irene, "I'm definitely obtuse."

That year, students voted Teresa the second prettiest girl in the school.

Soon after the announcement, Teresa spotted Agnes striding across the lawn, headed right toward her. Agnes, a trim, tall girl, expected to win, but she didn't place in the top three. Teresa wasn't surprised. Agnes was too tall and willowy to be a serious candidate in a school where boys were crazy about little girls. The boys considered "cute" only girls who measured five foot two or less. Indeed, the girl who won, short with curly hair, looked a lot like Teresa.

Agnes, frowning, stopped in front of Teresa. "None of the girls voted for you. You're small and your hair's curly, but if the boys looked at your face, they'd see you're not pretty."

Teresa agreed. She couldn't understand why anyone voted for her. She didn't mix with students, she never had time for school socials, and, except for the dress Mrs. Combs bought her, she didn't wear stylish clothes. So she smiled and shrugged, "Maybe you're right."

In May, three years after she completed her first year of high school, Teresa finished her sophomore year. She earned good grades, in part because she dropped that pesky geometry course. She wanted to stay with the Mandevilles, but she needed money, especially for clothes, so when Mrs. West of West Dairy Farm offered her $7 a week plus room and board for helping in the dairy, she accepted.

That June, Mrs. West drove Teresa one mile east of Hays to the dairy farm. Within days, Teresa saw that the work wasn't taxing. She loved the furry brownness of the cows, their warmth, and the way their jutting pelvic bones shaped their skin. She noticed that Mr. West, a meek man with snow-white hair, seemed content to let his wife run the farm, which she certainly did.

The only problem Teresa encountered was Udolf, Mrs. West's repulsive-looking brother who worked there. Udolf seemed smitten with Teresa. He pestered her from the time she left her room until she went back. He followed her so closely she had to hurry and slam the door to her room or he would come right inside.

Finally, Teresa spoke to Mrs. West. "Can't you tell your brother to stay away from me? He frightens me, the way he follows me everywhere."

"Oh, that's because he likes you so much. Can't you be nice to him?"

"No."

Teresa hoped her "no" would settle the matter, but Mrs. West didn't stop her brother.

In order to avoid Udolf, Teresa spent her spare time in her room, sometimes pacing like a caged animal.

By midsummer, Teresa spotted another problem. Her salary. She never received it. Each time she asked Mrs. West about it, her employer had some excuse for not paying her yet.

"You need clothes more than you need money," Mrs. West said when Teresa inquired again. "I'll buy you some clothes with your wage money."

This offer excited Teresa, but on shopping day, Mrs. West took Teresa to the Classic Store, a high-priced, high-powered clothing store in Hays owned by a Mr. Bissing.

Inside Teresa saw stylish dresses that cost more than any dress she'd ever owned. She felt like an imposter. Unable to resist Mrs. West's enthusiasm, Teresa tried on several. She liked none of them. They were old lady dresses, nothing she'd choose for herself. Nevertheless, Teresa let Mrs. West select a mottled green dress in a shade she'd never wear; it turned her face sallow. She listened while her employer told Mr. Bissing that she'd assume responsibility for the debt. However, a few weeks later, Mrs. West handed Teresa a bill from the Classic Store. "Here. You can pay for this out of your wage."

When Teresa noticed that the store had made out the bill to her, not to Mrs. West, a sober truth hit her: *I'm never going to draw my wage.* She retreated to her room and sat erect on her bed, her door locked against Udolf's urgencies. *Here I am, dogged by this creepy man, worse than broke, owing money but*

*having none and not likely to get any. And owning an expensive
dress that I hate. What a mess!*

Convinced that Mrs. West would never pay her, Teresa left
West Dairy Farm. Fall was coming, and again she had no idea
how to return to Hays and enroll in school. Local farmers, now
harvesting, were eager to hire workers to help feed harvest hands.
One such farmer, Mr. Blender, hired Teresa and paid her, but not
nearly enough to retire her debt.

After she worked for the Blenders a few weeks, two young
men and three women asked her to join them for a dancing
party. The following Sunday night, they drove to an isolated spot
on the prairie that belonged to one young woman's family. A
blond man, who reminded her a bit of Gilbert, stroked his fiddle,
and there by the light of the harvest moon the young bodies
swirled and stepped. One schoolgirl knew the Charleston, so she
taught them the swift-stepping dance. *What a silly dance, the
way you grab your knees and knock them together!* Teresa was in
her element. She danced nonstop until they headed home. Then
she was appalled to discover the hour: nearly midnight. *I'll have
to sneak in.* However, when she tried, the dogs barked, waking
up the Blenders and their workers. She rushed to bed.

A short time later, an intense abdominal pain woke Teresa.
She moaned until Mrs. Blender walked into her room. "You
come home late and wake up everybody, and now you keep us
awake with this groaning. I don't think anything's the matter
with you."

Teresa swallowed her moans, but her pain didn't diminish.
Near morning, Mrs. Blender looked in again. "I think you really
are sick." She called Dr. Middlekauf, the county doctor.

When he saw Teresa, he rushed her to his car and headed to
Hays. Teresa screamed with each bounce of the doctor's auto.
At Saint Anthony's Hospital, strong hands carried her into the
emergency room. Barely conscious, Teresa didn't notice the
surgeon, Dr. Charles H. Jameson. She did feel a mask settle on her

face, and she smelled the sweet scent of ether. Then she counted backward—ten, nine, eight—until the world turned black.

The next thing she knew, she swam up out of ether's night. To her surprise, she heard a voice that she recognized as hers cry, "I'm all alone. I don't have any brothers or sisters."

7

A MARRIAGE
OF CONVENIENCE

T
he next morning, Teresa lay immobile, hoping to avoid the pain that whacked her abdomen if she moved. Her eyes closed, she heard someone enter her room and stand by her bed, but she did not stir. She recognized the women, friends of Coach Mandeville, by their voices. *They think I'm asleep.*

"It's too bad the little girl can't die," Mrs. Weidlein said.

"Yes," "Zippy" replied. "She has no one. No one cares."

Teresa concurred. She knew no one cared.

After the women left, Zippy's voice rang in her ears.

Dr. Jameson brought her appendix that afternoon. Teresa stared at the limp pink worm floating innocently in a container. The doctor set it beside her, and then took her pulse. "You gave us quite a scare."

"I'm sorry." Tears rushed down Teresa's cheeks, spiking spasms in her belly. "I don't know how I'll ever pay you." The indignity of her debt for that putrid green dress overwhelmed her and now a hospital bill, so large, no doubt, she'd scrub floors the rest of her life to settle it.

"Don't worry." The doctor checked her heart as Teresa lay stiff under his intimate hands. "I'll see the hospital doesn't charge you. But where will you go when you're well enough to leave?"

"I don't know." Teresa's shoulders shook, agitating her stitches. *What if they send me back to Judge Gross?* "You must know I'm an orphan."

"I tell you what." Dr. Jameson patted Teresa's hand. "Why don't you stay here until you're healed?"

"Oh, could I?"

"You could and you shall." The doctor folded his stethoscope. "Now get some rest."

Teresa sniffled and blew her nose, although blowing her nose was an agony. Her spirits lifted as she realized someone did care for her: Dr. Jameson. She didn't know why he did, an intelligent educated man like him. It made no sense, but she basked in the knowledge that she had a secure place to convalesce.

As Teresa mended, she made friends with a good-looking young actor, Ben Dunscomb, who was in the hospital with a cast on his leg. He traveled around the country for Laugh More Comedy Company, a stock show, leading an adventurous life that appealed to Teresa. She laughed when he showed her how he could pretend to be angry or stupid, happy or bereaved.

A short time later, Jess Binder visited Teresa, his head awkwardly tilted to one side, as usual. Seeing Jess in the hospital surprised Teresa. She hadn't expected anyone to call on her, but his presence proved Zippy wrong. Someone did care. Besides the doctor.

Teresa inched along with Jess to a hospital balcony bench where they sat side by side, leaving a polite space of about a foot between them. Then Ben spotted her, hobbled over, and plopped down right between them.

"The nerve!" she said to Jess after Ben left.

She was joshing but he seemed angry. "That Ben's nothing but a goddamn patsy."

During her hospital stay, both Ben and Jess proposed to marry her, but she declined. Both were good friends, but she loved neither. Besides, she was too young to get married. She needed to finish high school first and then marry someone she truly loved.

A few days later, the Wooters, a couple in their thirties, visited Teresa.

"We've heard a lot of good things about you," Mrs. Wooter said. "Why don't you come live with us in Fellsburg? It's not far, only eighty miles south. The work isn't hard, just taking care of the baby and cleaning the dishes."

Mr. Wooter nodded. When he took off his hat, Teresa saw that the top of his head was white but his face ruddy from the sun. "We'll pay you with room and board plus time off to go to Fellsburg's high school."

School's fine. But no money. And I'll have to wash those despicable diapers. Since Teresa lacked any other offers, she accepted the job.

In the Fellsburg high school, Teresa performed commendably in all her classes except geometry, a class she was required to repeat since she'd dropped it at Hays High. She hated geometry with a passion. No matter how hard she studied, she couldn't seem to grasp it.

Since Teresa was a conspicuous new girl in the tiny school, many boys asked her out. One young man treated her to a boat ride; another took her dancing. Having so many dates delighted her. She loved being popular.

At home, the Wooters treated her decently, but they disapproved of her dating. Soon they told her not to date at all. Not date? What was she supposed to do: just sit and grow old? *If I stay with the Wooters and go to school, I'll have to study geometry, which I hate, and I can't have dates. Stuck in the house night after night.*

Then another possibility crossed her mind. Both Ben and Jess had proposed to her. Why not marry one of them and become a housewife? But which man should she marry? Good-looking Ben who could pretend to be happy or sad? Or truck driving Jess with his mouth full of profanity? She had no romantic feelings for either, though perhaps a few more for Ben, but neither affected her like Heinrich and Gilbert had. Deep down, Teresa wasn't sure she deserved a good-looking confident man like Ben. *But Jess, with his crippled back and neck, he probably isn't so popular with the girls. He'll be so grateful to marry me that he'll let me do whatever I want.*

Having decided, Teresa wrote: "Jess, if you still want to marry me, come and get me. I have no fun here. If you let me run around and do as I please, I will marry you." Teresa hedged her acceptance because she didn't want to be bossed around like Grandma.

Once she mailed her letter, Teresa wavered. Sometimes she could hardly wait for Jess to say "yes," but at other times, she yearned to hear his "no."

Before long, Jess, wasting no time, drove to Fellsburg to collect Teresa. She hastily packed her belongings, but before she stepped in the car Jess had borrowed to pick her up, she said, "Now, Jess, I won't go unless you promise to let me run around and do as I please after I marry you."

He agreed. Satisfied, Teresa climbed into the car, and the young couple left for Hays.

However, from the beginning, Jess ignored their agreement. Being Catholic, Teresa expected to be married in the Catholic church, but Jess wanted the nuptials in his Baptist church. They fought vehemently until they agreed on a civil marriage. *At least we'll be married in the eyes of the law, and maybe later I can arrange to have a priest bless our marriage.* Teresa struggled not to think what Sister Gertrude or Sister Rosina would say about marrying outside the church.

A few days later, on October 28, 1924, Jess's brother, Al, and his wife, Nora, drove the couple to nearby Russell, Kansas, where a justice of the peace married them in the courthouse. Jess was twenty-two; Teresa, eighteen. The ceremony was short, a far cry from a Volga German wedding that might last two or three days. After the quiet ceremony, the marital party ate at a local diner. This impressed Teresa. She had rarely eaten out.

On their wedding night, Jess sat on the edge of the bed and watched Teresa burrow in her satchel for the nightgown given to her by Saint Joseph nuns in Abilene. She seldom wore it, but her wedding night seemed to call for it. Using the nuns' system for undressing privately, Teresa put her nightgown over her dress, and then removed her dress so adroitly that Jess never saw a stitch of her body even though he stared. When she finished, he said, "Damn! I didn't know a person could do that."

"Do what?" she said, unconscious of anything unusual.

Teresa enjoyed being married to her hot-tempered foul-mouthed Jess, partly because his earnings as a driver for Felten Dreyline seemed a fortune. The most money she'd ever held was $5 she earned working for the Blenders, and she held that only a short time. When a harvester said, "I'll take care of that for you," Teresa handed it over and never saw it again. But Jess earned what seemed a huge amount: $24 a week. So when they inspected an East Eighth Street apartment and the landlady asked $6 a month rent, Teresa said, "You have lots of money, Jess. You can pay $8." Jess elbowed her too late. When they rented that place, the $8 a month stuck, even though they used an outdoor toilet.

A few weeks later, Teresa hired her young friend, Elaine, to clean house. Elaine loved to earn a quarter by mopping the floor or washing the dishes. While she cleaned, Teresa lay on her bed, eating a cracker, saying, "Elaine, do this. Elaine, do that." Pretending to be rich enchanted her until Jess told her he didn't have enough money to pay Elaine.

"What? You've got plenty of money. You're just cheap."

When Jess stood his ground, she fumed.

Next Teresa bought blankets and a linen tablecloth on the installment plan. Then she purchased a smart dress for $1.98. Oh how splendid to be modern! Next Teresa bought silk stockings, all the vogue, even though they were terribly expensive, 49 cents a pair, enough for nearly five movies. Then she punched a coin in the nickelodeon, chose "It Ain't Gonna to Rain No Mo', No Mo'," and danced. What rapture!

Not surprisingly, Teresa's debts multiplied. Among them was the money she owed Mr. Bissing for that ugly green dress. Jess, thank goodness, paid that bill for her, but he groused at her installment buying: "Don't you know? A dollar down is a goddamn dollar forever."

After a while, she learned to handle money more realistically.

⌇

Marriage liberated Teresa. Ever since she came to Kansas, no matter where she lived, she always feared that, like Albert, she would be told to leave. Counting orphanages, she'd lived in a dozen places, but until she married Jess, she never had a home. Marriage provided her with security. It felt like paradise.

But Jess kept telling her what to do. One night at supper he told her to wear no lipstick.

No lipstick! He must be joking. Whoever heard of such a thing?

The next day, she put on just a little lipstick, and he didn't notice. So the following day, she put on a little more, surprised at how the action exhilarated her, and the next day, still a little more, expecting to get caught, but Jess said nothing. On the fourth day, she became prudent. She knew her days of lavish makeup were history.

The Binders, from the left, Wolfgang (the father), Clyde, Al, Roy, Jess, George and Walter ("Petey"). Fred and Jim are not shown. (Courtesy of Teresa Martin)

After she married Jess, Teresa discovered that she'd also "married" his numerous relatives. His father, Wolfgang Binder, was German but not a Volga German, to Teresa's relief. Jess's Irish–American Indian mother had died when Jess was seven. His fourteen siblings, all older than he, married people like themselves; Teresa disdained them. To her, Binders were crude, rough-acting people. "Uncouth vulgar barbarians," as Ben once said. One sister-in-law chewed food, plucked it from her mouth, and fed it to her younger children. That particularly grated Teresa.

She learned to curb her tongue around the Binders. They didn't like the way she "showed off her book learning," as they put it. With her ninth-grade schooling, she was by far the most educated in the family. Jess with his fourth-grade education was typical. Not one Binder had the slightest interest in knowledge or reading, while Teresa read voraciously, mostly confession magazines and newspapers, especially the weekly *Ellis County News*. Her studiousness, like her Catholicism, was one more characteristic that set her apart from her in-laws. But what really galled Teresa was their belief that Jess, in marrying her, had married beneath him.

~

Teresa had been married about five months when she went next door, as usual, to light her landlady's fire. Mrs. Marshall and Teresa were friendly, so she didn't mind lighting the fire for the older woman, but this morning, nothing went right. Three matches in a row were duds, the paper lit only to blow out, and Teresa bit her lip to keep from snarling. Then, before she could get the fire going, Mrs. Marshall asked her to address some envelopes. Teresa often addressed her landlady's envelopes in French, not knowing what she was writing, but this morning, irritated, Teresa snapped, "After all, I light the fire for you."

"You're in a fix," Mrs. Marshall cried. "You're in a fix."

"What do you mean?"

"You're pregnant, aren't you?"

She was, but she didn't know that yet. As soon as she knew, Mrs. Marshall counseled her "don't reach up" and "be sure to get everything you crave or it will mark the baby." Teresa didn't believe these old wives' tales, but Jess did. Not wanting his baby marked, he did everything in his power to get whatever Teresa wanted, so she accommodated her husband by wanting things, mostly candies, especially chocolates.

Mrs. Marshall's cute little next-door apartment was too small for three, so Jess and Teresa moved a few blocks away into a two-room house on Allen and Ninth. Teresa didn't like the house, but Jess's stepmother owned it, so they rented it at $8 a month: a whole house for the price they paid Mrs. Marshall for her tiny apartment.

As her due date approached, Teresa felt apprehensive about giving birth. She had no one to consult but Jess who knew even less than she did. Oh, they enjoyed talking about the child they would have; Jess definitely wanted a son. But Teresa dared not discuss with him her fear the baby might be colored. She had no idea who her real parents were and her black hair curled so extremely. Was a parent or grandparent a Negro? Who was she? A person of no importance, she knew that. But did she carry colored blood that might leap out at any moment? She shuddered. How despicable being an orphan!

Jess never knew Teresa's concern about the color of their baby. When her labor began, he took her to Saint Anthony's Hospital, and then went home to wait as husbands did in those days. Teresa screamed all night long, even after a nun reported that an irritable patient said, "Tell that mother to get her baby into this world. I want to get my sleep." Finally, the next day, November 28, 1925, she gave birth to her first child, a girl.

"What color is she?"

She felt relieved to hear the nurse call the baby "all right."

When Teresa first looked at her daughter, she saw a sorry-looking little newborn with dark hair pasted to her head and her face all scrunched and red. An enormous burst of love coursed through Teresa's body. As she touched her baby's soft cheek, she saw not only her first born but also her only known blood relative.

A part of her self that withered after her mother relinquished her began to bud. Rapturous, she turned a corner of the squirming blanket aside to show her mother who seemed to stand at the edge of the bed, peering at her grandchild.

The ugly duckling infant transformed into a pretty, dark-haired girl with blue eyes. Jess and Teresa named her Mildred, a popular choice. They decided not to baptize the baby, which left Teresa heavy hearted. She wished a priest could baptize Mildred Roman Catholic, but she knew Jess would never agree. He would be happy to have Mildred baptized a Baptist, which Teresa couldn't condone, even though both parents now attended the Baptist church. Teresa went to church to please Jess, but sitting in a Baptist pew felt uncomfortable; she'd been taught that only Catholics know the truth about God. Although she no longer attended Saint Joseph's, she still longed to have a priest bless her marriage. Religiously speaking, she lingered in what Catholics call Limbo.

Teresa held high expectations for her daughter, a good baby who slept a lot and cried rarely. She wanted Mildred to rise above her humble origins, so she read baby books by the dozen and struggled to live up to their advice. Teresa rapidly became the sort of mother Marianna Wheeler describes in her popular book of that day, *Before the Baby Comes:* "A large number of babies, especially the firstborn, suffer from lack of proper knowledge on the part of the mother, who, in her anxiety to do right, frequently overdoes it."

Teresa particularly wanted Mildred potty trained by the time she was a year and a half, but although she continually lifted Mildred up over the hole in their privy, the child didn't seem to catch on, certainly not as quickly as Teresa wished.

Teresa, on right, with her friend Monie.
(Courtesy of Teresa Martin)

Nearly every afternoon, Teresa's best friend, Monie, dropped by the apartment, and they would go walking. Monie, short for Monica, was a bit of a tomboy. She wore her hair in a masculine cut that failed to conceal her good looks. Like most flappers who disdained conventional dress, Monie wore straight frocks with no waistlines and the popular "cloche" hats.

One afternoon, delighted to see pert Monie as usual, Teresa dressed her daughter and combed her shiny dark hair. Mildred enjoyed having her hair combed, but her curls were loose, not tight like her mother's hair.

"Any day now," Monie observed as she watched Teresa lift Mildred into her buggy, "she's going to be too big for that conveyance."

Teresa agreed as the three headed downtown for their daily walk.

Teresa with her firstborn, Mildred, in 1926.
(Courtesy of Teresa Martin)

Whenever someone on the street stopped to look at Mildred, Teresa couldn't wait to hear a compliment. "Don't I have a pretty baby?" she'd ask. Naturally, the person would agree, and Teresa's pride would swell.

By the time Mildred was two, she indeed had outgrown her buggy, so Mildred rode in a stroller when Teresa and Monie went downtown to dance to the nickelodeon. Teresa loved to dance the popular shimmy, even though the Catholic Archbishop condemned it.

"Listen to the way this guy describes the shimmy," Teresa folded back the newspaper.

"I'm listening." Monie kept playing horsey with Mildred.

"Quote, 'to jig and hop around like a chicken on a red-hot stove, at the same time shaking the body until it quivers like a disturbed glass of Jell-O, is not only tremendously suggestive, but it is an offense against common decency that would not be permitted in a semi-respectable road-house.'"

"Well, that's news to me," Monie said. "I didn't know a road-house could be semi-respectable."

One day in late September, 1929, Teresa and Monie stood on Chestnut Street, loafing around with Mildred. Mildred, almost four, was quite the little lady, but Teresa, five months pregnant, had gained an inordinate amount of weight. To her dismay, she fit her fattest sister-in-law's clothes.

Then Teresa noticed a shiny, late-model Studebaker a few blocks north. "Hey, get a load of that!"

"Oil money," Monie said.

"Probably."

They stood still, Teresa jiggling Mildred's stroller and watched the long lean car pull to the curb and stop.

"What are they doing?" Teresa said.

"Asking directions?"

Moments later, as the car drew alongside them, Teresa saw two stylishly dressed women inside. A sweet-faced woman at the window beckoned. Teresa heard the driver say, "The pregnant one."

The sweet-faced woman leaned out of the window. "Is one of you named Jessie?"

"No," Monie said.

Teresa scrutinized the woman's face, her broad nose, and her ready smile. She looked to be in her forties.

"Are you Austrian?" she asked Teresa.

"I don't think so."

"Are you sure? You look Austrian."

"Maybe I am. I don't know much about my parents."

"I see." The woman turned back in the car. Then she handed Teresa a used envelope with the address circled. "That's where I'm staying. In Mission Mound. Do you know it?"

Teresa nodded. Everyone knew Mission Mound, a fine residential area.

"Come see me," the woman said, "and bring your friend if you like. You'd both be welcome."

The car pulled away. Teresa stood on the curb, waving. She turned to Monie. "That could be my mother."

"Oh, don't be foolish."

"I'm sure she is. She looks just like me. Here, watch Mildred." Teresa grasped her big belly and started to run after the car, but Monie grabbed her arm.

"Don't be a goose! That couldn't possibly be your mother. She was too young."

"But her hair was so curly," Teresa insisted.

"Why would your mother be in Hays, worm-brain?"

"Looking for me."

Monie rolled her eyes skyward.

"Well, she invited us to her house," Teresa said. "Will you go with me? Tomorrow? It's too late to go this afternoon. I've got to get Jess's dinner ready."

"I'm waiting tables tomorrow, but Thursday I could."

"Okay, Thursday."

But Mildred came down with a cold Thursday morning, and Teresa couldn't risk taking her outdoors.

A week passed before they arrived at Mission Mound, an intimidating section of town, its brick houses large and far apart.

When they found the address, they stood and considered the huge door, the shuttered windows, and the wide front porch.

"Dingbust!" Monie said. "Looks like the governor lives here."

"You go first." Teresa gave Monie a little push. "I'll wait with Mildred."

"It's your mother not mine, ninny." Monie unwrapped Teresa's hand from the stroller handle. "Go on."

Teresa edged up the steps, stooped to render her big belly less conspicuous, and pushed the doorbell. She jumped when a five-toned bell rang inside the house. Soon the door opened and there stood pretty Mrs. Cochran, wife of one of the town's bankers. "Yes?" she said.

"That woman with the curly hair, in a Studebaker, she told me to come see her here."

"Rosie, you mean." Mrs. Cochran brushed her hair away from her cheek. She'd plucked her eyebrows, Teresa noticed. Penciled ones arched high over each eye. "I'm afraid she's gone back to New York. So sorry."

As the door shut, Teresa turned and lumbered down the stairs. "You see? New York. She could have been my mother."

"Right. Or my great-great-step-aunt-twice-removed."

Teresa punched Monie.

The door closed behind them with a heavy thud.

❦

One day when Teresa sat with Mildred in a coffee shop, reading the *Ellis County News,* a headline made her gasp: Judge Gross was dead.

Not long after she married, she heard that the judge resigned because of ill health, but she didn't realize he was that sick. The paper said he had been "confined to bed for the past two years."

What a sorry thing, death, even for such an awful man. So why did she want to dance?

Judge Gross is dead!

She'd never again avert her eyes when she saw him on the street, she'd never again force a stiff smile and pretend that nothing happened.

Judge Gross is dead!

Suddenly she stood, and even though she was as big as an elephant, she plucked Mildred out of her stroller and twirled her around and around, her startled daughter grabbing handfuls of Teresa's curly hair as they danced.

～

"You know, Tootsy," Jess said one night, "I for damn sure want to buy this frigging little house."

Teresa recoiled. She and Jess still lived at Ninth and Allen in the two-room house they rented from his stepmother. Teresa hated the house. It sat near the railroad tracks in a lower-class neighborhood. Their neighbors, Mexican track workers, lived in trailer houses. However, Teresa, knowing how sensitive Jess was about being lower class, said only, "Oh, no, Jess. It's way too small."

"Hell, we can manage."

Teresa protested, but Jess refused to listen to reason. Furious, she watched him put aside every penny he could spare, hoping to make a deposit.

Then one morning her friend Irene dropped by. "Better you hear this from me than from someone else," she said. "My husband's bought this house."

"Petey? His own brother? Jess will be furious."

So he was.

Not long after, Petey, angry that Jess opposed his purchase of the house, stopped by to shake the official sale paper under Jess's nose.

"I want you and Teresa out," Petey said, "and I want you out immediately."

"For Christ's sake, Petey. At least let us stay until Teresa has the baby."

But Petey refused.

Soon Teresa and Jess were apartment hunting, to Teresa's delight, although she carefully hid her satisfaction from Jess. Then unexpectedly another of Jess's brothers, George, who worked at the George Philip and Son Hardware, arranged for Teresa and Jess to move into a cheerful three-room apartment above the store.

"You'll like it," he told Teresa. He was right. She adored it. Sunlight poured through its big kitchen windows that looked out on the town's busiest intersection.

Teresa and Jess hadn't lived in the apartment long before their second child arrived January 27, 1930, a hairless baby girl who weighed nine-and-a-half pounds.

"Well, we didn't get a boy," Jess said when he visited, "but, damn, we got a big healthy girl. You and the baby are okay, and that's all that frigging matters."

They took the baby home to their sunny apartment and called her Doris, a hugely popular name, even more popular than Mildred. Both names pleased Teresa. Having known derision, she wanted her children to fit in.

～

The longer Teresa lived in the apartment, the more she loved it except for its one flaw: a long straight narrow staircase, Teresa's daily obstacle course. Each afternoon, as the weather warmed, she put Mildred in the buggy with Doris and crept down the stairs, balancing her heavy load step by step. But Teresa never complained about the treacherous descent. Even with the stairs, this apartment was the best place she and Jess had lived.

Doris looked cuddly and cute, but she had Jess's high forehead so she wasn't really pretty. Although she slept little, she had a wonderful personality. The whole family loved her, particularly Mildred, who called Doris "sista," not "sister."

Mildred, now four, struggled to learn to talk. When she spoke, she was unintelligible. Finally, Teresa realized that her daughter had a speech impediment. Shocked, she spoke slowly and exactly whenever she talked to Mildred.

Teresa still attended Jess's Baptist church, but she refused to have Doris baptized there. One day, scowling, she returned from a Baptist service and told Jess, "I've bent over backwards to please you, but I'm not going to that church of yours. Either I go to my own church or I'll go to none. And that's positive."

Faced with her ultimatum, Jess let Teresa return to the Catholic church, but he wouldn't let his daughters be baptized there. Elated to return to Saint Joseph's, Teresa attended regularly even though her civil marriage meant she couldn't take communion or confess.

That summer, Doris, only five months old, became deathly ill with pneumonia. Jess and Teresa rushed her to Saint Anthony's Hospital where they watched Sister Myra save their daughter's life by putting a finger down her throat so she could vomit up the poisonous phlegm. After that, nurses administered drops of whiskey to Doris every few hours. Teresa stayed by her daughter's side as often as she could. When she had to go home, she walked as fast and hard as possible, trying to pound into the pavement her fear that Doris might not be alive by the next visit.

Teresa's daughters, Doris (left) and Mildred, in 1931.
(Courtesy of Teresa Martin)

Teresa's old friend, Euphersine, who visited Judge Gross with her, often dropped by the hospital. Teresa was proud of Euphersine. After high school, she'd gone to nursing school and had become Ellis County's first nurse, but that did not make her too uppity to walk Teresa home.

"Don't worry," Euphersine said. "Your baby will pull through."

Teresa hoped her friend was right. *She ought to know. She's a nurse.* However, Teresa prayed for her tiny daughter just the same. After six long weeks, Doris healed enough to leave the hospital.

Jess and Teresa, so grateful that their perky Doris wasn't dead, did everything in their power to keep her happy. Soon she was spoiled tremendously. She didn't want Jess to leave the apartment, and he left often, still driving a Dreyline truck despite his worsening rheumatism. On nights without Jess, Doris cried to get attention. Then Teresa and Mildred walked the floor with Doris or rocked her.

One night when Doris woke them up, crying, Mildred kissed her and said, "Oh, you foiled darling." Teresa stopped, then recognized that Mildred meant "spoiled darling." She laughed and tousled the little girl's head. She had two darlings, maybe both of them a little "foiled."

~

When Jess's brother, George, married Sarah Lewis, Teresa lost her status as the best-educated Binder. Sarah, a high-school graduate, was a college student. Not only was she educated, she had striking good looks and stood so tall she towered over Teresa, who couldn't like this new Binder no matter how she tried.

Then George, who still worked downstairs in Mr. Philip's hardware store, wanted Jess and Teresa's apartment for himself and Sarah. Since Jess acquired the apartment through George, he and Teresa agreed to move again.

Jess finally found an apartment for them at 410 Fort Street, a loathsome basement apartment, the ugliest place Teresa ever saw. An armpit, Jess would say.

Even worse than the apartment were the nosy upstairs neighbors—a Bieker family of tall, skinny distant relatives of Bappa. When one of them accused Teresa of bringing men home while Jess was at work, Teresa lost her temper.

That night she told Jess, certain he would take her side. But he didn't. He believed them, which really angered Teresa. She had done nothing to deserve this. Why didn't Jess trust her?

For a few days, she vowed to leave him, but as time passed and she could think of no way to support herself and her two daughters, she decided to stay. She kept humming a Volga German song, "Du, Du Liegst Mir im Herzen." Bit by bit the words came back to her, and she danced around the apartment singing: "You, you give me so much pain./You don't know how good I am to you./Ja, ja, ja, ja,/Don't know how good I am to you."

Goodness! I'm as bad as Mrs. Denning! At least I don't dance with a broom.

◦

That autumn, Doc Maximus's Marvelous Medicine Show unfurled its colorful tent a few blocks from the Binder apartment. Curious, Teresa took her daughters and investigated.

The gaudy, noisy show cheered her. Inside a tent, many booths sold strong medicinal drinks. The red-headed show owner, Doc Rufus Maximus, speaking through a megaphone, claimed his medicine made people feel much better. She bought a small bottle, thinking it might relieve Jess's arthritis, and tucked it in the buggy alongside Doris. Other booths offered prizes. Oddly enough, when they were awarded, Teresa always got one, even if she hadn't registered.

Then Doc Maximus, a short dapper fellow, approached her and asked her to go on the road with him, to dance with him on the stage.

"Let me think about it," Teresa said, just to be polite.

Then he mentioned pay, almost as much as Jess made. Before she turned to leave, she won another prize, a cute teddy bear dressed like a Scotsman.

That night Teresa showed her prizes to Jess. Skeptical, he claimed that the medicine she bought for him was nothing but alcohol and cherry flavor. When she told him of Doc Maximus's strange offer, Jess took the news badly, calling her a whore and shaking her. She felt her insides tie into knots. Then they fought in earnest halfway through the night, so they all—Jess, Teresa, and the girls—woke frazzled and short-tempered.

As Jess limped to work that morning, he turned and said, "You stay strictly away from that show, you hear me."

I should have known. Teresa watched Jess leave. *He's so quick to believe the worst of me and other men.* She did like to flirt, she admitted that, but she never ran around the way he thought she did. Not because she was pure. No, she was too afraid of his temper to cheat on him.

Their fight made Teresa want to join the medicine show. To get paid for dancing exceeded her wildest dream. She loved the idea of people watching her swirl. She knew she would be good and, wonder of wonders, earn money, too—as much as Jess. Just think how rich she would be. What delightful things she could buy for the girls!

However, as long as Jess remained in Hays, Teresa knew she must avoid the medicine show. She dared not ignite his anger. So every day she asked him, "Are you driving out of town for Felten?" Every day the answer was, "No."

The instant Jess left town, Teresa readied the girls and rushed to the show. But she was too late. Doc Maximus's Marvelous Medicine Show had departed. Her loss made her sick to her stomach.

8

"MAYBE I LOVED HIM"

N ot long after the medicine show left town, Teresa's bowels locked so badly that Dr. Jameson, who had removed her appendix, operated on her to remove part of her intestine. Afterward, suffering from peritonitis, Teresa swam in and out of consciousness. Sometimes Jess was at her side when she surfaced, sometimes not.

After nearly thirty days of hospitalization, she woke to see the top of Jess's head by her bed. Despite his arthritis, he knelt beside her, his body listing.

"Don't die, Tootsy, don't die. Please get well. If you get well, I'll frigging marry you in the Catholic church or anywhere you want, but you have to get well. When you get out of this goddamn hospital, we will have our marriage blessed. I give you my word."

Teresa thought she must be hallucinating. She rolled closer to him. "Say that again."

Jess did.

Before a week passed, Teresa was home, convalescing in the vile basement apartment with its horrid memories. As she improved, Jess's often poor health declined. He suffered from rheumatoid arthritis, which ran in his family; the arthritis caused his old swimming hole injuries to plague him. His whole body tilted to one side.

Teresa hated to see Jess suffer, so when Clyde, one of Jess's brothers, dropped by with an incredible offer, she agreed. Just divorced, Clyde wanted to live with Teresa, Jess, and the girls in a larger apartment. He would pay the rent so Jess, with his worsening arthritis, would not have to work so hard.

The Binder brothers chipped in and moved Teresa and her family to a comfortable apartment on the second floor of a landlord's house. Tears welled as she saw the place, located at Seventeenth and Oak. She would actually live in a pleasant residential area, not in some dank basement or some hut by the railroad tracks.

As soon as they were mobile, Jess and Teresa arranged to go to Saint Joseph's to get their marriage blessed, Teresa as excited as a bride. Jess still worked, but his illness forced him to walk bent over to his right; the stitches for Teresa's operation were healing, so Teresa had to walk bent over to her left. Neither could walk the seven blocks to Saint Joseph's, so Jess borrowed George's fancy Model A to drive Teresa and the girls to the church.

"What made you decide to do this?" Teresa asked Jess on the way. "You always were so set against it."

"That rosy-cheeked little nurse of yours." Jess pulled across the intersection. "Hell, I was all balled up, can hardly walk, and who'll take care of the girls if you go? So I asked her what to do, and she said, 'Well, maybe if you marry your wife in the church, she might get well.'

"And hell," he flipped off the ignition. "She was frigging right."

Teresa expected the priest to sprinkle them to bless their marriage. That would take only a few minutes, so she left Mildred, four, and Doris, a big baby, in the car. Teresa figured they'd be fine. However, Father Raphael Engel didn't sprinkle them. Instead, he remarried them as though they had never been married.

Jess seethed.

Then Mildred honked the horn. *My God! What if that baby falls!* Teresa's worry obscured the words of the service.

When they started to leave, Teresa realized she had no money.

"You're supposed to pay the priest," she told Jess.

He refused. "That priest smiled like a cat eating sour mush."

Teresa didn't think the priest smiled, but she said nothing. He had blessed her marriage. Now she could take the sacraments and go to confession. What a triumph, especially when she found Mildred and Doris alive and well in the car.

Gradually Jess became too ill to work steadily. One day he could walk but the next day he couldn't. He never complained, but Teresa could calculate his distress by the set of his jaw. As he became bedridden, Clyde and Teresa heard that boiled ants could draw out pain. They found a sizable ant pile down by the tracks, hauled a boiler to the tracks in a wagon, and shoveled the anthill into the boiler. Then they hauled it six blocks home and cooked it. When the anthill cooled, they plastered Jess's arms and back with it, but nothing helped, not even wiring Jess in copper.

Jess's doctor cautioned Teresa not to provoke her husband. "With his weak heart, if you rile him, he could die," the doctor said. Just like that, Teresa's freedom to blow up at Jess evaporated.

Not wanting to be responsible for his death, she curbed her temper in earnest.

A proud man, Jess held tight to an idea Teresa considered old-fashioned—that he, not Clyde, should earn the family's keep. She felt she could bring home a salary, but she dare not rile Jess by asking. In addition to paying the rent, Clyde bought groceries, so she, Jess, and the girls had shelter and plenty of food, although she did tire of eating all the cabbages Clyde bought.

Teresa never had a cent to call her own, not even a dime for the movies. So she crocheted a hat and sold it for a quarter, more than enough "moolah" to see *Hot Pepper*. Enough "moolah" to treat her friend, Mabel Bieler, to the talking movie. They could see for themselves its star, Pola Negri, the actress who sent four thousand roses for Rudolph Valentino's bier.

Mabel agreed readily, but Mabel's mother, knowing Jess was bedridden, said, "Don't you think you should buy bread with the money you earn?"

"No, that's not my job. When Jess gets well, he will take care of it."

Mrs. Bieler shook her head, but Mabel went anyway.

When Teresa got home from the movie, Clyde was waiting for her. "You may think I'm supposed to pay for your food because I'm Jess's brother. But I don't have to pay for anything. I buy groceries of my own free will, not because I have to."

Clyde's angry words confused Teresa. She expected Jess to get well and take care of them, as he had before, but he wasn't improving. She knew how strongly Jess opposed wives working, but maybe she should. So she crocheted another hat, this one to profit the family.

Soon Teresa sold her hats to Scheer's, a fancy dress shop on Hays's Chestnut Street. When the store featured her hats in its window, she stood outside admiring them. *Pretty nifty!*

Teresa spent her profits from her hats on food for everyone. To her surprise, Jess didn't object. He simply ignored her crocheting.

Jess remained an invalid during 1932, but then he began to recover, walking on crutches or with a cane. When he was strong enough, he resumed occasional driving for Felten Dreyline. He didn't attempt long-distance driving but drove the flat wagon in town. Each day during the noon hour, Teresa surreptitiously brought Jess a fresh pair of shoes. He didn't want his boss to know he needed to change shoes, but fresh shoes relieved the pain in his feet enough so he could go on working.

Eventually Clyde, tired of spending so much money on Jess's family, moved out. After he left, Teresa and Jess rented a house on Sixth Street, just east of Chestnut, now called Main Street. Shortly after they moved in, a car rolled up and stopped. Out stepped a man from Felten Dreyline to tell them that Mr. Felten, Jess's boss, was dead. He had wrapped his car around a telephone pole.

In the face of such horrible news, Teresa froze but Jess seemed beside himself. He would jump up and pace the room at a fast limp or rush from the apartment, staying out for hours.

Teresa knew how kind the late Mr. Felten had been to Jess and how doggedly Jess worked for Felten Dreyline. But now, battered by the Depression, the struggling truck line would be run by Pete Felten, the son. Teresa believed Pete would treat Jess decently, but she knew Jess could not count on Pete for favors the way Jess counted on his father. The older Mr. Felten called Jess and Teresa "a couple of kids" and treated them like family. However, Jess was nobody special to Pete.

Because of Mr. Felten's death, the need for Teresa to earn money became clear to her and amazingly even to Jess.

Teresa knew finding a decent job would be difficult without a high school diploma. House cleaning positions were plentiful, but she despised being a domestic servant. After fruitlessly applying for other jobs, she swallowed her pride and answered housekeeping ads.

Many women turned her down because of her diminutive size: she stood four feet, eleven inches and weighed ninety pounds. Mrs. Homer Reed, for instance, opened her door, looked at Teresa, and said, "What can you do?"

"Try me!" Teresa cried but Mrs. Reed's door closed.

Just as she despaired of finding any job, Teresa found one. However, her pay didn't stretch far, no matter how hard she scrubbed and polished.

One day George Philip, the hardware store owner, stopped her on the street.

"How are you doing, you and Jess?" he said.

Teresa wondered why he asked. Surely he knew Jess was too ill to work, but she told him anyway.

"You know what you should do," he said. "You should go see the county about getting on welfare."

Welfare! The very word turned Teresa's stomach. She wasn't the sort of person who went on welfare. Since she left Judge Gross's house, she never asked anyone for financial help. *I won't do it. I'll manage somehow.* Eventually her meager earnings forced her to apply.

The welfare interview seemed to last for days. Teresa struggled to answer the multitudinous questions that Mr. Giebler, social welfare director, asked, but her shoulders tightened as one question followed another.

As usual, Teresa was hungry. She habitually ate less so Jess and the girls could have more. Suddenly the room swirled, and she blacked out.

She revived to find Mr. Huser, a courthouse official, hovering over her. "Don't worry." He placed another cool wet cloth on her forehead. "We put you on our roll."

She had accomplished her mission, but how her success diminished her!

For one month, the Binders lived on government money. The actuality proved worse than Teresa imagined. She believed that people in the street looked at her differently, that somehow they could tell by seeing her that she was on welfare. Sometimes when she went to sleep, she didn't care if she woke. She could hardly wait to be taken off the roll.

Each morning she told herself, today I'll earn enough to get off welfare. However, that day never came. At last her pride puffed up so stubbornly she went to the courthouse and declared that she didn't need any more county help. Saying that cooled her flushed face like a spring breeze. Somehow, the county's removal of her family from its roll vindicated her, even though Jess continued to be too ill to work regularly.

For a while, Teresa managed to support her family. Then one month when she couldn't pay the rent, a social worker told Teresa that she and her family ought to move to a rent-free Ellis County apartment on East Thirteenth Street. Not knowing what else to do, the Binders moved into a former poor house there.

Their second-floor apartment wasn't bad, but the area was despicable. Among their sleazy neighbors were thieves, prostitutes, and bootleggers. A bootlegger lived below the Binders and a low-class prostitute across the hall. The area seemed so primitive that Teresa called it "The Jungles."

Most people who lived in The Jungles were delighted to receive free rent, but Teresa despised being poor and dependent. Each family agreed to pay its rent by working one day a month for the county, but the workday was not required, so most residents didn't bother. Not Teresa. Her pride at stake, she worked one day a month as long as she lived there, muttering, "If only Jess let me dance in the medicine show, I wouldn't be reduced to this."

Of course, if Teresa had never worked for stylish families like the Mandevilles and the Combses, then she wouldn't have known what she was missing, but experiencing that cultivated lifestyle raised her standards. Refined people, she knew, considered living in The Jungles degrading, so she did, too. She understood that she and Jess were not well-bred, but she hoped for something better for their children than growing up low class and using bad grammar. She vowed she would do whatever it took to leave The Jungles. However, in order to move out, Teresa would have to earn more money than she could by cleaning houses. But how?

Soon the Works Progress Administration (WPA), a federal program started by President Roosevelt to help counteract the Depression, hired Teresa as a seamstress. In 1933, the WPA sent her to work in a mattress factory. Unfortunately, she lacked the strength needed to pull the threads tight. The factory boss didn't fire her, but he treated her with scorn. Sometimes he shouted at her, "I hate little women!"

Eventually Teresa joined another WPA group that sewed clothes for needy people. Stitching on buttons, a task she completed successfully, required no strength. She sewed well, thanks to restyling dozens of clothes for herself and her children.

In the summer of 1935, Teresa cleaned churches for the WPA. What a job that was! One day six women started cleaning the large Methodist church, washing walls and ceilings, scrubbing out cupboards. After a while, four worn-out women left, but Frances Phannenstiel and Teresa kept on cleaning. Then Frances left, but the head woman wouldn't release Teresa. "You are small. You can crawl into the bottom of cupboards, so stay until you're finished."

Teresa considered leaving, but she remembered hearing people call WPA workers "lazy" as though they lived off govern -ment dole. What a lie! She knew how WPA women labored, but she feared someone might see her leave early and call her lazy; she had too much pride to risk that. So she stayed, twisting and scrubbing so fiercely she tore a kidney loose and was hospitalized. Again, Dr. Jameson took care of her, again free of charge.

Shortly before Teresa left the hospital, her childhood playmate, Regina Bieker, Fred's daughter, visited her.

"Bappa's dead," Regina said. "Heart attack. I thought you'd want to know."

"Yes." Teresa tried to catch her breath. Tall skinny Bappa who'd caused her such agony, Bappa dead? It hardly seemed possible.

After Regina left, Teresa lay with a damp cloth across her eyes. Bappa treated her so foully, she knew she should feel elated but she didn't. His dying didn't erase the past; it just brought it into sharper focus. Now he could never come to her, in that slow shuffling walk of his, hat in hand, and say, "I'm sorry, Teresa. Can you forgive me?" Not that he'd ever apologize. She supposed that if Bappa had it all to do over again, he'd do pretty much the same things.

Tears trickled down her cheeks, warm beneath the coolness of the damp cloth. Bappa would never be dead for her. His treatment of her lived on inside her, coiling and churning in her stomach at the oddest moments. She knew she could never forgive him. His death did not elate her, but she did rejoice knowing that she'd never see him again.

When Teresa recovered enough to return to work, she refused to clean any more churches. Instead, she did general housework and continued to sew on buttons. She also cared for sick people and pregnant women—work that the WPA reimbursed.

With the additional money earned from these care-taking assignments, Teresa talked Jess into leaving The Jungles. They rented a second-floor apartment at 1711 Pine Street in a lovely residential neighborhood. The place delighted Teresa, primarily because of its distance—both literally and figuratively—from The

Jungles. She didn't mind working an extra day to pay the rent or crocheting hats in the evenings, "borrowing" a few groceries until she could pay for them and cleaning an occasional house to make ends meet. Living in a decent place made the extra work worthwhile.

One night Jess came home elated. "Tootsy, guess what. My frigging brothers are building us a house."

Teresa winced. Build them a house? Why would his brothers want to do that? Where had they been when she and Jess needed them? If only they had lent her money to pay that one month's rent, she might have kept out of The Jungles, but now she didn't need help. She had a good job and lived in a decent area. Besides, what kind of a house could they possibly build, as uneducated and boorish as they were?

"Don't let them build that house," Teresa begged, but when Jess resisted, she lacked the will to fight. By this time, her husband worked as a night guard for Pete Felten when he could, which wasn't frequently. Jess could no longer drive, so he hated to watch anyone drive his old truck. A new house would not change that, Teresa knew, but Jess wanted to own a house so badly she finally yielded.

Eventually the brothers hammered together a house at 98 Ash Street, next to a trailer park. Jess loved it, even though the house was only one large rectangular room divided into two by a curtain. Teresa hated it. What a stigma, living in such a hovel! The ugly thing looked like a shoebox to Teresa, so she called it the "Box House." Although not a trailer, the house looked like one. It satisfied none of her desires to be respectable. She no longer wanted riches; she knew they were beyond her, but how she wished she had stayed in her reputable apartment.

No matter how long the Binders lived in the Box House, it never seemed like a real home to Teresa. She tried to console herself by noting that the neighborhood on the side away from the trailer park was lovely. In that neighborhood lived Dr.

Burnett, a professor of sociology; Teresa's pride bloomed when she discovered she had such a refined neighbor. She taught manners to her daughters. Soon they consulted an Emily Post book to make sure they had placed each fork as correctly as the Mandevilles had.

Teresa wanted her daughters to be well-mannered but not snobbish, so she told them about the man who went to a banquet at the royal palace. There he poured his coffee into his saucer, blew on it to cool it, and drank it. Guests up and down the long banquet tables snickered to witness such a violation of good manners, but the king did not. Instead, he poured his coffee in his saucer, blew on it, and drank it.

"Don't be sloppy about eating," Teresa told her daughters, "but don't follow the etiquette books about every little thing. Just do your best and be kind, like the king."

As Teresa cared for the Ellis County sick, she decided to advance herself by training to be a practical nurse. The requirement—to take an on-the-job course—was minimal so, in 1936, she took the six-week WPA home-nursing course. She scored exceptionally well on the final exam, receiving the highest grade in the statewide class. Kathryn O'Loughlin McCarthy from Hays, the first Kansas woman to serve in the United States Congress, noticed Teresa's achievement. The congresswoman knew that Sara Fields, head of the Hays Public Library, needed a helper, so McCarthy recommended Teresa as "a bright young woman." Mrs. Fields hired Teresa on a three-month trial basis as a "glorified errand girl."

Teresa felt ecstatic to have the job even though libraries seemed foreign, but not as alien as they had when Sister Rosina described "rooms full of books." Still, Teresa didn't understand how books were cataloged until Mrs. Fields taught her to shelve books. *"Frisch begonnen,"* Mrs. Fields said, *"ist halb gewonnen."* Teresa agreed that well begun is half done.

Teresa's need to keep the job pushed her to work exceedingly hard. She knew she must; the Depression created more workers than positions. Her paycheck also motivated her. At the library, she earned more than a minimum wage for the first time, markedly improving her family's finances. She could not bear the thought of returning to work for the WPA with its low pay.

After Teresa had worked at the library a few months, she overheard Mrs. Fields tell Congresswoman McCarthy, "Mrs. Binder's doing fine. We'll keep her."

Teresa blanched; her stomach tightened. She had forgotten that Mrs. Fields had hired her "on trial." Just as well. Being on trial for anything made her nervous. Her palms would sweat, and she made stupid mistakes. If only she weren't an orphan. She knew people looked down on her, that they considered her "among the lowest of the low." She wanted to better herself, but no matter what she did, she never felt better. Still, the library job seemed to help.

By 1938, Teresa's library career appeared secure. Her weekly paycheck had grown to $30 for a forty-hour week, which was $14 more than the minimum wage. She considered herself blessed and set aside any thoughts of returning to nursing.

Later that year, Mrs. Fields told Teresa she needed someone to type.

"I can't type," Teresa said.

"Well, neither can I," Mrs. Fields said. "What are we going to do?"

They decided to send Teresa to typing class at the high school.

"As long as you're taking typing, you might as well take some other classes," Mrs. Fields said. "In fact, you should finish high school. You're too bright to flunky around."

In 1939, Teresa and Mildred, now a freshman in high school, "took up books" together. Mildred went full-time, Teresa attended as she could.

Teresa hadn't entered a classroom for twelve years, but she bolstered herself by remembering Mrs. Fields' saying: *"Frisch begonnen ist halb gewonnen."* Despite her determination, typing class proved difficult. She typed so slowly that her teacher, George Gatschet, said, "You'll never make it. You're too old to learn to type." However, Teresa knew lack of practice, not age, slowed her down. The typewriter's clatter made Jess nervous, so she couldn't practice at home. Finally, she practiced in the basement of a neighbor, Mrs. Zimmerman.

Despite daily practice, by semester's end Teresa typed only thirteen words to the minute. She knew she would fail, but instead, to her relief, Mr. Gatschet gave her a "D."

⌒

"Come into my office," Mrs. Fields said to Teresa a few weeks later. "We must talk."

Sweat broke out on Teresa's upper lip as she followed her boss into the small cluttered room. What had she done?

"Sit down, Mrs. Binder." Mrs. Fields lifted a pile of papers off a chair. Teresa sat, her back as straight as her ironing board. "A woman came into the library today and asked for your job. Of course, I told her, 'No.' But she pressed me, so I put it more clearly. I said, 'I'm satisfied with Mrs. Binder's work. I don't want to replace her.'"

Teresa took a deep breath. At least the problem wasn't losing her job.

"Then the woman said, 'But she wasn't even born in the United States.'"

Mrs. Fields stopped talking.

"Of course, I was," Teresa said. "I was born in New York City."

"But can you prove it?" Mrs. Fields looked at her sharply. "Because this woman isn't going to stop here. She knows that you have to be a citizen to work for the government. So you better get an affidavit, if you can. Maybe they'll give you one at the courthouse."

Shaken, Teresa asked her friend, Euphersine, to come with her to the Ellis County Courthouse to ask an official to vouch for her citizenship. By this time, Volga Germans, who had learned to vote as a block, occupied the courthouse. Since most people who worked there knew her, having her citizenship verified would be a simple matter, she thought. However, the official she asked, Bappa's cousin Karl Bieker who'd known her since she was four, drew himself up and, in garbled English, said he wouldn't consider it.

Teresa stared at him, remembering how Bappa used to say, in German, "You can look on a person's forehead but not read his brain." That's how she experienced Karl.

Beside her, to her amazement, Euphersine exploded. "You retard. You can't even speak English but you're an American citizen. Why can't she be one?"

Afterward she and Euphersine laughed about it, but Teresa knew her friend's outburst closed the testimony avenue. She wrote the Foundling and asked for proof of her birth. But the Sister in charge of records wrote that Teresa's case was closed. Teresa seethed. How could the Foundling close her case? She wasn't dead.

Undeterred, she wrote to New York City's Department of Health, asking it to search for her birth certificate. To her surprise, she received notice that the department had found no record of her. No record? How could that be? It seemed as though she was the only person who knew she was alive. She and her mother. Her breath shortened as she contemplated losing her job.

Teresa decided to write once more to the Foundling, saying, "I've got to know." This she did.

But the nun again wrote back, "Sorry. The case is closed."

Teresa became alarmed. What if she didn't prove her birth? What then? Maybe, she thought, the nun doesn't understand how much rests on this information. So one night, she composed a detailed letter to the Foundling. She told the nun that her library job supported her semi-invalid husband and their two children. "If I can't prove my citizenship," she wrote, "I will lose my job."

The Foundling nun's reply—that Teresa's mother had named her Jessie, not Teresa—shocked her. Jessie! She had never known her name to be anything but Teresa. Quite unexpectedly, the nun had returned a name that Teresa didn't know she'd lost. Which name should she use? Which one was really hers? Or were they both hers? Eventually Teresa decided to use "Teresa" since so many people knew her by that name.

The nun suggested Teresa search for information about Jessie Feit, so she did. This research took months. Teresa had to pay a quarter each time she wrote to New York City's Department of Health, so she taped the quarter to her letter. She mailed a lot of quarters before she received her birth certificate, but eventually the certificate, stamped November 18, 1940, arrived.

Making sense of the inscrutable birth certificate took Teresa several hours because of the odd statement on the bottom of the page. The Registrar of Records of New York City's Department of Health had printed: "NOTICE: In issuing this transcript of the Record, the Department of Health of the City of New York does not certify to the truth of the statements made thereon, as no inquiry as to the facts has been provided by law." Teresa read that and reread it. Finally she concluded her birth certificate was bogus, which didn't matter to her as long as Mrs. Fields accepted it as proof of United States citizenship.

Even though Teresa believed her birth certificate was fraudulent, she hesitated to examine it for fear it might be true. She now knew her given name; she knew that her mother had placed her in the Foundling and presumably paid for her for fourteen months, so she didn't care to know any more about what had happened more than thirty years ago. But her past simply refused to disappear.

If her birth certificate were true, then her mother gave birth to her on May 25, 1906, in New York's Lying-in Hospital. When she read that, her heart jumped. For the first time, she knew when she was born. Before, even though she celebrated her birthday on May 26, she actually knew only that she had been born somewhere between May 23 and May 30. She didn't even know what year, but now she knew she was thirty-four years old. If the certificate were true.

Teresa next learned that her mother, Rosie Breitowich Feit, had been twenty-one when she gave birth to Teresa. "Rosie," Teresa said. "Your name is Rosie, isn't it?" Teresa repeated the name, rolling it around her mouth. What a treasure, knowing her mother's name! Rosie had listed her address as "No Home" and her birthplace as Austria. Austria! Hadn't those two women asked if she were Austrian? What if one had been Rosie, seeking her? What if Monie were wrong?

The prospect sat like a lump in Teresa's throat. Determined not to cry, Teresa pushed her thoughts away. She couldn't consider Austrian ladies right now; right now she had to read her bogus birth certificate.

Teresa's father, Wolf Feit, a twenty-two-year-old baker with no address, had been born in Russia. This news devastated Teresa. To her, "Russian" meant "Volga German," and all she knew about Russians were the prejudices she had learned in Ellis County. "Dumb Roosians" and "dirty Roosians" were words that leaped to her mind, so she couldn't believe her bad luck in having "Roosian" blood. Only the notice stating that the facts might not be true gave her comfort. Still, she couldn't bear giving Mrs. Fields a certificate that stated Teresa Feit had half-Russian blood. So she took her pen and, as carefully as she could, changed the "R" in Russian to "Pr." There. Now she had Prussian blood. That felt auspicious.

So did Mrs. Fields' acceptance of the "fake" certificate, making Teresa's job secure.

On December 7, 1941, the Binders woke to news that Japanese planes had attacked the United States naval base at Pearl Harbor. Stunned, Teresa and Jess listened to the radio. More than two thousand people dead, eight U.S. battleships lost and the base suffered immense destruction, the broadcaster said.

The next day, President Roosevelt declared war against Japan. When Jess heard, he cried, "I'm going! I'm going to fight." Teresa looked at him, astonished, for there he sat, crippled, obviously unfit to join the army. Determined to enlist, Jess registered despite his 4-F classification. The army declined his services.

Soon Germany and Italy declared war on the United States, Congress voted to declare war on them, and World War II became official on both fronts. Like many Americans, Teresa held her breath.

For the next six months, Japan beat the United States repeatedly in Guam, Wake Island, Hong Kong, Malaya, and Singapore. Each loss made Teresa flinch. The gloomy war news troubled her—so many young men losing their lives.

Still she could not help but love how the war had changed Hays. Streets teemed with GIs from the nearby Walker Air Force Base. Teresa volunteered to wash dishes at the United Service Organization, a group designed to help soldiers. Some soldiers asked her for dates, and Jess said, "Oh, no!" but other married women dated the soldiers. Sometimes local women fell in love with the young energetic air force boys. Teresa envied these women, not their boyfriends but the way they typically met, at the dance hall for soldier boys. How she wished she could whirl around the big polished floor with men who might fly U.S. missions! Of course she couldn't. Jess would have a hissy.

At the library, thanks to regular practice, Teresa now typed fast enough to handle all the typing chores, including the catalogue cards. In fact, she typed so well she passed a civil service exam; Walker Air Force Base offered her a job.

"I think I should take it," Teresa told Jess. "The Air Force could use me." She was just as patriotic as Jess, in her own way.

"Why do you want a frigging job out there?" He looked up from the comic strips. "Folks say the goddamn base will hire any baboon who can tell a typewriter from a washing machine. You're better off at the damn library." He would not let her leave.

Jess's stubbornness didn't disappoint Teresa too much. If a job at the base was no big prize, she did not want it. Still, she wished her teacher, George Gatschet, saw how fast his "D" student typed.

During the war, the government issued stamps to ration gas, shoes, coffee, meat, butter, and sugar, but the Binders didn't suffer much from rationing. Since Jess owned no car, gas rationing didn't affect them. Between Jess, too sick to eat much, and Teresa, perpetually dieting to keep her slender figure, the family had plenty of food. Coffee rationing affected them most. Jess loved to drink coffee but Teresa didn't, so she guaranteed plenty of coffee for Jess by pretending she, too, was a coffee drinker when she picked up the coffee stamps. She did not like to lie; dishonesty made her queasy, but better a small lie than Jess's angry face over an empty coffee cup.

Inflation hit the Binders harder than rationing. Prices rose rapidly. What cost fourteen cents on Monday might cost nineteen cents by Thursday. Wages didn't keep pace, so Teresa's earnings seemed to dissolve. As she bought fewer and fewer groceries home for the same amount of money, Jess complained, "You son-of-a-bitch! Where's the frigging money going?"

Teresa tried to show him. "Everything's so high," she said, "even the Post Toasties."

Talking failed to convince Jess. His stubborn anger so frustrated Teresa that she retreated into the bedroom, closed the door and cursed Jess under her breath. Then she pulled her curly hair until she calmed down. She had to keep calm. Since that doctor said that riling Jess could cause his death, she'd managed to curb her quick temper—at least most of the time.

In May 1944, Teresa graduated from high school, one year after Mildred. How difficult going to school, working full time, and taking care of her family had been! Accepting her diploma, Teresa swore that she would never go to school again, but she soon took a library-science correspondence course from the University of Chicago. Kathryn O'Loughlin McCarthy, who had recommended her to Mrs. Fields, paid for the school—$40, an impressive amount. Eventually Teresa completed the fifteen long lessons, received an "A" in the non-accredited course, and earned a certificate in Library Technique. How that pleased her!

Teresa mentioned to her former neighbor, Dr. Burnett, a Fort Hays State College sociology professor, that the correspondence course lacked college credits. He suggested that she study library science at the college, so in the fall of 1944, she enrolled. Hearing that a grown woman was a college student excited a few people. In 1944, nontraditional female students were rare, especially one with a family and a job. Most supported Teresa although some, primarily Volgas, told her she shouldn't waste time getting an education. She wondered what they imagined she should do—stay at home and scrub floors?

Teresa's high school graduation picture. She was 38.
(Courtesy of Teresa Martin)

At first, Teresa took only subjects she wanted to study: German, English, and all the library courses she could find. Enrolling in German courses was easy; during the war, few wanted to study German. Those who did chose their hours, which made courses convenient. Not surprisingly, Teresa and three other students, all German majors, became close friends.

Frau Golden, a short fat professor with a heavy German accent, taught them. Teresa enjoyed studying with her, but the number of C's she received surprised her. After all, she had spoken High German since she turned four years old. What was she doing wrong? Had she offended the teacher? She asked Vince

Rufus, a fellow student, who told her that he got straight A's after his wife did Frau Golden's laundry.

"Give her some of your rations," he said. "Your grades will go up."

Teresa recoiled. Bribe the teacher? Surely, Frau Golden wouldn't change her grade for sugar stamps. Or would she? Finally, Teresa tested her. She gave some spare sugar stamps to Frau Golden, who seemed appreciative. When Teresa's grades jumped right up, she kept on giving her teacher extra stamps and received nothing but A's and B's after that. Having justified it with herself, Teresa continued to argue the issue with her mother who now had a name. "There's nothing wrong with that," she told Rosie. "She needs the sugar, and I deserve those grades."

Teresa enjoyed her college classes; she never knew when she would learn something unexpected. For instance, when a history professor, Eugene Richard Crane, said, "There are still people who believe in Adam and Eve," Teresa jumped, recognizing herself. She always believed that Bible stories were true. After that class, though, she wondered.

Another day, a student making a speech in class said horrible things about Japanese women. Teresa shifted in her seat. During the war, everybody talked against the Japanese, including herself, but in a public setting, the student's words made Teresa uncomfortable. She expected her professor, James R. Start, a well-liked, down-to-earth sort of man, to speak against the Japanese, too, but instead he changed the subject. This confused Teresa. Why hadn't he spoken out? Didn't he consider the Japanese people the enemy?

Once thing was clear: college made Teresa think.

Then in August 1945, the United States dropped atomic bombs on Hiroshima and Nagasaki, leaving her with mixed feelings. So terrific that we'd beaten Japan, but so awful that thousands of people died such gruesome deaths. When Japan surrendered on August 14, Teresa knew the war would not be over until the

Japanese signed articles of surrender on September 2, but around her, an enormous spontaneous celebration erupted. Even though it was Tuesday, stores closed as people poured out into the streets rejoicing the end of the war.

*The Binder family, 1947. From left, Teresa, seated, Mildred, Doris, Jess.
(Courtesy of Teresa Martin)*

One Sunday morning that fall, Jess yelled, "Dammit, I can't get any air!"

He's just being cranky. Then Teresa realized that Jess actually was struggling to breathe. Hands shaking, she called his brother George who drove them to Saint Anthony's Hospital. All the hospital's doctors were attending a convention except for one who admitted Jess; when he realized his new patient had an asthmatic heart, this doctor declined to care for him. *What kind of a doctor is he? I thought all doctors had to swear the Hippocratic Oath.* To her relief, nuns immediately stepped in to nurse Jess, especially Sister Myra who'd saved Doris's life when she was a baby.

Knowing that Teresa and Jess had a mixed marriage, some nuns decided to convert Jess to Catholicism, which irritated Teresa. Why should they bother her suffering husband about religion? This wasn't the place. Jess tried to put the nuns off by saying that he would become a Catholic "when I get out of here," meaning when he left the hospital.

One day when Teresa walked into his room, Jess picked up a newspaper. Smiling, he said, "See. I'm getting better. I'm reading the frigging funnies." He didn't know he held the paper upside down, but Teresa was not fooled. She knew Jess was fighting for his life and had been since they'd arrived at the hospital a week earlier. Believing he failed to understand the severity of his illness, she considered talking to him about the possibility that he might die. However, she didn't want to be pessimistic. She wondered if he knew when he said, "Should something happen to me, be careful, but I am going to be all right."

Sister Charles, who worked hard with Jess, seemed determined to baptize him before he died. When the family continued to refuse her, she asked if she could baptize him right after his death.

"For two hours after a person dies," she said, "the soul does not leave the body."

"After Jess is dead, you can do whatever you want," Teresa said. "Just do not trouble him while he's alive."

On the night of October 15, 1947, at the age of forty-five Jess's asthmatic heart gave way. Shortly after his last breath, Sister Charles baptized him Catholic. Teresa, watching, shook her head. Still in shock from Jess's death, she couldn't decide whether to be amused or amazed or angry. Certainly, she'd never met such a zealous Catholic as Sister Charles.

Afterward, Teresa called a taxi to take her and her daughters home, but in the flurry of last minute goodbyes, she forgot she'd called one. They walked the seven blocks home through a pitch-black night so still Teresa swore she heard her heart beat.

Doris, now seventeen, snuggled close to Teresa. "I'm your mother now," she said. "Daddy said if anything happened to him, I should look after you."

Teresa squeezed Doris's arm. "Hush. I can still take care of myself."

Although Sister Charles baptized Jess Catholic, his funeral was held in his Baptist church. Watching people pour in gratified Teresa. So many mourners crowded the service that the church set up extra chairs. Many people respected Jess for his bravery in the face of his pain from rheumatoid arthritis. *Well, Jess was no angel by any means, but his courage obviously inspired people.* How awful to be left with the knowledge that Jess thought she didn't love him. She did really care for him, but he was so strict, so set in his ways, he seemed more like her father than her husband. When she wasn't losing her temper at him, she was struggling to please him. Truly, what surprised her about Jess's death was her pride in him, a feeling he rarely invoked in her when he lived. *Ah, Rosie, mother mine. Maybe I loved him more than I thought.*

9

OH, TO BE LEARN-ED!

On January 6, 1948, Teresa became a grandmother. Her older child Mildred had married Jack Rosell and now gave birth to her first child, Sharon. Teresa adored having a grandchild, but at forty-two, she felt too young to be a grandma. She peered into the mirror to see if she looked different, but her curly hair was still black and she had hardly any wrinkles, just little crow's feet at the corners of her eyes. *Those don't matter. Those come from laughing.*

That fall, after Jess had been gone nearly a year, Teresa started to go to dances. Soon she dated. Eighteen-year-old Doris, still living with Teresa, abhorred her mother's dating. "Don't you bring any of your 'male friends' inside this house," Doris said, and Teresa agreed, but she continued to date. She couldn't let Doris rule her life.

Besides, she loved to dance. She never drank at dances, but my, she did enjoy dancing and flirting! *Goodness!* she thought as she refreshed her lipstick in the dance hall bathroom. *I'm as bad as a teenager, living just to doll up and cut a rug.* However, she carefully kept her active dating life from interfering with her college classes and library work. And Doris.

Some time later, Irene Binder, now running with the oil-field crowd, urged Teresa to meet a friend.

"I'm not interested," Teresa said. By then, so many dates had become tiresome that she recoiled from meeting still another man.

A few days later, Irene turned up at the library at closing. "Hurry up. Let's go for coffee at Kent's Café."

"Why? I don't want to meet any of those big fat greasy men with their oily clothes." But Teresa went anyway, to please Irene.

While they drank coffee, Teresa noticed a classy-looking man—handsome, well-dressed—sitting by himself. She pointed him out to Irene, "I'll bet that man's lonely."

Irene laughed. "He's the big fat greasy oil field worker I wanted you to meet."

So Teresa met Lawrence "Frenchy" Martin. No oil worker, Frenchy ran a string of cigarette machines and owned half of a Hays supper club, the Golden Acres.

On their first date, Teresa noticed his well-kept, late-model Buick, a Roadmaster. She liked the way he held the car door open for her as though she were royalty. Frenchy had manners, and he danced exceptionally well. She loved to feel the lightness of his hands as he held her; she loved the swift sure way he moved around the floor when they waltzed, and she loved the way he smiled down at her from time to time. Frenchy also had a beautiful crooning voice. He enjoyed singing, especially after he had had a bit to drink.

Soon Teresa dated no one else.

Doris objected. Of all Teresa's dates, she particularly disliked Frenchy. His drinking disgusted her.

Lawrence "Frenchy" Martin.
(Courtesy of Teresa Martin)

"I've heard you preach against drinking so often," Doris said, "I can't understand why you would go out with a man who comes to the door reeking of alcohol."

Teresa, who preferred to focus on Frenchy's assets, listened patiently. She knew Frenchy drank too much, but at least he drank legally. That November, Kansas had repealed its sixty-eight-year-old state prohibition law. Teresa laughed to read that only eighteen Ellis County residents, fewer than any county in the state, voted to keep Kansas dry. She bet none lived in Schoenchen!

Still, as time passed, nothing changed the fact of Jess's death. Teresa might forget it for hours or even days; then suddenly a memory would bring Jess to mind. She missed his constant presence. Not hearing his voice, not being told what to do, not being occupied every moment seemed strange to her. How could she be lonely with Doris and Frenchy around all the time? But she was. Lonely for Jess.

⁓

One afternoon, Mrs. Addison, head of Hays Business and Professional Women's Club and a dynamo in the community, approached Teresa. She knew Mrs. Addison to be a formidable woman. Mrs. Fields once hinted that Mrs. Addison's pull enabled Teresa to graduate from high school as rapidly as she did.

The intimidating woman laid a thick manuscript on Teresa's desk. "I'm a strong Episcopalian, you know, and we're looking for someone to type this history of the Episcopal church in Hays. Mrs. Fields says you type well. Won't you type this for us?"

"Oh, I don't know." Teresa eyed the thick handwritten manuscript. "I really don't have much time."

"But you don't have a husband at home anymore, do you?"

"No, but I'm taking courses at the college and sometimes I work overtime."

Mrs. Addison nodded. "I'll speak to Mrs. Fields about the overtime. You must remember that you are an orphan. You're fortunate to have this good library job and to be so well accepted in town. Now don't you think you could find a few moments here and there to type this for us?"

Teresa crumbled and took the copious manuscript home.

After Teresa finished the project, Mrs. Addison sponsored her into the Business and Professional Women's Club. She reminded Teresa how fortunate she was, as an orphan, to join this group. Soon Teresa had accepted an officer's position, and each month after she gave her report, Mrs. Addison would pat her and say,

"My, how much can those little shoulders carry?" So, despite the woman's pomposity, Teresa almost liked her.

Teresa met Mr. Addison, a genial unpretentious man. "You know, I saw you come into Hays from New York," he said.

"You did?"

"Yes, I was in the station that day watching this one and that one pick you up. My, you were popular! If I'd had my say, I'd have brought you home to be a little sister to our two boys."

This unexpected prospect of life with Mrs. Addison as her mother made Teresa flinch.

❧

Teresa experienced a disruptive recurring nightmare. In the dream, she shook a piece of laundry, a sheet or sometimes a towel, and a baby fell out. The dream petrified her; she woke short of breath, her heart pounding. She dimly remembered the Foundling's basement laundry where huge machines washed clothes, where white sheets hung on long lines. Such a disquieting dream. Was she that baby falling out of a sheet? That orphan? *Why won't my past leave me be?*

❧

Despite Doris's protests, Teresa and Frenchy continued to date. Before long, he asked her to marry him, but she refused. He was too spoiled, he drank too much, and when he sobered up, he became wretchedly ill. So Teresa turned down his repeated proposals.

Then one morning after Doris left for school, Frenchy came to Teresa's home to eat breakfast. With him, she had broken the rule about no male friends in the apartment, but she only let him in when Doris was away.

Noticing his hangover, Teresa fixed Frenchy some coffee, and then sat beside him at the table. When he attempted to scoop a spoonful of sugar, his hand shook so badly the spoon rattled against the sugar bowl. Teresa helped him hoist the sugar into his cup. *I took care of Jess. I might as well take care of him.* She watched him lift his shaking cup with both hands. *At this rate, he won't live out the year anyway.* So she agreed to marry him.

Before they could marry, Teresa entered the hospital to have a nonmalignant fibroid tumor removed from her uterus, a tumor that Doris insisted Frenchy caused. When Teresa needed a blood transfusion, Frenchy offered to donate blood, but their types didn't match.

"Doris," Teresa said, ever mindful of her fiancé's virtues, "wasn't it nice of Frenchy to offer his blood?"

Doris demurred, "His blood would be no good; it would be full of alcohol."

Knowing Doris would protest their wedding, Teresa and Frenchy married secretly on March 26, 1951, in nearby Russell so they could avoid a notice in the Hays newspaper. When the newlyweds returned, they continued to live separately, hoping Doris would suspect nothing until after her upcoming July marriage to Donald Crippen, a college boy.

At work, Teresa continued to be "Mrs. Binder," although Frenchy objected. "Let's let people know you're Mrs. Martin." However, Teresa, afraid of Doris's anger, refused.

❧

At the library, the new director, Lucy Cole, hired after Sara Fields died, resigned. Teresa was glad. Miss Cole stood over six feet tall, and she lied to board members about Teresa's work. She said Teresa knew only how to shelve books, as if she hadn't been cataloging books and supervising the children's library for years under Mrs. Fields. Fortunately, board members ignored Miss Cole and promoted Teresa to children's librarian.

After the new director resigned, Teresa received calls suggesting she apply for the position. At first, she dismissed the idea. She never dreamed of becoming head librarian and certainly couldn't apply now; she needed time to heal from her tumor operation. As more people encouraged her to apply, she decided to try.

On the day of her formal interview, Teresa arrived at the library unusually edgy, having downed only several cups of coffee for breakfast. As she walked into the familiar boardroom, she seemed to step back in time. The board members' familiar faces encircling her transformed into the faces of her Volga German classmates on the playground. A sense of helplessness rose in her. Everyone seemed to shout; she couldn't hear what anyone said. She felt battered.

One man asked her about ordering books, which she'd done for years, but she couldn't think how to answer him. Another asked about cataloguing, but she forgot everything she knew, including her courses in library science. She did remember that Miss Herriot, her Fort Hays instructor, considered her unusually good at library work, but she didn't know how to mention that.

Finally she stuttered, "I guess I don't know a thing," and fled the way she'd run from her tormenters when they cried, *"Das geschickte,"* "The sent-for one," the mail-order kid.

In the ladies' room, she wept. *I knew the answers! I knew them. Why did I clam up?*

The board selected Dorothy Richards for the position, even though she had only two hours of library science. Teresa feared Mrs. Richards would fire her for her behavior in the boardroom, but the new director didn't. That was a relief. Teresa needed her paychecks to help Doris finance a fine wedding.

To her surprise, Teresa felt no jealousy of Mrs. Richards. Instead, she liked the brash outspoken woman. *How can I feel bitter? She applied for the job and got it fair and square.* But Teresa cringed when the new director bragged about how easily she'd aced the interview. However, Mrs. Richards knew how to put Teresa at ease. That, as much as anything, led to their friendship, although it helped when Teresa showed the new director many aspects of the library that she didn't know.

Teresa (left) and Dorothy Richards in the Hays Public Library.
(Courtesy of Teresa Martin)

Several months passed before Doris discovered Teresa and Frenchy's secret marriage. As planned, the Hays newspaper did not write up the marriage, but Russell's newspaper did, and someone mentioned it to Doris. Infuriated not only about Teresa's marriage but also about her deliberate secrecy, Doris confronted her mother. Earlier, when Teresa became a grandmother, Doris excitedly called her "Gross," short for "*Grossmütter*" or Grandmother. Now Doris sobbed, "You aren't my Gross anymore!" and yanked a fur coat, a gift from Frenchy, off her mother's back and jumped up and down on it.

Because of her daughter's fury, Teresa lived separately from Frenchy the next six weeks, until Doris married Don. That July after the Crippens returned from their honeymoon and relocated to Lenore, Kansas, Teresa gathered her belongings and scurried to Frenchy's upstairs apartment at 413 West Eighth Street.

What a relief, being with Frenchy at last, after all that deception and the strain of bad feelings with Doris! Teresa could hardly contain herself. Frenchy wasn't as handsome as Clark Gable, but almost. And he was such a character. Putting a cow in the classroom. Having a shotgun marriage. Just like him.

Teresa's warmth for Frenchy rushed to the surface. She felt certain this marriage, based on love instead of convenience, would be fulfilling, but she soon regretted her move. Living with Frenchy lacked the ease she had known when she lived with Doris. Oh, he let her do what she pleased, at least usually, but nothing could duplicate the bliss of being her own boss.

Worse yet, Frenchy, such a boring drunk, found innumerable reasons to "hang one on." He drank to celebrate the Yankees winning, and he drowned his sorrow when they lost. One day Teresa bought a pair of cheap shoes for $12. She didn't realize they were made of straw until they fell apart in a rain storm later that day. When Frenchy heard, it drove him to drink to think Teresa bought shoes that lasted only one day.

Dancing provided one more reason to drink. The Martins danced every Saturday, and Teresa usually enjoyed it. People often asked Frenchy to sing, for he sang beautifully. However, Frenchy's drinking often drove them home early. Teresa hated being his handmaid, especially since she knew that in the morning he'd have a hair of the dog that bit him to launch his weekend drinking.

～

On July 30, 1954, Teresa, now forty-eight, completed the college education she had started ten years earlier. During that decade, she attended school as she could, not at all some semesters. Money was never a problem. She could easily pay the $8-an-hour tuition from her library salary. Finding time proved more difficult. Teresa almost gave up school until Stanley Dalton, the registrar, said, "If you stop taking just the courses you like, and take a few courses you don't like, then you could graduate."

So Teresa earned a degree with a dual major in English and German and a minor in library science. She wished Sister Rosina could see how she'd set herself apart from her eighth-grade classmates, and this time, not with white stockings.

Many in town including *The Hays Daily News* considered Teresa's graduation unusual. Few older women went to college, and even fewer did so while working full-time. The newspaper published a feature on her accomplishment: "Grandmother of Four to be Graduated from Ft. Hays State." The headline was true. Mildred and her husband, Jack, had produced three more children: Johnny, in 1949; Susie, 1951; and Bill, 1952.

College administrators arranged for Teresa to march down the commencement aisle alone to make her unique achievement visible. This made her nervous. What if she stumbled? Her clammy hands stuck to the black robe and mortarboard she had donned. They certainly weren't the most stylish garments she'd worn, but they were highly satisfying, for she looked like every other graduating senior.

At home that night, Teresa remembered how proud she was to be "educated" when she graduated from eighth grade. How tiny her eighth-grade knowledge looked now! Even her baccalaureate seemed insufficient. She wished she had a library science major, but Fort Hays State didn't offer one; Emporia College had a franchise on library science in Kansas.

If I could just get a master's degree. But where?

The only close schools offering graduate degrees in library science were Denver University and Emporia College in Emporia, Kansas. Emporia College, which had invited Teresa to study in its library school, was about two hundred miles away. That was closer to Hays than Denver, but how could she get there? She had no car and didn't know how to drive. However, the Union Pacific stopped in Hays on its way to Denver, making transportation easy, so Teresa applied there.

When Denver University accepted Teresa, she resigned from the Hays Public Library after having worked there for eighteen years. She was eager to leave even though she enjoyed working for Mrs. Richards, now her close friend. However, to Teresa's dismay, Mrs. Richards let her teenage daughter "help out" in the library. The young woman busied herself in the children's department, butted into Teresa's business, and tattled every time Teresa waived a two-cent fine. Her nosiness nauseated Teresa, but she could not bear to mar her friendship with Mrs. Richards, so she never complained. Leaving the library solved that problem.

Teresa had another reason to move to Denver: Frenchy. She longed to get away from him, especially from his drinking. Since he had to tend his cigarette machine business in Hays, he couldn't move with her. Sorry that she had married him, she still was Catholic enough that she did not want to divorce him, but she wanted to put some distance between them. Three hundred miles seemed about right.

Before Teresa's last day of work, Ed Wilson, who had ridden the train to Hays about 1901, came into the library looking for her. Mr. Wilson, a rare tall orphan, received a lucky placement with the Wellbrooks in Victoria. They gave Ed an excellent education, making him one of the few New York orphans in Ellis County to earn a college degree. Now he worked in a Hays bank and dabbled in insurance, finance, and real estate.

Highly respected for his intelligence, Mr. Wilson remained proud and aloof. He never came to the library and never spoke to Teresa, so his presence surprised her.

"I hear you've resigned," he said.

"Yes."

"I sure hate to see you leave. I never paid much attention to you, but I feel there's a kind of bond between us."

Teresa understood what he meant. She, too, felt a bond with other New York orphans—Pete who died of Spanish flu, Mary Childs who'd ridden with her on the train, and, yes, even Mr. Wilson whose career she had followed so closely and with such pride.

~

In Denver, Teresa found a room on busy East Evans Avenue near the university. What a relief! That first quarter, she carried a full load of studies, worked part-time at the school, and occasionally took care of children for pin money.

Denver University, unfortunately, turned out to be less than congenial. Students whose ample allowances enabled them to attend movies and plays that Teresa couldn't afford intimidated her. Listening to them talk made her life seem paltry. Her sense of self-worth, never high, seemed to sink daily. Worse yet, Dr. Bailey, head of the library science department, seemed to dislike her. She could not imagine why. She had never done anything to him.

Still, Denver felt distinctly better than Hays. No one in that huge city knew that her parents had given her to the Foundling. Her past hadn't followed her. What a blessing!

On the evening of November 17, 1954, Teresa, in her room, heard the phone ring downstairs.

"It's for you," the landlady, Mrs. Dekker, called. "From Scotts Air Force Base."

That would be Doris, her husband is in the air force now! She must have delivered their baby!

As Teresa raced downstairs, her foot caught between two banister slats, and she fell. She limped to the phone and watched her foot balloon as she heard Doris's good news—a boy, Galen.

When she hung up, Mrs. Dekker said, "I don't want you to call the doctor."

Afraid to anger her, Teresa agreed. She went to bed pleased about Doris's news, but she slept poorly. Pain from every twist and turn kept her awake.

The next day, scared to limp downstairs and face Mrs. Dekker, Teresa stayed in bed until a classmate, Martha, visited her. "Why aren't you in school?"

"Something's wrong with my foot." Teresa pulled the covers aside.

"It looks awful! You've got to see a doctor."

"I can't. I promised the landlady I wouldn't."

"Nonsense." Martha grabbed Teresa's coat. "Here. Put this on. I'll go with you."

With Martha as a shield, Teresa limped by Mrs. Dekker. The two visited a doctor who pronounced Teresa's foot broken and put a cast on it.

Teresa tried to think ill of no one, but she did wish her landlady would break her foot, be forced to climb a flight of stairs, and lie in bed twenty-four hours with her ankle throbbing. How could she be so cruel?

Learning to walk on her cast was not that difficult. Once she got used to walking on it, she moved around almost as freely as usual. Why she even danced on it when she went back to Hays to visit Frenchy!

Weeks later, Teresa found the courage to ask Mrs. Dekker why she didn't want her to see a doctor.

"I was afraid you would sue me," the landlady said.

Teresa laughed. "Unfortunately, I'm too kind hearted to be the suing kind."

⁓

At the end of the second quarter, Dr. Bailey tried to block Teresa's "A" in an audio-visual course taught by another faculty member. "She doesn't deserve an A," he said.

Teresa knew she was no audio-visual expert, but she crammed to earn that grade. Finally, to her relief, Dr. Bailey let the grade stand, but their disagreement unsettled her, especially when her counselor, Dr. Post, told her Dr. Bailey didn't like her.

"Go to another library school," Dr. Post said. "Bailey will never let you pass here."

However, Teresa refused to quit. Why should she? Dr. Bailey may not think she was graduate-level material, but others did. Teresa had done exceptionally well during her library practice at Colorado State Library, so well that after she finished her practice, the library director hired her full-time. A short while later, the director reluctantly let Teresa go when the state cut library funds, but she recommended Teresa to Mercy Hospital for a full-time job as medical librarian, a field she never considered.

"I don't know a thing about medical literature," Teresa said at her interview, but Mercy Hospital hired her as a full-time faculty member. Her monthly salary was only $150, a sizable drop in pay from the $300 a month she received from the Colorado State Library. Still, being a medical librarian pleased her—such a prestigious job, as important as any job she could hope to land with a master's degree.

Despite Teresa's successes in the field, her relationship with Dr. Bailey deteriorated. In his catalog class, he humiliated her so often she crumbled whenever he looked her way. He unnerved her so she couldn't settle into her desk without spilling books or dropping her pencil.

Teresa dreaded final exams, scheduled for spring. Her final would be in cataloging, an exam designed to test everything she knew about the subject. She had no reason to fear the test for she'd earned B's in all her catalog courses, both in Hays and at Denver University. However, the exam—a verbal one—would be given by several professors, including Dr. Bailey.

On exam day, Teresa's digestion flared up, so she ate no breakfast. She knew she needed to eat, but food seemed unappetizing. Finally, she ate a few peanuts, which seemed to settle her stomach.

When she walked into the exam room, she felt a tickle in her throat. Ignoring it, she talked to herself, trying to lift her spirits as she waited for the exam to begin. *Remember, Teresa, you've studied diligently. You know quite a bit about cataloging. You will do okay.* Because she reminded herself that several teachers—not just Dr. Bailey—would question her, she wasn't prepared for Dr. Bailey to ask the first question.

He did, saying, "What is the purpose of the card catalog?"

Teresa, to her surprise, blanked. She knew she knew the answer. However, facing Dr. Bailey, her knowledge disappeared. Had she ever heard of such a thing as the purpose of a card catalog? Not that she could remember.

Unable to answer that first question, she stiffened. Other teachers posed more questions, but she bungled her answers.

When the questions stopped, she fled the room in tears. In the hall, she remembered that the purpose of the card catalog was to serve as the index to the holdings in the library. Of course. Other answers also became obvious as she crossed the campus.

Shaken, she stopped to eat at an East Evans Avenue restaurant; those peanuts had not been enough. After lunch, she went to her room and packed her suitcase. Planning to visit Frenchy and Doris in Hays, she returned to East Evans Avenue to wait for the bus. As she stood at the bus stop, her stomach churning, she blacked out, falling on top of a garbage can. When she revived, she lay in the back room of a nearby drugstore under the gaze of a concerned pharmacist who took her to Saint Luke's Hospital. Doctors told her she was suffering from "complete exhaustion" and recommended bed rest.

Lying in her hospital bed day after day, Teresa found ample time to reflect. She knew stress exhausted her. Dr. Bailey was the obvious source of stress, but his hatred alone hadn't put her in the hospital. No, what put her here was a series of stresses, his included. Another was lack of sleep; she slept fitfully before her final exam. Then she not only carried a full-time load of graduate credits at Denver University but also worked full-time at a new job in Mercy Hospital. On top of that, she worked part-time caring for children.

That part-time work helped her financially before she got her job, so she felt obligated to those mothers. She couldn't just leave them in the lurch. Maybe she should stop babysitting; the mothers surely had other help now. Teresa felt she could not drop her new job at Mercy. That would be financial ruin. Besides, she liked the Mercy job. No, she must change her relationship with Denver University if she didn't want to faint on top of another garbage can.

Perhaps she should relinquish her ambition to have a master's degree. She didn't really need an M.A. now since she'd landed as good a librarian job as any master's degree could get her.

Giving up the degree would please Dr. Bailey, and he would stop harassing her. She knew he didn't think she was master's degree material, so if she gave up that goal, she still could take a few more courses here and there, as time passed. Surely, he wouldn't mind that.

The thought of pulling back at Denver University saddened Teresa. After all, she'd accomplished so many goals: learning High German as a child; finding housekeeping jobs; supporting her family through the Depression; learning library skills; learning to type; graduating from high school and then from college. She was not a quitter. The very idea made her squirm.

Still, if she gave up her goal of getting a master's degree, she could concentrate on her new job at Mercy with its emphasis on medical literature. She'd have time to study and learn about that unknown field, a goal perhaps more important than a master's.

During Teresa's several-week stay in the hospital, she became convinced this was the realistic course of action. She knew it partly because of her deep sense of satisfaction when she imagined never coming into conflict with Dr. Bailey again. Never.

The following school year, 1955–56, Teresa continued to study at Denver University but only part-time. Dr. Bailey gave her no grief. To learn about medical literature for her new position, she took physiology and medical terminology courses at the University of Colorado's extension campus in Denver. She performed well in her classes and felt comfortable at Mercy Hospital.

Then someone knocked on her door.

She opened it to see Frenchy's slender body and bright smile, a sight she never expected to see in Denver. Suspicion tempered her joy. "What are you doing here?"

Frenchy said he had sold his cigarette machines, traded in his old Buick Roadmaster for a newer one, and driven to Denver. "I just want to be with you."

Despite her tiny room, she agreed to let him live with her. He was, after all, her husband, but she knew how weak he was. He never could resist a snoot full. She prayed she wasn't making a mistake.

At home, Teresa decided to spoil Frenchy; she let him have his way 98 percent of the time. She enjoyed making him happy, and she needed little in return. She had her own friends, doing research for doctors satisfied her, and at night she read a lot, studied, or crocheted. Later, after they purchased a TV, Frenchy watched it, especially the Westerns. Sometimes Teresa looked at *Gunsmoke* with him, sitting by his side, crocheting little favors for the doctors during commercials.

Except for the TV, Frenchy couldn't stand noise, so Teresa kept their home quiet. But oddly enough, after a few drinks Frenchy became voluble himself, filling the silent air with the sound of his voice. At such times, Teresa despaired.

When Frenchy didn't drink too much, he and Teresa got along unusually well. Teresa looked forward to those times, even though they were fleeting; they refreshed her like ice-cold milk in a tin mug.

She and Frenchy had little in common except they both loved to dance. They went to dances almost every week, twice a week sometimes, cavorting to songs like "Alexander's Rag Time Band" and the "St. Louis Blues," pieces Teresa relished. She and Frenchy also loved to waltz, especially the Viennese waltz. Frenchy still danced magnificently, his body moving like a lithe, lean cat. Sometimes Teresa wondered if she married him so she could claim him as her dancing partner.

Teresa's job as a medical librarian at Mercy Hospital satisfied her, especially working with prestigious doctors. Whenever a doctor entered the library, she thrilled to watch the nurses stand up as a sign of respect. At first, Teresa's awe of doctors hindered her. She expected them to act superior, like Mrs. Addison, but they did not. Their grief over lost patients surprised her. Gradually, as she understood they saw themselves as human, she felt comfortable working with them. Then she noticed that the doctors acted like her Hays library children; when they asked for a book, they wanted it instantly. So she decided to treat them as she'd treated her Hays children. Rather than attempt to impress them, she acted naturally. Her tactic worked well. The doctors grew appreciative of her.

Professionally, 1956 was a year of achievement for Teresa. When the National Accreditation for Schools of Nursing team came to Mercy Hospital, it gave Teresa a 100 percent positive rating. This delighted her, but even more moving were tributes that Mercy students wrote about her in *Chart*, the school of nursing paper.

"Small in stature, large in unceasing benevolence," wrote one student, "she is our guide to the wondrous world of unending knowledge."

Teresa wished Sister Rosina could see how well her little orphan was doing in her "rooms full of books." Clearly, life—except for Frenchy's drinking—was good.

Even though she loved working in Mercy Hospital, in 1962 Teresa left. As she saw it, she had no choice. When students used the library, Teresa treated them with the same deference that she treated the doctors, so students came in droves. That created a problem. A pharmacology teacher in a nearby office complained that the students' noise interrupted her work. The situation seemed impossible to resolve. Teresa couldn't change the way she treated students, but she feared a confrontation with the complaining teacher. Much as she wanted to blow up, tell the professor what she thought of such niggling insistence on a pristine quiet, Teresa dared not. Who was she to stand up to a professor? Only an orphan with no master's degree.

Then, Presbyterian Hospital, at that time the most prestigious hospital in Denver, offered her a position with higher pay. The offer flattered her. It made leaving easy.

Teresa enjoyed her work as a medical librarian in Denver.
Such prestige, doing research instead of reading to children in Hays!
(Courtesy of Teresa Martin)

PART III:
AGENTS OF CHANGE

10

ORPHAN TRAIN RIDERS

S ecular Frenchy respected his wife's Catholicism. Teresa liked to attend Mass even though her civil marriage prevented her again from being an active Catholic. On cold or rainy days, Frenchy drove her to church. She liked pulling up in the big Buick Roadmaster, waiting while Frenchy rounded the car and opened her door. He still was gallant.

While he parked, Teresa chose an aisle seat close to the exit. She knew that Frenchy, after the middle of the service, would whisper, "Is it communion?" Catholics could leave after communion and still feel they'd attended Mass, so when Frenchy drove, he and Teresa never stayed for the blessing.

Then one rainy day while Teresa waited inside for Frenchy to bring up the car, she spotted a slim publication, "Mater Dei," on a church table. Noticing that the Foundling Hospital published the pamphlet, she picked it up and flipped it open. Inside was a photograph of the Foundling building where she'd lived. The sight chilled her. Then she recognized a photo of the hospital administrator; Sister Teresa Vincent, wearing her odd black bonnet, gazed at Teresa again. When Teresa saw Frenchy's Buick slide along the curb, she slipped the publication inside her suit jacket to protect it from rain and ran to the car.

At home, she devoured the pamphlet. It focused on an April 1, 1962, reunion in Grand Island, Nebraska, a reuniting of children that the Foundling had shipped there fifty years ago. The pamphlet said fifty-two of the fifty-seven children sent to Nebraska by the Foundling May 20, 1912, came to the gathering from five different states. Teresa was astounded. Fifty-two "children" like her and Pete, and Mary Childs, and Mr. Wilson, people who had experienced being dressed in new clothes, boarding a train, and walking into an unknown world of new "parents." Not in Kansas but in Nebraska.

She read that the orphans showed one another "treasured possessions," the tiny suits and dresses they'd worn, faded photographs, baptismal certificates. Teresa wondered if any had saved a numbered tag. Then the orphans "traded tales" of their lives, but the pamphlet didn't describe what they said. Had their childhoods been as horrible as hers had? Better? Worse?

Mrs. Howard Kingdon of Grand Island, an organizer for the event, had written to the Foundling and asked a representative to attend. Three did: Sister Marie Catharine, Foundling administrator; Rt. Rev. Daniel A. McGuire; and Sister Thomasina.

Sister Marie Catharine, reporting on the event for her Advisory Board, described how the orphans, mostly unknown to each other, had been drawn to the reunion by a common need—the need "to try to fill the void in their hearts created by the absence of knowledge about their identity," including parents and siblings. For each of them, she said, the Foundling had been "their first known home." Slowly the nun realized that she, Monsignor McGuire, and Sister Thomasina had become like parents to these people.

"Eager to be near their parents," she reported, they surrounded each Foundling representative, "and since we were father and mother to each and to all, they became, as if by one impulse, brothers and sisters of one another."

Brothers and sisters? Teresa brushed away tears as she remembered her appendix operation, coming up from the ether and crying, "I'm all alone. I don't have any brothers or sisters." Feelings she'd stifled for years leaped to the surface. She sobbed. Thank goodness, Frenchy was glued to the TV; how could she explain her tears? If these people really felt like brothers and sisters to each other, she wanted to be part of their family. Indeed, she felt as drawn to these orphans as a hairpin to a magnet.

Teresa wondered if this group planned another reunion. The pamphlet printed only the Foundling's Office of Closed Records address, and she remembered how difficult her correspondence with that office was. Fortunately, she had honed her research skills. Soon she had the address of an organizer, Mrs. Kingdon.

A reply to Teresa's letter came swiftly. Yes, another reunion was set for spring 1963. Mrs. Kingdon had placed Teresa's name on the mailing list. The letter contained a photocopy of a news article about the 1962 reunion. The Golden Jubilee reunion, they called it. And yes, many orphans arrived wearing "Shipping Tags," which bore their names and the names of their sponsors. For the first time, Teresa wished she had hers.

～

Teresa didn't attend the spring 1963 reunion. Frenchy's older sister, Nettie Starnes, died, throwing her plans out of kilter. Mrs. Starnes, twenty years older than Frenchy and his last living sibling, had visited them in 1956. She called Frenchy by his given name, Lawrence, and spoiled him almost as much as Teresa did.

One day when Teresa came home late from the hospital, Mrs. Starnes said, "Where have you been? Lawrence had to get up on a chair and put in a light bulb."

Mrs. Starnes liked Teresa, especially the way her care had mellowed her headstrong brother, so she said, "When I die, you and Frenchy will inherit that house of mine in Colby." True to her word, when Mrs. Starnes died, she left her Colby, Kansas, home to the Martins, so Teresa went to Kansas with Frenchy instead of attending the Nebraska reunion.

However, in spring 1964, Teresa boarded a train in Denver and headed to Nebraska to go to the Third Annual Nebraska Reunion, this one in Primrose, population about 200. Teresa thought it looked like a Kansas town with its grocery store, service station, bank, and many small square houses, all flanked by two tall grain elevators.

Since Teresa arrived late, she went directly to bed in the small room provided for her. She slept poorly, especially after a dream woke her about 4:00 a.m., a dream she used to have, the dream where she shook a baby out of a towel. She woke petrified, her heart pounding. In the dark room, she almost smelled the Foundling laundry.

In the morning, she rose early, dressed, and slipped over to the big brick auditorium. Someone had cracked open a set of double doors, so she slipped in. The auditorium was huge; it looked as though it could hold everyone in town and then some. She thought she was alone until she noticed someone unpacking brochures and placing them on a table. The woman looked up. What a pinched face she had, but when she smiled, it didn't matter.

"Looking for the orphans' reunion?" the woman said.

Teresa nodded, "I came from the Foundling to Kansas."

"Ah! You're one of us!" The woman set down the brochures and held out a hand. "I'm Mary Tenopir. I came to Nebraska when I was two."

The women smiled and held hands for a moment. Tears dampened Teresa's eyes.

"Well," Mary loosened her hands. "Why don't you help yourself to coffee and sweet rolls on the table over there? We won't start for a while."

Teresa turned to see breakfast laid on what looked like a linen cloth with a stunning array of flowers in the middle.

"How pretty the table is!" Teresa walked slowly toward it, taking it in.

"You like it?" Mary looked up from her brochures. "I learned how to set a beautiful table when I worked in the homes of doctors and judges and a well-to-do ranch family."

Teresa stopped, "You worked in people's homes, too?"

"I sure did. You learn a lot doing that, don't you?"

Teresa nodded and told Mary about snooty Mrs. Brown who said things like "I have place mats for four, but now we are five."

Mary laughed. "You never know who you're going to find inside a house until you work there. Most of my families were good to me, real friendly, like the judge who let me bring my boyfriend in for special occasions. But in the doctor's house, I had to eat alone in the kitchen after I'd served the family."

"How awful!"

"It was degrading, that's what it was." Mary returned to her brochures. Teresa poured a cup of coffee and watched other adults, many about her age, enter the room, greet each other, and help themselves to breakfast. Soon she stood with a group of orphans comparing their lives. Mass was scheduled at 11:00 a.m., but 11 came and 11 went and no one stirred.

"Are we going to have Mass in here?" Teresa said.

"Oh, no." The tall loosely built man who answered her had heavy jowls. "We'll go over to St. Mary's."

"Shouldn't we go?"

The man laughed and patted her on the shoulder. "Might as well wait here where we can refill our coffee cups. Gettin' places on time isn't one of Father Fangman's virtues. He probably heard of a farmer wanting to sell some junk and just had to go see."

Moments later, a tiny priest, almost as small as Teresa, stuck his head in the doorway.

"Here we go." The heavy-jowled man led a procession of participants down the street to the church.

Seeing how small Saint Mary's was, tiny and white and square, startled Teresa. She had expected another Saint Anthony's, huge and built of stone. How could such a small church serve 200 Primrose people when fifty people in Schoenchen needed a Saint Anthony's to serve them? As she waited for Mass to start, she looked around. The light, airy interior was pretty with tall stained glass windows. *Wait a minute.* She squinted. *That's not stained glass, it's regular glass with something, maybe decals, on it.* She understood then how devoted the Schoenchen Catholics were, giving to the church first and themselves later.

When Teresa and the others returned to the auditorium, a buffet table sat waiting. They gathered their food and sat, eating and chatting, at long tables covered with white paper. The main speaker was a psychologist from Hastings, Nebraska, who specialized in post-traumatic stress disorders resulting from adoption. His topic was "Genealogical Bewilderment."

The psychologist stood, a tall thin man with graying red hair and intense blue eyes. "If you are a typical orphan," he said, "you tend to feel disconnected from the past. That's because your birth parents left you without clues to your identity."

Teresa noticed a general sort of stirring in the audience.

"You may notice this loss of your parents and your extended birth family at critical times, like birthdays," the speaker said. "For instance, you may have met your first blood relative when a son or daughter was born." Teresa jumped, remembering the incredible glow of love she experienced when she first saw Mildred.

"To lose your parents and your extended birth family like this is more global than a divorce or death. So your search for your parents becomes broadened to a reconstruction of an entire culture, missing for most of your life. When the New York Foundling brought you out here, you not only lost your parents, you lost your origins. Your sense of self has been damaged, and it's this loss of self that you grieve for."

The group burst into prolonged applause. Teresa turned to speak to the man beside her, but she noticed his wet cheeks so she remained silent.

Next orphans rose, one by one, to tell their stories. No two were alike, and neither were their attitudes. A Mr. Lang had a terrible time as a youth and never got over it.

Fred Swedenburg, the big-jowled man, said, "Sometimes you hear sad stories during these reunions. As we grow older, many of us research our pasts, only to find bitter secrets, and sometimes children lived in sad homes after they were placed." He seemed calm about it, almost resigned. Then came an orphan who had been adopted by a banker and had a good life. He was quite cocky.

Mary Tenopir had asked Teresa to speak. She agreed, and then sat twisting her handkerchief; she'd never told anyone her story. As she listened, she noticed that the orphans who spoke usually told about riding the train and what happened in the home assigned to them. When she imagined standing up in front of all those people and talking about the Biekers, she nearly told Mary Tenopir she couldn't speak. But before she could contact Mary, it was her turn.

Looking at the inquisitive faces made Teresa open her speech as she planned in Denver, "I was born on May 25, 1906, the same year as the electric washing machine, the Victrola, milk cartons, permanent waves and Greta Garbo." Audience laughter reassured her. As she spoke, time passed quickly, like a spring breeze. When she finished, she feared that she'd rambled until

Mary Tenopir and others told her how beautifully she spoke, how her story moved them.

Then Mary Tenopir described the seventeen years she'd worked taking care of mothers and their new babies, washing, baking, and ironing with a flat iron heated on a stove. Just as Teresa ironed.

Next, up stepped Father Fangman who had celebrated their Mass. Teresa didn't know he was an orphan, but he was. People in Raeville, an unincorporated village, took him. A skinny little man, Father Fangman didn't talk long, although he said he was born Jewish but raised Catholic. Teresa stirred. She wondered how he knew he was Jewish. The priest seemed nervous. He shook a lot and rushed through his words. Mostly he spoke about how he never tried to find his folks. Teresa wondered if he thought he should. Those who knew him seemed to love him. They called him Father Paulie.

At last orphan Mary Buscher rose to great applause. She described, for the new orphans, how in 1960 she read an article about orphans who went to New York to visit the Foundling thirty years after the Foundling had placed them. The paper quoted one orphan as wondering if any other Foundling orphans lived near her Nebraska home.

"I was so excited, I just tracked down her phone number and called her," Mary Buscher said. "Together we planned and advertised the 1962 Golden Jubilee, which, as you know, received national news coverage. It seemed like every mail delivery brought the name of some orphan somewhere in the United States. So we made our Nebraska reunion an annual event."

After hearing everyone's stories, Teresa realized that the Biekers weren't the only caretakers who had good intentions but became sorry they had taken a child. Maybe her life hadn't been so bad after all. True, the Biekers had expected her to help with chores, but she hadn't worked nearly as hard as some of these orphans had. She always had plenty to eat, even if it was coarse, unappetizing food, and she went to school. Of course, not everyone had to deal with a caretaker with octopus hands like Bappa.

Then musicians started to play on the stage, and suddenly everyone danced. *Oh, joy!* Mary Tenopir grabbed Teresa's hand, and they danced polka after polka after polka. Teresa liked Mary. So friendly, so at ease. She felt like the sister Teresa wished she had.

Riding on the train back to Denver, Teresa savored her experiences. Mary Tenopir seemed particularly close, but Teresa felt connected with all these orphans who rode to the Great Plains—even the cocky orphan adopted by the banker and nervous Father Fangman. Somehow, she knew them more intimately than she knew most people. In a way, the orphans did seem like family but not blood relatives like Mildred and Doris. These orphans were family of another sort, men and women bonded by their common train ride and by the similar threads in the patterns of their lives. Adopted siblings. Perhaps the brothers and sisters she longed for when she came out of the ether. She no longer felt, as she had then, so alone.

11

A Foundling Orphan

I nitially, Teresa enjoyed the novelty of working at Presbyterian Hospital. At that time, Boris Pasternak's novel, *Dr. Zhivago*, was the rage. Teresa jumped when she heard Dr. Zhivago paged over the hospital intercom, but then everyone giggled, and so did she.

As time passed, Teresa grew to dislike Presbyterian. The library holdings disappointed her, she hated the rampant snobbery, and she didn't trust Mrs. Beaten, her director, a stolid woman whose voice box trouble made her rasp. When she interviewed Teresa, the woman promised to put Teresa in charge of the nurses' library, housed separately in the nurses' dorm, while Mrs. Beaten would manage the doctors' library. Actually, Mrs. Beaten ran both libraries, pressing Teresa into service at any time.

Worse than Mrs. Beaten was the snobbery, which wore Teresa down. It reminded her of grade-school days, when children treated her like scum. It reminded her of the Biekers, of Judge

Gross, and of the women like Mrs. Addison who made sure she knew her place. It reminded her that no matter how high she rose, she could never shed her past. No one at Presbyterian knew she was an orphan; she had made certain of that. No one in Denver knew but Frenchy. Still, at Presbyterian, she felt like one.

In 1968, Porter Memorial Hospital, a Denver hospital run by Seventh-Day Adventists, asked Teresa for an interview. She went, although she knew nothing about Seventh-Day Adventists.

At the interview, she said, "Why are you interested in me? I'm a Catholic."

"But you are the nearest to a Seventh-Day Adventist that we could find," the interviewer said. "You don't drink and you don't smoke."

When Porter Hospital offered Teresa a salary better than her current one, she accepted the offer. Porter proved to be a good place to work, much better than Presbyterian was. Porter had an excellent reputation, the administrators believed in keeping the library up-to-date, and no one seemed particularly snobbish, thank goodness.

Teresa and Frenchy bought a house at 2570 South Marion, only three blocks from her new job. They used money from the sale of his sister's house as a downpayment. Frenchy, who was much better at budgeting money than Teresa, handled all their money. Teresa turned over her paychecks to him, letting him pay bills and deposit the remainder in her savings account. Thanks to Frenchy's good management, they were able to own their new home with a mortgage of only $100 a month.

❧

One day, Teresa slipped home for lunch to find her husband there.

"What are you doing here?" she said. She expected Frenchy to be at work for the Cole Company, a manufacturer of keys, in Woolworth's key department. He had taken a correspondence course in making keys, liked the task, and found himself good at it. At last, Teresa had thought, a job he likes.

Frenchy's key shop.
(Courtesy of Teresa Martin)

"I quit."

"What happened?"

"They got smart with me." A man brought a key to Woolworth's that he wanted remade. When Frenchy examined it, he saw that the Cole Company made the key but not in this Woolworth store.

"You didn't get the key from us," Frenchy said, "so I'm not going to fix it."

The men quarreled.

When the Woolworth floor manager told Frenchy to make a new key, Frenchy refused. "I'm not working for Woolworth's. I'm working for the Cole Company." He walked off the job.

Holding a job seemed impossible for Frenchy, Teresa thought. In Denver, he took up and then gave up TV repair. After managing five different apartment houses, he quit that line of work. He lasted only a few months at the Villa Shopping Center. Now he had thrown in the towel on making keys. How could he continue this way?

Fortunately, Teresa now earned enough money at Porter to provide for them both, thanks to their low mortgage and to Frenchy's frugal financial management. "You are a good cook," she said, "and you love to keep house. Why don't I bring home the bacon and you fry?"

Frenchy loved being a gentleman housekeeper, content to stay home and watch baseball, basketball, and football on TV. He kept the house spotless. He cooked good meals and even drank less.

When Teresa returned from work, she waited on him, grateful not to keep house, which she despised. They watched whatever TV program Frenchy wanted to watch. Sometimes Teresa brought her husband little presents. With Frenchy keeping house and Teresa coddling him, their marriage improved markedly.

Teresa still despaired of Frenchy's drinking, but she never gave up. Since she knew he liked to be treated like a little boy, she said, "Instead of drinking this Tuesday, try not to." Then she had him skip Saturdays. She praised him lavishly on weeks he stayed sober, and finally he stopped drinking altogether. Perhaps his failing health helped. When he drank now, he got much sicker than he had when he was younger.

After Teresa attended the Nebraska orphan reunion, she felt differently about being orphaned—less lonely, not so ashamed. For the first time, she talked to people in Denver about her past.

"Are you Jewish?" Mrs. Rosenberg said. "You look Jewish, that's certain."

Teresa knew Mrs. Rosenberg only slightly, but she answered honestly. "I don't know if I am or not. The Catholic Church baptized me and then placed me out as an orphan."

"No! Then of course you can't be Jewish! Jews don't put their children in orphanages. We take care of our own."

Teresa didn't reply. She just shrugged and thought, "One more argument against my being Jewish."

Eventually she confided in Dr. Ken Moon, a friendly colleague and neighbor. He seemed fascinated with her history, especially her desire to know more about her mother.

"Why don't you go to New York and find out?" he suggested.

"Oh, I don't think I'd find out much there. When I wrote to the Foundling for my birth information, the nun who replied said, 'The case is closed.'"

"It might be different, face-to-face."

"Maybe. You know, I'd love to go to New York, but how expensive that would be! The airfare, the hotel room. I don't see how I could swing it."

"Well, let's think about it, shall we?" Dr. Moon patted her hand.

That night Teresa said to Frenchy, "It's been two years since we wiped out the savings account buying that new Buick of yours. Do you think I have enough to go to New York?"

"Maybe," Frenchy said. "We can probably swing it, but it might be tight. I'll take a look." He pulled out the savings account book and discussed prices with a travel agent before he told Teresa she had enough money to go. Barely enough, but enough.

The next time Teresa saw Dr. Moon, she said, "I'm going to New York! I've decided to go even if it breaks my bank!" She thrust both fists in the air like a champion boxer and laughed.

"Great! A good decision! You won't regret it."

A week later, Dr. Moon came into the library with an envelope. "Here. For you. We doctors took up a collection to support your trip."

"For me?" Puzzled, Teresa opened the envelope to see a row of what looked like fifty-dollar bills.

"For your trip. All of us doctors chipped in."

Teresa burst into tears.

"Now, now! This is supposed to make you happy, not sad." Dr. Moon whipped out his handkerchief and handed it to her.

"Oh, it does! It does!" Teresa's tears subsided as she lay down the envelope to wipe her cheeks and blow her nose. "Oh, thank you. Thank you so much. Oh, how can I ever thank all of you?"

"Please, Teresa, it's only a small token of our gratitude for all the work you've done for us," Dr. Moon laughed. "And the shamrocks you knit for us for Saint Paddy's day."

He left before she could reiterate her gratitude. When she picked up the envelope, she noticed she still held Dr. Moon's handkerchief. She used it to wipe her damp cheeks.

❦

About a month later, Teresa flew to New York. Her trust in revealing her past to Dr. Moon was justified. The doctors' money paid her airfare and then some.

When she arrived at the New York airport, she couldn't wait to see the Foundling, so she took a cab directly to the orphanage. She stepped out and looked up at enormous modern buildings, nothing like the ones she knew as a child. Could this be the place? Then she remembered Mary Buscher talking at the Nebraska reunion about the Foundling moving, in 1958, into new quarters.

"I saw it happen right there on the evening news," Mrs. Buscher had said. "The Foundling moved out of its old buildings on Sixty-Eighth Street and into its new ones nearby. My heart just sank. If ever I wanted to go see my first home, the home I moved into when I was eight days old, why it would be gone. Used by someone else perhaps. And the new buildings, of course, they didn't look like anything I remembered."

These modern buildings, then, must be the new quarters. Teresa shook herself and entered, found the main desk, and identified herself. She showed the nun in charge letters that the Porter doctors wrote for her, letters attesting to her popularity as a medical researcher.

"Thank God," the nun said, "someone came back who was cheerful and didn't complain."

Teresa started. *I could complain, too! My Schoenchen home wasn't the greatest.* But she said nothing.

Wanting to stay near the Foundling, Teresa rented a room in an inexpensive old hotel on East Sixty-Eighth Street. The place looked a bit seedy but that didn't concern her until the hotel man said, "You won't go out at night, will you?" Then she wondered if she had stumbled into a sleazy neighborhood, but she didn't care. Her room and the lobby were comfortable.

Across the street from the hotel stood the Lenox Hill post office, which looked more familiar than the orphanage had. Curious, Teresa entered the building the next day and saw that the spacious interior seemed familiar, too. She located an older postal worker.

"I was a Foundling orphan," she told him as he made change for her purchase of stamps. "It's strange, but this post office seems familiar."

"Maybe you remember the nuns bringing you here. In the old days, they often wheeled orphans over here."

The postal worker also told Teresa that the Foundling hired people to "love" the orphans, to hold them and caress them so they wouldn't die of lack of mother love. So perhaps orphanage life wasn't as bleak as Teresa supposed. For the first time, she imagined someone cuddling her when she was a toddler, an infant. She wondered who had loved her, who had wrapped her in strong, warm arms. Maybe the same person who taught her to hold up her arms when she wanted to be picked up. A sudden burst of warmth hit Teresa, as though a cloud dissolved to reveal the sun.

Later that day, Teresa returned to the Foundling for a closer look. She saw the original basket that, in 1869, sat outside the front door to collect babies. She saw Sister Irene's desk. She met Sister Mary de Sales who knew the history of Kansas riders.

"You weren't the only one," Sister de Sales said. "We placed about 5,000 children in Kansas."

"Five thousand!" Teresa felt astounded. She knew the Foundling had placed some hundred children in Ellis County, but she had no idea so many children had been placed all over the state.

Later, she sat in a pew in the huge modern chapel and watched. Most nuns who worshiped there dressed in street clothes, none particularly fashionable, but a few wore the same kind of habits and bonnets that nuns wore in Teresa's day. Seeing them excited Teresa. She remembered women who'd cared for her, their warmth, their odors, pungent and spicy. She remembered most vividly their strong insistent hands washing her hair. *I must have been a handful.* That pleased her.

Still later, Teresa asked to see her records, but the nun in charge refused. This disappointed Teresa even though it did not surprise her, not when she remembered their frustrating correspondence about her birth certificate. Still, the nuns' refusal stirred up unanswered questions. *Did my parents try to find me?* Sometimes she wondered if they had come to Kansas seeking her, and the Biekers refused to tell them anything. Or maybe the woman who asked her if she were Austrian was Rosie. Preoccupied, she barely heard Sister de Sales describe Teresa's mother as a "small proud little woman."

"What did you say?" Teresa said.

The nun repeated her words.

Just like me, but I'm not so proud. I wonder why she was. Her fantasy that Rosie came from a rich family never vanished, so Teresa thought Sister de Sales's words might prove that Rosie was well-born.

Maybe I can find out if I'm Jewish. Turning to the Sister, she said, "You know, a woman in Denver thought I was Jewish. When she asked me about it, I told her the Foundling baptized me in the Catholic Church and then placed me out as an orphan. Then she said, 'Oh, no! You can't be Jewish! Jews don't put their children in orphanages. We Jews take care of our own.'"

Sister de Sales's face was impassive, her voice quiet but decisive. "They don't always know what their girls do."

Maybe they don't. Maybe I am Jewish. The nun didn't say I wasn't.

Teresa remembered reading that some Catholic orphanages refused to return Jewish children to their parents. The Catholics supposedly did this because they wanted Jewish children, in particular, to be converted and raised Catholic. Teresa wondered if the Foundling had done that, if she were Jewish and her proud mother came to get her and the nuns refused to give her back.

Perhaps that's why the payments stopped.

She almost asked, but she dared not.

Next Teresa went to the Lying-in Hospital where she had been born, even though the old hospital had been replaced by the New York Hospital–Cornell Medical Center. She visited the hospital's fine medical library and the library at Columbia;

she owed at least that to the generous doctors. Then she simply became a tourist, inspecting the Statue of Liberty, the United Nations building, and Saint Patrick's Cathedral.

Teresa loved New York. She loved to watch the people, especially the stylishly dressed women. She knew she must look dowdy alongside them. If she had stayed with Rosie and grown up here, would she too have looked so smart and self-assured?

The city seemed surprisingly like home even though the crowds sometimes frightened her. Once as she waited at a bus stop during rush hour, someone in the crowd started shoving. Suddenly a person pointed at Teresa and shouted, "Look at that pushy Jew!"

Then a rider on the bus called, "Don't you say that. Can't you see she's scared to death?"

A pushy Jew! Maybe I really am Jewish.

Too soon, she was back in Denver.

❧

On Teresa's sixty-fourth birthday, Mildred gave birth to her eleventh child. Eleven children! Teresa could weep! Such excess! At least Doris and Don had the good sense to stop ten years ago, after three sons, but not Mildred. She was worse than her mother-in-law who gave birth to eight. They both scorned Teresa's two.

"What's the problem?" the mother-in-law said. "You get only one at a time."

Still, Mildred couldn't drop children forever. Already forty-four, if she didn't stop soon, Mother Nature would halt her.

❧

When Teresa turned sixty-five on May 25, 1971, she continued to work at Porter even though she could retire. But why take out Social Security now when her good salary would only increase it? Besides, she didn't want to stay at home; she liked being busy, so she continued to work.

Even by her own tough standards, she was a successful medical librarian. She knew because nursing students at the hospital named her employee-of-the-month over and over. The local *Newsmakers* reporter wrote that choosing Teresa for this honor was "almost an annual custom." One student, Lane Casey, gave her a rose representing the students' appreciation. These honors warmed Teresa, but she knew they weren't entirely her own doing. Porter Hospital should take some credit. It provided the warm safe soil in which she could flourish. At the hospital, she could be who she was, without apology. No one ever put her down, not even after learning she was an orphan.

By this time, Frenchy and she rarely went out. To keep him from drinking, they avoided the dance halls—a sacrifice Teresa happily made to keep Frenchy sober. Sometimes she missed waltzing to the dance band's rhythms, sliding with Frenchy across a shining dance floor, their bodies swaying as one. They even stayed home on New Year's Eve, a significant change since they always celebrated Frenchy's most beloved holiday. Now they turned on TV, listened to Guy Lombardo, and danced, just the two of them. Even in the confines of the living room, Frenchy still was a marvelous dancer. Teresa felt herself melt in his arms.

⌒

One blistering July day in 1978, Teresa came home for lunch to find that Frenchy had mowed their lawn when the hired man didn't show up.

"How could you, honey?" she said. "In this terrible heat. You know you need to take good care of yourself." Frenchy, on his dentist's advice, had stopped taking his blood thinner, Coumadin, to prepare for some extractions.

"Frenchy, I'm going to be late for supper," she said after lunch. "I'm planning to work late."

"Come home at five instead. You can eat and go back to the hospital. I want to see the game."

Teresa agreed, knowing how Frenchy loved his evening sports! He never missed those games.

A little after five, Teresa went home. The house seemed unusually quiet. No TV blared. No supper simmered on the stove. Teresa looked for a note but found none. *That's strange. Frenchy never goes anywhere without leaving a note.* She looked all over the house but couldn't find him. When she went down the basement, there he lay on the floor, his leg at an odd angle. She put a pillow under his head and said, "Did you break your leg? Oh, Frenchy."

Then she noticed his eyes. She knew something terrible had happened, so she called Dr. Moon, the doctor who had raised money for her New York trip. He lived across the street; he and his wife, a nurse, came right over. They took Frenchy to Porter Hospital to resuscitate him, but the doctor couldn't. At the age of seventy-three, he was dead from arteriosclerosis.

Finding Frenchy dead was excruciatingly painful. The pain seemed to gather in Teresa's chest, around her heart. Concerned hospital doctors gave her an EKG test. That night severe pain pinned Teresa to her bed, but she refused to call for help. She knew the pain came from losing Frenchy. *Just imagine. Yesterday he was mowing the lawn, but today he's lying stiff in the morgue.* If only she had found him earlier!

The next day, the hospital doctors told Teresa that she had had a heart attack, but she refused to believe them.

"No, I didn't have a heart attack," she said. "I'm just in great pain because I lost Frenchy."

The doctors insisted, but she denied it until they showed her the results of her EKG test. It clearly showed her heart attack, so she agreed to take Papaverine to improve her circulation.

Since Teresa worked for the Seventh-Day Adventists, she chose Pastor Christian of the Seventh-Day Adventist Church for Frenchy's service. Mildred came from Seattle with two of her eleven children and Doris, leaving her three boys behind, came with her husband from Hays. Surrounded by her family reduced Teresa's sense of being badly bruised. When the organ belted out "The Old Rugged Cross," Teresa almost heard Frenchy chuckle. He knew that tune well. When he was young, he sang it over and over for the folks at his local barber shop. They gave him a free beer just to hear him sing it.

HORSE THIEVES

E ach morning after Frenchy's death, Teresa told herself she must buy a scrapbook to hold the dozens of condolence cards she'd received, but she never bought the book. Instead, she tucked cards away in odd places until she couldn't open a drawer or pull a book off the shelf without finding a card.

At bedtime, unwilling to lie alone between the sheets, she lay on top of the covers to sleep—or read. She read voraciously, especially in the evening when she missed Frenchy keenly. They spent so many hours in the TV's twilight, talking or watching *Columbo* or dancing. Reading blunted the reality of Frenchy's death, so Teresa often read half the night.

But she agonized over paying bills. When she reached for the checkbook, she saw Frenchy writing checks, calculating their debts, calibrating how much money to set aside for her savings. This memory nearly did her in, so she shoved the bills aside until shut-off notices arrived.

Then shortly before Christmas, Teresa noticed a TV listing for a three-hour CBS special called *Orphan Train*. She'd never heard of an orphan train, but she felt it must have something to do with her, so she determined to watch it. On the broadcast day, she planted herself before the TV, expecting to watch a film featuring nuns tending a trainload of little girls in white dresses.

Instead, the movie featured dirty orphans off the streets of New York. Tough street boys and girls. *Hoodlums.* Teresa wrinkled her nose. This was nothing like her experience. Where were the nuns? The children didn't wear tags bearing the name of their caretaker. Instead, agents lined them up like cabbages in the grocery store so people could look them over and pick one. Or not. Teresa shuddered. *So, it could have been worse.* She remembered the calling out of numbers when the nuns gave her to the Biekers.

Of course, the film was not meant to be true, and it wasn't, with its fire and its train wreck and romantic undertone, although the hostility the orphans received from respectable people seemed accurate enough.

Afterward, Teresa stared at the dark screen. How disappointing! She was so certain the show would dramatize a life similar to her own. She thought CBS made a mistake showing orphans as a bunch of hoodlums. Holding her head up as an orphan had proved difficult enough without negative publicity.

Later, Teresa noticed that broadcasters and others referred to this relocation of children as "the orphan train movement." Obviously, the CBS movie made an impression, for the name stuck.

〜

When Doris heard about the broadcast, she urged Teresa to search for her relatives, but Teresa demurred. "My birth certificate tells me all I need to know."

Doris persisted, "Let's go to New York and see what we can dig up."

"We won't find anything. Whenever I contact the Foundling, the nuns always tell me, 'Your case is closed.'"

"We can look other places."

"Besides, what if my birth certificate's wrong, and I was born out of wedlock?" Teresa asked Doris. "It would be awful to visit a woman who didn't want to see an illegitimate daughter she gave away." Although imagining her mother fascinated Teresa, she feared an actual meeting.

"But you're seventy-three now. Chances are your mother isn't alive. Even if she is, you don't need to protect her. You can't possibly hurt her now," Doris insisted.

"That's not all. Suppose we do find my relatives? You don't know who they might be. Given my luck, they're probably a bunch of horse thieves."

But Doris persevered until her mother yielded. Maybe going to New York would be better than mooning around about Frenchy. So Teresa went to the bank to withdraw money to buy two round-trip tickets. As she waited in line to receive funds that Frenchy had so carefully amassed, she experienced the now-familiar pang that accompanied any thought of her husband. Her grief was dimming, but her memory of finding him on the basement floor still tortured her.

～

Early that June, Teresa and Doris arrived in New York, checked into their hotel, and then left to visit the Foundling.

As Teresa predicted, they learned only that her case was closed, but she did remember to ask about the Foundling laundry. Her memory proved correct: the Foundling's laundry was in the basement of the building she knew as home. Securing this morsel of information satisfied her.

She'd turned to leave when the lanky nun in charge said, "I can make a copy of your baptismal certificate if that would help."

Teresa and Doris exchanged startled glances. "Oh, please!"

Soon the nun handed Teresa an ornately decorated document. As she walked toward the door, she squinted at the slick gray paper. The type was so fuzzy she couldn't read a word.

"Here." She handed the page to Doris. "You read it."

Doris scrutinized it. "It shows that Teresa Feit, born May 26—Hey! They've got your birth date wrong, Mom."

"And my name. I was Jessie then, until they baptized me."

"It says the nuns baptized you in the Church of St. Vincent Ferrer on Lexington Avenue on July 31, 1907."

"How many months old would I have been?"

Doris ran a quick finger calculation. "A year and two months."

"Just what Mrs. Spallen said. Somebody paid my keep for fourteen months." Teresa folded the precious document and tucked it in her purse. "Probably my mother."

Then she remembered what else Mrs. Spallen told her, that she was a favorite of Sister Teresa. "Doris, do you think they named me after Sister Teresa?"

"Maybe. Or maybe after Saint Teresa."

"Oh, I don't think they'd name a little orphan after such a great mystic."

Stepping into the spring air and heavy roar of traffic, Teresa sighed. "Didn't I tell you this would be a wild goose chase? We've come all the way from Colorado just to hear, 'Your case is closed.'"

"But it wasn't closed entirely. At least you got your baptismal certificate," Doris said.

"True. But we don't know a thing about my relatives."

"Not yet. We've barely started to search. You're the librarian. Where should we look next?"

Teresa thought a moment. "Maybe we could find a phone book."

"Great. But where?" Doris said.

They glanced up and down the long Manhattan avenue until Doris spotted a YWCA sign dangling from an old brick building. "Let's go there." The closer they got, the more rundown the building looked. "Oh, Mom, I don't think we should go in. It looks too seedy. Let's go somewhere else."

"But where, Doris? Let's just step in the lobby and see if they have a phone."

Both felt relief to see an old-fashioned wooden phone booth with New York City's telephone book, as thick as an unabridged dictionary, dangling at its side. Doris turned to the "F's," looking for Teresa's birth name, Feit.

"Oh, my gosh, Mom, will you look at this?" Doris flipped page after page, each filled with lists of Feits. "Why your name's as common as Smith!"

"In New York, anyway. Why don't you look up my mother's name?"

"How do you spell it?"

"B-r-e-i-t-o-w-i-c-h," Teresa spelled out.

Doris scanned the B's, ran her finger down a column, then stopped. "Success! Only two Breitowichs listed." She stepped into the phone booth.

"Oh, I don't know. Maybe we shouldn't bother anyone."

But Doris dropped a coin into the slot, checked the dial tone, and handed the receiver to her mother. Teresa reluctantly dialed the first listing.

To her surprise, a man answered. He told her to call Etka Slota. "She'll be able to tell you."

Disappointed to learn so little, Teresa wrote down Etka Slota's phone number and started to put it in her purse, but Doris wanted to call immediately.

"Come on, Mama! We haven't come all this way to stop now."

So Teresa handed Doris the number, "You call, then."

Standing beside her daughter, Teresa heard the phone ring twice. When a woman's voice answered, Teresa started. *Why, she sounds just like me!* That seemed impossible, until Doris covered the mouthpiece and whispered, "She sounds just like you!"

Doris and Etka Slota talked for a long time, maybe ten minutes, as Teresa marveled at how much that woman sounded like her. Mrs. Slota told Doris that a cousin, Arthur Weinstein in Chicago, had researched the Breitowich family tree and might be able to answer her questions.

"She doesn't seem to know anything about the Breitowichs," Doris said after she hung up. "But she mentioned that she and Arthur are 'double cousins.'"

"I expect that's all we'll find out."

But Doris disagreed. "I'm sure we're on the right track, Mama. We just have to reach this Arthur."

"Oh, I don't know. I don't think there's any point in that, really. He can't be interested in us."

But when she heard Doris's eager, "Don't worry, I'll contact him," Teresa gave in. If Doris wanted to find her ancestors that badly, at least let her try.

❧

Back in Denver, Teresa immersed herself in work, friends, and other activities, soon forgetting the New York trip. After sleeping between the sheets in the hotel bed, she slept between them at home now. Though picking up her checkbook still pained her, she paid the June bills on time. She also joined the Lady of Lourdes senior citizen group, and she noticed Captain Korb. She had met the captain in the Porter Hospital library where he came to research the cancer that had hospitalized his wife of fifty-eight years. Teresa could tell that he adored her. When she died, he was distraught.

After his wife died, Captain Korb dropped by the library to chat, and Teresa discovered he was an aviation doctor during World War II. *That's why he carries himself so erect. It's that military training.*

Then he asked her out to dinner, but she couldn't date him, she just couldn't. She knew he was lonely; so was she, but it hadn't been a year yet since Frenchy died, not until July 17. Maybe she'd agree after that. She did like him; he displayed so much integrity.

On July 18, she started to date Captain Korb. They had delightful times together, as she knew they would, even if he did reminisce about his wife. He soon proposed marriage, and Teresa was tempted. Her house sometimes felt so empty, but she couldn't bear to relinquish her freedom again. She turned him down, but they continued to see each other.

During this time, Doris, at home in Hill City, Kansas, heard from Arthur Weinstein. She mailed Teresa a copy of his book, *Our Exodus,* which detailed the history of the Feit, Weinstein, Breitowich, and Fenig families. Teresa flipped through the opus; its pages seemed crammed with genealogical charts and stories about people she didn't know. Unimpressed, she set the book aside.

Then Doris called. "I wrote Arthur again, and sent him all the information you've given me about your relatives. But then I didn't hear from him all during July."

"Slow down. I can hardly follow you, you're talking so fast," Teresa said.

"Well, I just got his letter! Listen to this—he says he didn't write because he had to review his notes and call up other relatives to 'stretch their memories.' He says he'd hoped one of them might remember hearing of a Rosie Breitowich or a Wolf Feit or, for that matter, a Jessie Feit, but nobody had."

"A Jessie Feit." How odd to hear someone use that name. But that would be my name if I grew up in New York.

"Here. Listen to this." Doris read Arthur's letter. " 'From the first I thought that Jessie must be a rather close relative, because we don't know Breitowichs that are not related. The astonishing point is that you have come up with a Breitowich and Feit background.' Mama! He's really helping us!"

Teresa saw that Doris was excited about this letter, but for her part, she couldn't understand why this man found a Breitowich and Feit background so astonishing. After she hung up, she promptly forgot Doris's call.

When Arthur called Teresa later that August, she didn't remember him. "Arthur who?"

"Weinstein. Your daughter wrote to me."

"Oh, yes."

"My wife, Bernice, and I want to meet you and Doris in Denver," he said.

Surprised, Teresa agreed.

"Do you know a good eating place?"

Teresa suggested Denny's; it would be good enough.

"No," Arthur said. "We don't eat at Denny's."

Teresa raised an eyebrow, wondering what could be so terrible about Denny's. Arthur chose an unfamiliar restaurant where they agreed to meet in a few weeks.

During that time, Teresa wasted no energy speculating about Arthur. She agreed to the dinner primarily to satisfy Doris's desire to find her ancestors. Personally, she didn't think meeting this man would mean much. If seeing an unknown person who might be a relative didn't interest her, why would it interest him? *He's just curious. He'll see me and be satisfied and that will be that.*

On the day of the dinner, Doris and her husband, Don, picked up Teresa to drive to the restaurant Arthur had chosen. "How sophisticated," Teresa murmured as she saw glittering white trees around a palatial building. As they drove in, she spotted a couple standing outside the restaurant. *Probably Arthur and his wife.* The man appeared to be Jewish, sort of short and chubby with curly hair framing his baldness. He looked quite unlike the man Teresa expected: shorter, lighter skinned, and an entire generation younger. Since Arthur was Rosie's relative, Teresa had thought he'd be from that generation, not hers.

Teresa and her cousin, Arthur Weinstein.
(Courtesy of Teresa Martin)

As she walked toward this curly-haired man, who indeed was Arthur, she gasped; they looked so much alike he could be her brother. Waiting beside Arthur was his wife, Bernice, a pretty woman in her middle fifties. Teresa admired her stylish dress. Bernice, who didn't look particularly Jewish, was short but not as short as Teresa, perhaps five foot four.

"My God," Teresa heard Bernice say as they approached. "She looks exactly like your mother!"

"Yes," Arthur said. "She does."

How strange that I should look like his mother! Teresa couldn't believe that these fine looking, expensively dressed people might be related to her.

After introductions, Arthur said to Teresa, "Take your shoe off. Let's see your foot."

His request amused her. So unusual! She obediently removed a shoe. Arthur looked at her foot and said, "Oh, with that wide foot, you belong to us. Besides, there's such a strong family resemblance, we can't deny you. You look every inch a Breitowich."

As she slipped her wide foot into her shoe, she felt like Cinderella donning the glass slipper. Up from ashes. She could hardly breathe. After all those school children's taunts, after the years living with the hurtful Biekers, the years scrubbing floors, the lonely fight to be educated, after a lifetime of being a mail-order orphan, now, at last, in her seventies, blood relatives had claimed her. She blinked back tears.

As they turned to enter the opulent restaurant, Teresa experienced a surge of happiness, like bubbles in a fountain, clean and delicate, unlike any joy she had known, although similar to her feelings when she saw her firstborn. She wanted to pinch herself, to make sure this wasn't a daydream, but instead she followed Bernice into the restaurant to partake in what seemed, oddly enough, like a family reunion. The maitre d' seated them at a private table in a group of artificial trees.

A thick white cloth covered the table, and each place was set with heavy silverware and spotless glasses in a manner Emily Post would approve. The maitre d' lit two rotund candles on either side of an exquisite bouquet of real flowers. Soft music muted the bustle of the restaurant. *Well, this certainly isn't Denny's!* Teresa had never encountered such luxury; it made her apprehensive, as though she had no right to be there. *What in the world shall I order?* She picked up the massive menu, but Arthur solved her problem by ordering for her.

Then he and Doris talked, Arthur providing incomprehensible details of genealogical topics, and Doris telling Arthur more about Teresa's background. Teresa did learn that Arthur's mother, like hers, was born a Breitowich, and that Breitowichs were known for being short, plump, and frivolous. They also had wide feet and wide noses.

"Breitowich," Arthur said, "means 'son of wide.'"

Teresa giggled. "Thank goodness, I didn't inherit a Breitowich nose."

Arthur glanced at her quizzically, then smiled and said that the Feits, like his father and hers, were tall, slim, reserved people. Arthur used Weinstein as his last name instead of Feit because his father, the son of a Weinstein-Feit marriage, had taken his mother's name to keep the Weinstein name alive, so Arthur, like Teresa, had Breitowich-Feit parents.

"If your father was a typical Feit," Arthur said, "he was dark with a prominent nose. The Feits are intense, energetic people. Your father might have been a scholar, but definitely not a mixer."

As the waiter placed more food before Teresa than she could eat in three days, she considered what Arthur had said. Was she mostly Feit or Breitowich? Scholarly or frivolous? A little of both, she decided, suppressing a giggle and pinching herself.

As Teresa ate, she remembered her little dog. Last September, she had adopted a badly beaten Sheltie-mix named Sunshine. He was beautiful, tan and white like a full-blooded Sheltie, but he trusted no one. He wouldn't even let her walk him, so Teresa left her back door open—imagine, in Denver!—so he could relieve himself in her fenced-in back yard.

Then one night Teresa heard a noise in her bedroom. When she turned on her lamp, she saw Sunshine standing by the side of her bed looking at her, so she patted her blanket. He joined her. She caressed him and talked to him. From then on, they were close friends, so close Sunshine let no one near Teresa. She had to look sharp to keep him from nipping someone, but she didn't mind. Her house no longer felt empty.

When Teresa thought of her gorgeous Sunshine, she wrapped her uneaten meat, whispered to Arthur, "I'm going to save that for my dog." She whispered because she didn't want Doris to see her wrapping food for Sunshine. If Doris saw her, she would make a fuss.

After they finished coffee, Doris and Don drove to Kansas, while Arthur and Bernice took Teresa home and stayed to visit. As she opened the door, she saw how cluttered her house was, papers piled high and projects left half finished. She apologized profusely for her housekeeping, but the Weinsteins made light of it. She introduced them to Sunshine and told them his history, which they admired, but they said that keeping a dog wasted money. She saw they weren't "dog people."

Arthur and Bernice spoke highly of Doris—she obviously made a good impression—but Arthur continued to describe the four Feits who married the four Breitowichs. However, Teresa's new "cousins" fascinated her more than his genealogy. She liked Arthur and Bernice, but their refinement made her uneasy. She never really believed her grade-school teachers who told her she came from "good stock," so she doubted Arthur's claim to be her cousin. How could this cultured man be related to a nobody like her? Cousins? That seemed absurd.

As Arthur talked, she finally understood the significance of the Feit/Breitowich marriages. Arthur's grandparents, Hersch and Jachit Breitowich, had eight children. Three of these Breitowich children, Alter, Joe, and Anna, married Feits. Then Teresa's Breitowich mother, clearly a relative of the Hersch Breitowich children, also married a Feit. All this intermarriage, Arthur believed, made them "double cousins."

Teresa nodded politely. But as she closed her door behind the Weinsteins that night, pride surged unexpectedly through her. *I've found my relatives at last, and they're not horse thieves! Whoopee!*

❧

Teresa expected never to hear from Arthur again, but that September, the Weinsteins invited Teresa and Doris to their Skokie, Illinois, home near Chicago, to celebrate Rosh Hashanah, the Jewish New Year.

Doris declined. "I don't want to get to know the Weinsteins any better," she said.

"Are you sure?" Teresa pressed.

"Positive."

Just look at that, Teresa thought. *We've switched roles. Doris was so fascinated with our genealogy, but once she met her relatives, she was satisfied. But me, so bored with genealogy I met the Weinsteins just to please Doris, here I am fascinated by these new flesh-and-blood cousins. How curious!*

She laughed off Doris's shortsightedness and eagerly bought her ticket.

In Skokie, the Weinstein home looked ordinary. After all those swanky white trees at the Denver restaurant that Arthur chose, Teresa expected at least an artificial tree or two!

That night, Friday, she went to synagogue with Bernice, Arthur, and his sisters, Helen and Lillian. They attended the Yahrszeit, a ceremony to remember those who had gone before them. The service reminded Teresa of High Mass in Latin that Catholics used to celebrate.

Saturday, at breakfast, Teresa and the Weinsteins ate bagels and lox.

"This lox," Arthur said, "cost $14 a pound."

Unlike her cousins, who loved to eat, Teresa never ate a lot. Since the removal of much of her colon, she ate even less, so she didn't know what to do when Arthur pushed food on her.

"No, thanks so much," she said. "It's very good, but I really can't eat any more."

"Just because I say $14 a pound," Arthur said, "that doesn't mean you can't eat lox!"

Teresa's heritage, her Weinstein relatives.
Arthur is seated on the floor in center.
(Courtesy of Teresa Martin)

That Saturday, Arthur and Bernice hosted a large reception to introduce Teresa to her other cousins. The crowd, full of stylishly dressed women, arrived in a throng. She met cousin after cousin—so many she didn't remember much about them individually. Each seemed so happy to meet her. When she realized that most of her cousins worked as physicians, teachers, or lawyers, she burst with pride. They seemed so generous, too, supporting causes like the Jewish National Hospital in Denver, and they gave her many gifts, including a menorah.

Teresa (right) with her newly discovered cousin, Lottie Breitowich Sachs.
Teresa treasured the Star of David necklace that Lottie gave her.
(Courtesy of Teresa Martin)

One cousin, Lottie Breitowich Sachs, gave Teresa a Star of David necklace with diamond chips, which Teresa treasured. Lottie fascinated her. Tall and slender with colored red hair, Lottie dressed well. She didn't look her age—the mid-eighties— and she didn't look Jewish. Oddly, Lottie seemed proud of that.

"I worked for years as a secretary in a firm where no one knew I was Jewish," she told Teresa. "I had to swallow a lot, but I needed the work." She and her husband used her income to put their boys through medical school. "They took me for a Gentile," she bragged.

After the reception, Teresa felt strange yet happy, strange that she, an orphan, was related to these polished people, and happy with their refinement. That night tears dampened her pillow.

When her visit was over, Arthur drove her to the airport and helped her to her plane.

"I had to pay the airlines quite a bit of money to change my ticket," Teresa said as they waited. Before she left Denver, Arthur had called and asked her to change to a more convenient time.

Arthur examined her ticket. "Why, you only had to pay $67 more! You act like it was so terrible!"

But to her, $67 did seem terrible. She liked Arthur, but she saw he had no idea what it was like to stretch a dollar.

❧

On her next Chicago visit, Arthur showed Teresa that he had located, among his numerous relatives, a person named Rachel, the second child of thirteen children, twelve of them female. He believed Rachel was Teresa's mother.

"But how can Rachel be my mother? Her name isn't Rosie."

"True. But Rachel's Yiddish name is Raisa. Your mother probably used Rosie instead of Raisa because Americans understood it easily, just like women named Etka go by Esther. Doesn't sound so foreign."

"But look!" Teresa pointed to Arthur's chart. "This Rachel can't be my mother. She died in Europe."

Arthur smiled. "You don't know where your mother died, do you? Maybe she went back to Europe. Or maybe my information's wrong. The people I interviewed said they thought Rachel died in Europe, but they could be wrong." He shrugged. "See? I wrote that she 'probably' died in Europe. We can't be sure, Jessie."

Hearing herself called "Jessie" still gave Teresa a start.

"What we know is this. Rachel was the right age to come to New York and give birth to you when she did. Did you notice that five of her sisters died of tuberculosis? Where did they get it? Not from the Liba Breitowichs."

Both Rosie's parents—Liba and Mechel—were Breitowichs; they were cousins.

"Of all the Breitowich families in my genealogy, only one family mentions lung disease—Rosie's family." Arthur looked at Teresa. "You remember that her hospital record states that her father had a lung disease?"

Teresa nodded.

"Well, maybe Mechel brought tuberculosis into his family, gave it to his daughters, and then died of it himself. That could be. We don't know anything about his people, so we can't prove it one way or the other."

Teresa didn't know what to think. "So that's why Rosie went into the Lying-In Hospital so early, because she was sick."

Arthur disagreed. "There's no mention of her not being well," he said. "She's described as 'erect and cheerful.'" He smiled at Teresa. "Sounds just like you."

That rang true. "But why did she go to the hospital early if she wasn't ill?" Teresa said.

"Because she had no home. She was a pioneer. If the Feits or the Breitowichs had been in New York then, the family would have helped her, if they could."

Over the following months, Arthur searched for additional information about Teresa's family, but he found nothing. When Teresa realized she would never know, definitely, what happened, she felt empty. She remembered the psychologist at the Nebraska reunion saying that their relocation had disconnected them from their pasts. She certainly was disconnected. She had so hoped she could find out more about Rosie. Nearly any detail would do. In particular, she wanted to find out if the nuns had forced her mother to give her up because they were Jewish. That rumor haunted Teresa.

At home, she read everything she could find about Jewish immigration, pages upon pages, some in tedious tomes. What she learned was this: Rosie was hardly the first eastern European Jew to come to America. They had been arriving since the 1820s, packing America's ghettoes.

Then, between 1880 and World War I, when Rosie came, roughly a third of the eastern European Jews left their homes in an astonishing migration, equaled only by the rush to leave Ireland during the potato famine. Teresa liked the way one Yiddish writer described it, as though "a powerful storm-wind ripped us out of our place and carried us to America." That storm-wind, Teresa figured, clearly carried her mother and possibly her father to New York City.

Teresa couldn't know if anything she read was true of Rosie or Wolf, but at least it might have been. That seemed to satisfy her. She put the books away.

THE SCENE OF THE CRIME

O n January 29, 1982, after a working life that spanned sixty-one years, Teresa retired. From her unpromising beginning as a fourteen-year-old who scrubbed commodes, she had risen to be an accomplished medical librarian in Denver. Her achievement pleased her, especially her success as a research librarian where her "unbelievable tenacity," as Dr. James DeRoos called it, let her find almost any piece of literature in the medical field. Maybe Dr. DeRoos sensed how important to her finding every item was. Each time she filled a request, especially a difficult one, a doctor was pleased and that pleasure transformed her, momentarily, from "just an orphan" to "as good as any hospital worker."

After Teresa retired, she lived alone in Denver, a widow with an overprotective dog. Her close friend, Captain Korb, had died shortly before she retired, and she lamented his absence. Sometimes she paced the living room, unaccustomed to so much free time. Sometimes, when she looked in the mirror, she wondered where the Teresa she knew had gone. Oh, with careful eating, she had maintained her trim figure. The few extra pounds didn't show, but her face! How had she arrived at this old woman's face, as wrinkled as an apple left to dry?

As time passed, Teresa tired. When her daughters noticed, they insisted she see a doctor. He found a cancerous tumor, which a surgeon removed along with fourteen more inches of her colon.

Afterward, Doris, who lived in Hill City, Kansas, not far from Hays, and Mildred, who lived in Springfield, Missouri, argued that Teresa needed to move to Hays. Who knew what her health would be like? And in Hays, she'd be closer to them.

Initially she rejected this idea. *How can I leave Denver? It's been "home" for thirty-one years, and home in a way Hays never had been, perhaps could not be.* She had no idea how she could explain this to her daughters. Doris and Mildred seemed to believe she should move, but how could her "girls" possibly know? They seemed like such children.

However, Teresa finally decided to placate them. Perhaps living in Hays would be different now. She knew who she was: daughter of Rosie Feit who'd come to the States during the flood of Jewish immigration in the early 1900s; cousin to Arthur Weinstein and his many relatives, rich, bright Jewish people; Jewish by birth and Catholic by happenstance; medical librarian at the finest Denver hospitals. She no longer had to hang her head.

So in the spring of 1985, at the age of seventy-nine, she moved to Hays.

In Hays Teresa wanted to rent an apartment close to the main part of town. There she could walk to the public library and go to Fort Hays State University for various gatherings. But Doris insisted on renting an apartment in Saint John's senior citizen complex, not far from the area Teresa once called The Jungles, leveled now and replaced with modest homes.

Teresa didn't want to live in Saint John's. "It's so far away from everything."

"Look, Mother, at this button. If you press it, a nurse will come running. You don't have one of these in an apartment."

So, full of misgivings, Teresa moved into Saint John's with Sunshine. How lucky she owned a dog! Saint John's allowed dogs to stay only if they initially moved into the complex with their owners.

The first night, the phone rang about midnight.

Who can that be? The telephone company had installed her phone earlier that day, but not even her daughters knew her number.

She answered to hear a woman, "Get your damned dog out of my yard!"

But Sunshine sat right beside her. "It can't be my dog, he's right here."

The woman hung up, leaving Teresa rattled.

When she woke the next morning, on Good Friday, she decided to license Sunshine immediately, just to be on the safe side. She knew she must hurry, for Hays businesses close at noon on Good Friday. She called a taxi but when it arrived at city hall, nothing looked familiar. Clearly city hall had moved, but where? Neither the cab driver, a college student, nor Teresa knew, but together they found it. There she bought Sunshine's license.

Then she ran to the bank. While there, Mrs. Jeter, a woman that Teresa remembered as quite stuck up, greeted her and seemed interested in her return to Hays.

Then, in that la-de-dah way she had, Mrs. Jeter looked at Teresa's feet.

Surprised, Teresa glanced down to realize she'd run out of the house in her carpet slippers. Her face turned crimson. Later she wished she had told Mrs. Jeter which side of the bus to get off, but instead she said, "Oh my gosh! I wore my slippers by mistake." Mrs. Jeter's cool glance didn't change. *Oh, no! Is this what living here is going to be like?*

Living in Hays did prove difficult for Teresa. In Denver, people knew her as a medical librarian, but in Hays, few knew about her achievements.

One day when she visited the sick in nearby Saint John's Rest Home, she saw that Winola, a Schoenchen schoolmate, occupied a room. Winola had been hateful when they were children, but as an adult, she was civil, so Teresa walked into the sick room.

Winola looked quite ill. Friends and relatives, who were clustered around her bed, glanced up as Teresa entered; one said *"Geschickte"* or "sent for" and nodded toward Teresa.

A shock like ice water coursed through her veins. Could it be true that, after more than seventy years, these people still regarded her as the mail-order orphan? A choking sensation rose in her throat. She fled the room.

At her apartment, her stomach cramped. She wretched. The experience struck her so deeply that even remembering her rich, educated Chicago relatives didn't assuage her.

When Teresa visited the rest home another day, she met a Volga German man who had lived in Schoenchen. "I always remember how much fun I had throwing snowballs at you," he said.

This time Teresa's temper flared. "To think I let people like you hurt me. You were just a nobody. I don't know why I let you bother me so."

Shortly after she stalked away, she realized that reacting angrily damaged her less than fleeing in shame. Her stomach didn't churn. But she felt badly that she put the man down so quickly. She struggled to be fair. When she considered the suffering the Volga Germans had endured, pioneering twice, once in Russia and then again in Kansas, when she thought how hardy and stoic they were, why she couldn't help but admire them. However, she certainly was pleased to see that those heroic Volga Germans no longer gathered on Hays's street corners to jabber and jostle her when she tried to pass.

Teresa joined every organization that interested her: the Ivanhoe Club, Toastmasters International, Ellis County Historical Society, Friends of the Hays Public Library, the Senior Companion Program, and the auxiliaries at Saint Anthony's Hospital and Hadley Memorial. She became a life member of Saint John's Auxiliary of Hays, volunteered half days at Fort Hays State University's Forsyth Library, and brushed up on her German. She resumed her membership as a university alum, joined the American Association of Retired Persons (AARP) and the Western Kansas Association on Concerns of the Disabled. A charter member of Colorado Council of Medical Librarians, she kept up her membership there as well as her professional memberships in the Medical Library Association and in Special Libraries.

But no matter how many organizations she joined, she couldn't conquer a childhood emotion, more active since she moved to Hays. As she sat with others, maybe in a meeting, suddenly she experienced a deep certainty that these people didn't really want her.

I'm an outsider, she would think. *I have no right to be here.* And her body would melt with the shame of being nobody.

Rarely could she shake this feeling quickly. Sometimes she longed to return to Denver to live, or to relocate in New York, the city of her birth, for in the anonymity of the city, she felt as though she belonged.

⟿

One day Regina, Fred's daughter, came to see her. "Grandma's in a bad way. I don't think she'll live much longer. Why don't you go see her?"

See Grandma after all these years? Teresa certainly had mixed feelings about that, but finally her curiosity won.

She found Grandma ill in the county home. Teresa tiptoed into Grandma's room with trepidation. The old woman lay in bed. Her skin, shrunken and tight, left her looking more craggy and fragile than Teresa remembered. Grandma stirred, smiled, and held out a hand. *This isn't the same woman who terrorized me so.* Teresa walked to Grandma's side. *This is just her shadow. She's been broken. By life. Like so many.* She squeezed Grandma's hand and sat beside her.

The next day, when Teresa visited again, Grandma pressed the Bieker house key into Teresa's hand and asked her to find the property deed. "I think it's in the little trunk under the front window, but if it's not there, just look around." Grandma had managed to keep the Bieker house in Schoenchen, even though she had lived on welfare since she unexpectedly lost her farm.

Regina gave Teresa a ride to the Bieker house, then went next door to visit her mother. Teresa stood a moment looking at her old home and the nearby building that once contained the store. How small they seemed! She unlocked the door. When she entered the main room, she almost heard her screams and the sheriff knocking. She hurried to the trunk and threw open the lid.

Bolts of fabric, probably from the store, filled the trunk. Grandma must have saved them for dresses she never made. Beneath the bolts were bed linens, but nothing else. She reached to shut the lid when she spotted papers tucked along one side.

She pulled them out: the deed, and next to it, another document, her indenture paper.

She scanned the Foundling Hospital letterhead, the listing of the Biekers' duties; they were to house her, clothe her, feed her, school her, and treat her as their own child. *And look at this!* If they died before she turned eighteen, she was to inherit their estate as though she were their own child! *Imagine them agreeing to that.* She rubbed the indenture date: June 29, 1910, nearly two months after she'd arrived from New York.

She started to fold the paper, intending to put it back, and then read where the Biekers agreed to write the Foundling twice a year. But they hadn't done that. As soon as she could read and write, she wrote all their letters, and she never wrote to the Foundling for the Biekers. She smoothed the paper over her knee. Then she realized the Biekers' signatures were missing. They hadn't signed.

"I wonder," she spoke aloud. "Did they really indenture me? Or did they just keep me."

She folded the paper and put it in her purse alongside the deed. She intended to ask Grandma if she could keep the indenture paper, but when she returned to the county home, Grandma was sleeping so heavily Teresa dared not stir her. Within a few days, she was dead. Teresa had given the deed to Regina, but she kept the indenture paper.

One morning soon after Grandma's funeral, as Teresa walked her little dog, Sunshine, he leaped so vigorously to catch a squirrel that he yanked the leash from Teresa's hand. Free, he dashed into the path of a swift-moving automobile. Teresa screamed. The car braked. Its distraught owner carried Sunshine to the curb and laid him on the grass. Teresa tried to stop wailing long enough to thank the owner for his kindness, but she could not muster her speaking voice.

As the car drove away, Teresa ran to the nearby home of an animal-loving friend, Virginia. The two women took Sunshine to Teresa's veterinarian, Steve Mosier, who confirmed that the little dog was dead. Dr. Mosier, who knew Teresa, offered to cremate Sunshine at no charge. Grateful for his kindness, she could not bring herself to leave her little dog. She kept stroking his long beautiful Sheltie hair as she had stroked Fanny day after day by the river bank. Finally, Virginia placed a strong arm around Teresa's shoulders and turned her toward the car.

"You must get a new dog," Virginia said as they drove away.

"I can't. Saint John's only allows pets that you bring in with you when you move in."

"Nonsense. We'll find just the dog for you today, and they will be none the wiser."

With that, Virginia headed out of town. "I know the woman who owns a restaurant right off the Interstate. You know the one?"

"In Ellis?"

"Yes. And she told me her $400 pedigreed bitch, a bichon frise, had an 'unfortunate encounter with a dog of uncertain ancestry.'"

Teresa laughed.

"So she's giving away a parcel of pups. We'll take a look."

The only pup left was the runt, as ugly a dog as Teresa had ever seen. He was small and sturdy, as bichons frises are, but his thick wavy coat was gray and white instead of pure white. His ears did not droop properly and his tail didn't curl up, but when the pup licked her hand, Teresa melted.

"You two will be good for one another," Virginia said.

On the way home, Teresa held the pup, fondling his ears as though they were velvet. That night, she named her dog Timi because he was so timid. And Virginia was right: in the following days, not one Saint John official noticed that a new dog tugged at Teresa's leash.

"An Endangered Species"

I n 1988, Teresa received a mailing from a new national organization, the Orphan Train Heritage Society of America (OTHSA). Based in Arkansas, it published a newsletter, *Crossroads,* which contained stories of individual riders. Teresa joined and attended the First Annual OTHSA Reunion that October.

The stories she heard as rider after rider stepped to the microphone riveted Teresa. Big-jowled Fred Swedenburg said his first caretakers didn't let him sleep inside the house, but his second caretakers, Hazel and Arthur Swedenburg of Clarks, Nebraska, treated him well. Mrs. Swedenburg even wrote the Children's Aid Society, asking for information about him. She learned that the society had taken him from his home because of "scandalous neglect."

"You wonder what scandalous neglect would have been in those days," Fred said. "It don't take much for that today."

Teresa (seated third from right) with other orphan train riders at OTHSA's first national reunion in Springdale, Arkansas, 1988.
(Courtesy of OTHSA)

When Fred returned from serving overseas during World War II, he found two letters, one from his birth father, Frederick Engert, a farm hand, and one from his birth mother, Irene Brown. Fred threw both away, thinking "the Swedenburgs are my real family." But the next year he traveled to New York and spent Christmas with his father. Then he went to Canadiagua, New York, where his mother lived.

"I drove past her home, but I didn't stop," he said. "I just couldn't make myself do it."

Teresa understood Fred's hesitancy. What would it have been like to see Rosie, not the mother of her dreams but the actual flesh-and-blood Rosie?

When Mary Ellen Johnson, OTHSA Founder, introduced Toni Weiler, she mentioned that Toni often spoke to organized groups about the orphan trains.

"That's right," Toni said as she took the mike. "And my speeches aren't complimentary. For one thing, I'm convinced that the indenture system was just another form of slavery." She detailed her argument at length, and Teresa almost believed her, but not quite. *I was indentured, but I wasn't a slave.*

Teresa felt proud, and extremely surprised, of the number of orphan train riders who made something of themselves. Particularly successful were Andrew H. Burke, a governor of North Dakota from 1890 to 1892, and John Green Brady, appointed governor of Alaska Territory for three terms, from 1897 to 1905. Other orphans became members of Congress, district attorneys, sheriffs, mayors, a justice of the Supreme Court, judges, college professors, clergymen, and high school principals, members of state legislatures, railroad officials, journalists, bankers, physicians, lawyers, postmasters, contractors, teachers, and civil engineers. And a medical librarian! With pleasure, Teresa counted herself among those who succeeded despite inauspicious beginnings.

At home weeks later, Teresa opened up her new issue of *Crossroads* to read that she was a "short perky little lady with a smile and a kind word for everyone." That pleased her. "Short and perky" made her sound like Rosie.

Mary Ellen Johnson, editor of *Crossroads*, reminded readers to tune into the TV show *Unsolved Mysteries* January 25, 1989, to hear another rider story. The night of the broadcast, Teresa watched orphan train rider Sylvia Wemhoff tell her story. At first, it seemed ordinary. Sylvia was three years old when she rode from the Foundling to Nebraska in 1921. The John Miick family, farmers with two sons, took Sylvia. In 1943, she married a farmer, George Wemhoff; they had four sons and one daughter.

Then *Unsolved Mysteries* took an unexpected turn. When Sylvia's daughter, Laura, helped her mother find her birth certificate in 1988, Sylvia discovered that she had a sibling. Who was this person? That was the unsolved mystery.

Studio portrait of Teresa in her early eighties.
(Courtesy of Teresa Martin)

Teresa turned off the set. She envied Sylvia. Even though Sylvia didn't know who her sibling was, she knew she had one. That was more than Teresa knew.

Sylvia hoped to hear from that sister or brother after the TV broadcast, but she didn't. However, when the TV rebroadcast *Unsolved Mysteries* in August, her brother, Joseph Wolk, contacted the show. Five days later, the show united Sylvia, then seventy, and Joseph, seventy-two, in New York City. Teresa watched as the siblings pieced together their history.

The television broadcasters made a spectacle of filming the reunion, and disgusted, Teresa shut off the TV. *Such a hullabaloo. Why their story is no more interesting than mine!*

◆

In October 1989 at OTHSA's second reunion, Teresa met Phil Coltoff, head of the Children's Aid Society, and his wife. They were mutually pleased to discover they all were Jewish, so Teresa told Phil about Arthur and later told Arthur about Phil.

That December, Arthur stopped in New York to look up Phil. The two men visited the New York Hospital–Cornell Medical Center (once the Lying-In Hospital where Rosie gave birth to Teresa) to see if they could find any additional information about Teresa or Rosie.

With the help of Dan Cherubin, assistant archivist, they discovered Rosie had given birth to Teresa at 11:26 in the morning on May 25, 1906, after thirteen hours of labor with no complications, although she required three stitches. Discharge papers on June 3 described both mother and child as "well."

Arthur and Phil also found out that Rosie had been in the hospital for thirty days before giving birth to Teresa. Just as Teresa had suspected, Rosie was no pioneer. She was ill—with a lung infection.

Teresa refrained from telling Arthur, "I told you so."

◆

In 1990, OTHSA and the Children's Aid Society co-hosted a national reunion in New York City, a homecoming, really, for orphan train riders. What would it be like, Teresa wondered, to have the city of her birth, which had so cheerfully rid itself of her and tens of thousands of other children, welcome her back home? Naturally, she planned to attend; nothing could keep her away.

When Teresa arrived on November 19, she found the Penta Hotel lobby jammed with orphan train riders. More than one hundred riders or descendants, ranging four to eighty-four years old, lined up to register. Mary Ellen and Leroy Johnson of OTHSA, who greeted the riders, counted Teresa among the eighty-four-year-olds.

That evening, journalists crowded a festive reception. Television lights, cameras, crews, and reporters from Channels 4, 7, 9, 11, and the Associated Press edged around the tables or conducted interviews with orphans in the foyer. Teresa could scarcely believe the fuss. In her lifetime, attitudes about orphans had changed so much that riders like her were now novelties rather than scum.

After dinner, following custom, the orphan train riders, including Teresa, rose to share memories. Robert Petersen told how his father left him, then four, and his brother, Archie, thirteen, in a New York City park. Eventually, a Children's Aid Society agent placed him in Nebraska on a farm with a "big red barn just like pictures I'd seen," he said. There Jens and Pearl Petersen adopted him and educated him well; he became a lawyer.

"The day I was abandoned on New York City streets turned out to be one of the luckiest days of my life," Robert said.

On another lucky day, Robert, then twenty-one, sat in a barbershop, leafing through a 1939 *Look* where he read about a carnival man, Archie Gayer, who froze a woman in a cake of ice for the New York World's Fair. Since Archie Gayer was his brother's name, Robert wrote this man and found his brother.

Next Art Smith, a big fellow from Trenton, New Jersey, told his renowned story: he had been left in a basket at Gimbels department store. He was a healthy baby wearing good-quality clothes; the New York City Department of Welfare named him "Arthur Field." Art hadn't known his mother left him in a basket until a Children's Aid Society agent told him. Crushed, he refused to discuss it.

"I don't feel bad about my mother," Art said. "I assume she was in circumstances beyond her control."

But the mystery of his parents' identities haunted Art. He felt as though a "great door" had "shut and locked" when he realized he'd never know his original family.

Then a tiny red-headed lady, Marguerite Thompson, who sat next to Teresa at dinner, talked about mistreatment in her foster home. Teresa identified with her. They were nearly the same age, and Marguerite rode to Nebraska in 1911, a year after Teresa had gone to Kansas.

Marguerite lived in a beautiful ten-room house with the upper-class Larson family in Lincoln, Nebraska. The Larsons made her use the outdoor bathroom and sleep on the front-room couch. Marguerite had to scrub the three bedrooms the Larsons rented. They whipped her frequently, sometimes with a rawhide whip, and they never gave her enough to eat.

When fifteen, Marguerite joined a carnival, but her caretakers caught her and put her in a convent. The convent dentist told her that he had never seen a young person with such bad teeth.

"You certainly didn't get the right kind of food," he said, "or enough milk to drink."

That was true. After she turned five, the Larsons had given Marguerite no milk, even though they kept two cows and gave plenty to their sons.

When Teresa's turn came, her palms were sweaty at the prospect of facing such a large, important audience. She'd considered what to say, choosing to emphasize the positive in her story, so she described Volga German customs rather than detail her abusive home life.

Tens of thousands of children had ridden the orphan trains, but not many riders remained. Orphan Harold Williams called the still-living riders "an endangered species," which they were rapidly becoming.

After the banquet, the riders posed for a photo, then said their goodnights. Teresa's roommate, Toni Weiler, the woman who believed indenture was slavery, seemed happy to see her.

"My foster parents were lovely," she told Teresa as they got ready for bed, "but a little old—forty-two and forty-three—for raising a toddler." So she got into trouble. She tipped over the church collection plate. At her mother's party, she kept the little dish of peanuts instead of passing it. One night, in her prayers, she said, "God bless Mamma, and God bless Daddy's little honey bunch." She saw her father take off for the closet with a big smile on his face, but her mother scowled.

Years later, on Mother's Day, Leo, Toni's husband, helped their six-month-old son, Bobby, give a box of candy to Toni. She cried as she realized her mother lived somewhere in the world, but she couldn't even send her a card.

"There has never been a mother that was loved more than I loved my birth mother," Toni said.

Like Toni, Teresa loved her mother unreservedly.

"How do you know she was so nice?" Doris once said. "Maybe she met someone and thought, 'To hell with this little bastard, I'm going to give her away and marry this man.'"

But Teresa didn't believe that for an instant.

◦◦

The next day, the orphan train riders toured Franklin D. Roosevelt's Hyde Park home. They rode back to Grand Central Station on a train reserved for them. Journalists interviewed some riders who described how they felt riding away from New York so many years ago. Some wept as they described their youthful apprehension and wonder at sights beyond New York City streets. Teresa sat quietly, but riding on the train with the other orphans made her unaccountably sad.

As the train pulled into Grand Central Station, Teresa saw a crowd of journalists waiting for them. Teresa's hands flew to her hair as lights flashed, shutters clicked. A journalist interviewed her and several other riders, making VHS tapes for OTHSA to house in its library. Then Children's Aid Society representatives welcomed the riders with a proclamation from Governor Mario Cuomo declaring November 19–24 "Orphan Train Homecoming Week" in New York.

Next, orphan train riders chose among several possible trips. Some went to a special Mass at Saint Patrick's Cathedral, but Teresa chose not to go; she had gone there during her 1970 visit, and now she wanted to see the Children's Aid Society Community Center. After all, the orphan train movement really started there. When she arrived, the Center's huge size, including hundreds of files on orphans it had placed, startled her. She hadn't realized the organization's scope.

Next, Teresa went to Ellis Island to view the museum's list of people who had immigrated to the United States from the 1860s to the early 1950s. She wanted to find her mother's name. What a mass of names were listed! But no wonder. She knew that by 1910 when she rode the orphan train, three out of four people in New York City were immigrants or children of immigrants.

Teresa searched first for Volga German names on the long metal Wall of Honor, but found none. Then she looked for any of the Feits or Breitowichs as well as for her husband Jess's people—Binders who came from Düsseldorf, Germany. Teresa found only one name she recognized, Sid Feit, Arthur's cousin. She ran her finger over Sid's name. *All my other relatives must have arrived at other ports.* The metal cooled her fingertip. *"My relatives." I still don't believe it.*

She found no Rosie Breitowich Feit, but as she toured the exhibits, she imagined another Rosie, no longer tall and stately but short, perky, and dressed in typical immigrant clothes, including an unfashionable shawl. Imagine the indignity, Teresa thought, of being bathed and deloused before she could board the ship. The stink of the dining room. The crying of children. The thrill of arriving.

But what a gauntlet to run: inspectors, interpreters, doctors, nurses, waiters, con men with pamphlets about the marvelous prairies. *Rosie never knew I ended up there.* A little jolt shot through Teresa. "Ever in prison?" "Can you read?" Maybe here is where she chose the name Rosie.

How courageous Rosie had been, coming from a log house in a tiny hamlet, crossing the ocean to enter a new world, perhaps alone. Teresa left Ellis Island with a renewed pride in her mother.

Thursday, November 22, dawned bright and sunny, perfect weather for Macy's Thanksgiving Day Parade. In the hotel lobby orphans gathered to walk together to their viewing spot. Teresa looked for her roommate, Toni, but she didn't see her.

"Forget her and come with us," Mary Ellen said.

Finally Teresa did.

Police guarded the orphans as they pushed their way through crowds lined up to watch the parade. Even though Teresa knew Mary Ellen's husband, Leroy Johnson, was a sheriff in Springdale, Arkansas, she was startled to see him on the street, helping the New York City police.

All ten blocks to the viewing site, Teresa looked for Toni to no avail.

Finally, apologetic Children's Aid Society officials escorted the orphans into a junky, vacant building across the street from Macy's. "It was the best place we could find on such short notice." Teresa and the other orphans rode an elevator to an almost empty room, but its windows did face the parade route. Watching with them were about fifteen mentally retarded children. Teresa regarded them. *We're shut in with the outcasts. Typical.*

For two hours, they watched tiny floats, bands, and balloons glide along the avenue. Not everyone had a seat, and those who did found them uncomfortable. The children, restless and bored, behaved badly, and many riders complained, but Teresa didn't mind. She enjoyed the colorful spectacle unwinding below her, and their situation amused her.

Before they had come to New York, OTHSA told the orphans to plan to march in the parade, so they notified their friends and relations. Now hundreds of people from coast to coast, including Doris and Mildred, waited patiently before their TV sets, certain they'd see the riders walking in the parade.

Afterward, Teresa walked back to the hotel through the enormous crowd of spectators. She never did find Toni.

That night, riders gathered for Thanksgiving dinner in the hotel's rooftop ballroom. Two Children's Aid Society singing groups entertained them. Then Senator Patrick Moynihan compared the plights of children at the turn of century and today.

After dinner, to her delight, Teresa spoke to the senator, which excited her so she couldn't remember, later, what they said.

Shortly after, Teresa spotted her roommate. "Toni," she cried. "Where were you?"

"Oh, I had more interesting things to do." Toni winked. "I was flirting around with some policeman."

In their room that night as they lay talking, Toni said, "My foster mother and me, we were exact opposites. I was open and very—well, I don't know exactly what you would call it. I said pretty much what I thought. But she was the type that, you know, talks about the neighbors but doesn't let anybody know she's doing it."

"I know what you mean," Teresa said. "Grandma and I were opposites, too. Grandma seldom spoke, but I just couldn't be still. How my constant chattering grated her nerves!"

"Like mine?"

Teresa laughed. "I could listen to you all night."

But she didn't. Both women drifted to sleep.

After the reunion ended the next morning, Teresa packed reluctantly, knowing she'd miss her spunky roommate even though Toni could be blunt. "You're so concerned about other people," she had snapped yesterday, but this morning, she helped Teresa get ready to catch her flight.

"You're so helpless!" Toni headed out the door with her own suitcase. "You'll never make it to the airport in time!"

A few minutes later, Teresa called a cab only to discover that Toni had called one for her. She laughed. *I guess I'm not the only one concerned about other people!*

HOME AGAIN

B ack in Hays, Teresa's life settled into a pleasant routine. On Sundays she went to Mass where she wore her Star of David with its diamond chips as well as her Catholic cross. On Mondays and Fridays, she reported to her volunteer morning job as medical librarian. There she groaned at the inferiority of the Hays collection compared to the Denver medical libraries where she'd worked. Still, being able to use her specialized skills pleased her.

She read every day, and at night, she read herself to sleep, a habit she acquired after Frenchy's death. At least once a week she called shut-ins for St. John's Auxiliary, and once a month she made about forty telephone calls to remind Ivanhoe Club and LineWrights members of their upcoming meetings. She exchanged visits with her blood relatives, although not Arthur and Bernice. They were both dead, but she enjoyed her own offspring: two daughters, fourteen grandchildren, and more great-grandchildren than she could remember.

Teresa wearing her Star of David.
(Courtesy of Teresa Martin)

Despite her many activities, Teresa managed to find time to date. Not that she wanted to marry again, but flirting was fun. And finding boyfriends seemed easy, although Teresa wondered what they saw in her, so old and so wrinkled. She met Joe Luecke, a great big upbeat fellow, at Toastmasters. They found they could discuss anything with each other. Teresa loved the way he treated her as an intellectual equal.

After Luecke died, her next-door neighbor, Scotty Riedel, courted her.

"Oh, Mother," Doris said when she heard. "Not again!"

Teresa ignored her. She enjoyed having a man fuss over her, and she saw no reason to stop. Scotty couldn't replace Joe, but he kindled her sympathy, as Frenchy had. Scotty was a good cook and fed her well; in return, she listened to his interminable stories. And he loved animals. He scratched Timi's ears and laughed when the little dog danced on his hind legs.

Attending the New York orphan train reunion had changed Teresa. For days, people had treated her as a special person precisely because she rode the orphan train. New York journalists had interviewed her, a United States senator had shaken her hand, hundreds had listened to her story, and not one person had treated her like scum. Those days were over. Being an orphan train rider, once so shameful, no longer was.

At home, *Crosswords,* the OTHSA newsletter, arrived regularly, each issue crammed with stories of riders like her. How many orphan train stories had she heard or read? Hundreds, maybe. Dozens, certainly. The more stories Teresa encountered, the more familiar they sounded, the more they blended, even when their details didn't quite match hers. She listened to stories of parents who were happy to be rid of their children, of parents who couldn't wait to get them back but were too late, to stories, like hers, of parental desertion. Of children watching a parent die or going to the morgue to identify a parent. Gilbert Eadie's story of riding excitedly to his mother's burial in a carriage drawn by two black horses. Watching his father drop lumps of clay on his mother's coffin. Then Gilbert dropping clay. The drunkenness of parents, having to beg for them.

Apartments with crumbling plaster, leaking roofs. Claretta Brown, screaming as rats ran over her bed and through her hair. Living in a tent. Sleeping on the streets. Living in orphanages, the bland food, the overcrowding, and the rows of white iron beds. The punishments meted out: locked in a pantry, dunked in cold water, slapped on the soles of the feet.

The unexpected new clothes for the train. Riding the train. Teresa's memory of 1910 sometimes got mixed up with her recent New York train ride, and she couldn't remember which ride left her with such a chill. The ride itself: older orphans taking care of younger ones; Bertha Schukman, two years old, bottle-feeding babies "in exchange for half an orange." The weeping. And other orphans, so eager. Margaret Webber unable to sleep the night before. Lena Weast feeling so free, "like a bird out of a cage." Dreams of fame and ease of country life. The "gawking" at deep canyons and mountains. Sleeping in their seats.

Being stared at by the crowd of people. Being lined up, like walking the plank. The pinches, pokes and prods. Being refused by the chosen caretaker. Being taken by the scary-looking one. Being left over, having to be placed by the agent. Brothers and sisters torn apart. Leo Rodgers, running after his brother, hanging on the spare tire, trying to stop the car. Running down the track after the train, hoping to get away.

Going to loving homes, to indifferent homes, to abusive homes. The changing of names.

Not letting children write home. The change of environment: no street lights, no traffic, no noise. The strange animals: cows, pigs, chickens.

The loneliness, the incredible loneliness.

Unable to speak. Having to learn a new language.

Being indentured. Children becoming chore boys or kitchen drudges. Washing clothes, fixing meals, feeding animals, gathering eggs, chopping kindling, picking up corncobs, taking out the ashes, cleaning bathrooms, milking cows. Standing on a box to learn how to wash dishes.

Being adopted. Becoming the child the foster parents couldn't have, the child precious to the new parents.

Being treated differently from other children. "Stop calling us Mom and Dad." Silence. Not being part of the family.

Gobbling food, afraid long fingers would snatch it, afraid each meal would be the last.

Being slapped. Being beaten with a stick, with a rawhide whip. Being stripped naked and whipped with a broom handle with nine straps nailed on it. Being locked in a cellar.

Being rescued by a neighbor. Running away.

Being shunned, being treated like scum. Having "bad blood." Not fitting in. Being called names: bastard, mooncalf, mail-order kid.

Dealing with the visiting agent. Afraid and lying. Afraid of being taken back East. Being returned to the orphanage.

Living every day, as orphan Billy Landkamer said, "On the very edge of humanity."

Experiencing all these orphan train stories helped Teresa understand that she, like a displaced person after a war, had been caught in a tide so deep and swift that nothing she could have done would have changed the course of her life. She remembered Toni's question, "If you had it to do over again and you could change things, wouldn't you?" Of course, she would, but who lives her life over again? As impossible as being born twice. This was just as well. She certainly wouldn't want to repeat the life she'd led, but still, when she looked back at it, she saw that, despite its pain, it wasn't such a bad life for an infant given away by its mother.

Newspaper reporters called Teresa, asking to print her story. *Isn't it strange,* she thought as she answered their questions, *that instead of trying to hide my background, I'm revealing it.*

As stories about her life appeared, usually with her photograph, she became a local celebrity. Organizations seeking a speaker contacted her. She decided to speak whenever she could. Thanks to Toastmasters, she developed a certain way to tell her childhood story—full of detail, but not too grim.

As she grew more courageous about describing some of the grim aspects of her home life in Schoenchen, she was careful to end her talk something like this: "For years I was resentful, perhaps even bitter, about my foster parents, but as I matured, my anger seemed to go away. Now when I think of them I ask myself, 'What else could they have done?' Bappa probably agreed to take me because of his pride, and then regretted it. Grandma probably never did want me. Then, in all fairness, I have to say that I treated my foster parents with little consideration. I never wanted to be part of that Volga German culture, and I'm sure, in my youthful way, I made that clear. The Biekers didn't want me, and I didn't want them. Our situation was doomed from the beginning."

Teresa at home in her St. John's apartment.
(Courtesy of Teresa Martin)

Teresa, now ninety-three, slowed down. She no longer attempted to polish her German, she stopped her part-time volunteer work at the university library—and perhaps more telling—she no longer returned to Denver to visit every few months as she used to.

Some days she would wake up and long to stay in bed. "Maybe," she'd think, "I should stop working." But then she'd remember that working kept her mind active, so she'd pull herself out of bed and go to work—whether she wanted to or not.

Teresa continued as Hays Medical Center librarian and also made dozens of telephone calls for various organizations. After Timi's sudden death, she hated going alone to visit in the St. John's Rest Home building. She knew how much the residents had enjoyed Timi, so Teresa regularly borrowed a dog from the Hays Humane Society to accompany her when she visited. She also talked to journalists or student historians about her life as an orphan, and she accepted occasional speaking engagements. But she was clearly slowing down.

In October 1999, when OTHSA awarded the Sister Irene Award to Teresa for "her endeavors in preserving the history of the orphan train riders," she didn't feel well enough to go to Arkansas and receive it. But she was proud of the tribute. No other Kansan had received this honor. Teresa was praised for speaking so often about her orphan train story, not only at reunions and to other groups but also to journalists and students. Francis Schippers, son of orphan train rider Frank Rafferty Schippers, received the award in Teresa's name and brought it to her.

~

Soon Doris tried to talk Teresa into moving to Hill City into a nice assisted living community. "You know you haven't been feeling well," Doris said, "and your weight's under a hundred pounds, and the nurse at Saint John's is concerned that you're not handling your medications well."

Teresa felt her temper flare. "What's wrong with the way I'm taking my medicine?"

"Never mind that. Just think how much easier it would be for you to live near me so I could see more of you. We could go shopping for clothes together."

Teresa laughed. Doris knew her weakness. "Well, how much does this place cost?"

When Doris told her, Teresa was appalled. "It'll take every bit of my social security. I can't have that. Why, if I needed to buy stamps, I'd have to break into one of my CDs. You know I don't want to touch those." Teresa had purchased the CDs in Denver with the profit from the sale of her house, CDs that were to go to Mildred and Doris when she died.

By the time Doris came to Hays the following week to take Teresa to the doctor, she had discovered another solution, apartments for the elderly run by the Hill City Housing Authority. They were cheaper, but Teresa would have to do more for herself.

"That sounds better," Teresa said.

Late Friday afternoon Teresa finally saw her doctor. "I can't seem to eat or drink a thing," she told him.

"That colon cancer you had about a year ago must be acting up again," he said. "Didn't you have surgery then?"

Teresa nodded. The cold round metal of his stethoscope lay heavy on her chest. He kept poking here and there and listening. She wished he'd get it over with.

Finally he stood and placed the stethoscope around his neck. "Sounds like you've already got a stent in your heart. Here. I'll give you a few of these nitroglycerin pills, enough to keep you over the weekend. Then come see me on Monday."

When Teresa reported what the doctor said, Doris fumed. "He just doesn't want to be bothered during his weekend. Go get your pills and clothes, Mother. You're coming to Hill City to stay with me."

Once in Hill City, Doris drove Teresa to the emergency room of the Hill City hospital. There a doctor diagnosed her with colon cancer, but he refused to operate on her. "She's too old," he said. "She'll never survive the surgery."

"I don't believe you," Doris said.

Monday morning Teresa and Doris were back in Hays at her regular doctor's office.

"Forget about the surgery," Teresa said. "I don't want to be a burden."

But Doris and the doctor insisted. "We want you alive," Doris said.

~

When Teresa woke up after the surgery, both daughters sat in her room. She smiled and drifted off again. When she came to, she heard her girls arguing.

"She's going to be fine," Doris said. "She's survived the surgery and the tumor is out. She'll be okay."

"I know you want her to live, but she won't," Mildred, a trained nurse, said. "She can't. Look at her urine bag. There's nothing in it. They can't get her body functions going again."

As her death became imminent, Teresa and her daughters discussed the disposal of her body. She wanted cremation, but neither Mildred nor Doris would consider it.

"Well, then, bury me in Colby," Teresa said, "alongside Frenchy. He bought a space for me. My name is already carved on his gravestone."

"But Colby's so far away, Mama. Why don't you let us bury you here in Hays, beside Daddy?" Mildred looked as though she would cry.

"All right, then, all right. Bury me beside Jess. Why not. We started out together, we might as well end up together."

On Sunday, June 17, 2001, three days after her surgery, Teresa died. Many friends and forty-six of her forty-seven descendants attended her funeral, including Christopher Rosell Junior, who had made her a great-great grandmother when he was born March 17, 2000.

Her obituary headline in *The Hays Daily News* read "Last Orphan Train Rider [in Ellis County] dies at age 95."

How ironic that Teresa was remembered with the taunt that so curdled her life—the *geschickte,* the sent-for one, the mail-order kid. She arrived in Hays, Kansas, an orphan train rider, and now she exited there, still an orphan train rider to many. Despite years of hiding her origins, Teresa at the end of her life wore her orphan label as visibly as Hawthorne's Hester wore her scarlet A. However, she never hid her origins from herself. She always knew she was, as she put it, "the lowest of the low." That is why she had fought so hard to excel, so she would not be just a "nobody."

Judy Sherard, the *Daily News* reporter, must have phoned all over town to gather so many quotes from people who had known Teresa. Like the blind men and the elephant, each person stumbled on a different aspect of her. One admired her for being "always so pleasant and enjoyable." Another appreciated her pride in her Jewish heritage. One saw her as a "tiny, unassuming woman" who "epitomized kindness, independence and optimism." Another fell in love with her because "she was such a bright, interested little person."

Time transformed that curly haired temper-filled child who rode to Kansas. Circumstance forced the first change. Her marriage to Jess made her rein in her temper, but she bloomed after she went to work for Mrs. Fields in the Hays Public Library. There Teresa realized that, like Mrs. Fields and Sister Rosina, she possessed the power to help others blossom—and she did.

But Teresa didn't quite understand the love that flowed back to her. She could not lose sight of her position—her "lowly" position, she would say—as an orphan in the world. Her diminished self-esteem made her quick to credit everyone but herself.

Finding her relatives and discovering that they were not horse thieves but well-to-do educated Jews helped a lot. So did all those orphan train reunions she attended, especially the New York one, full of another kind of family, a family of folks who knew what it meant to work hard, to face mockery. Her shame slowly turned into a stubborn pride as she spoke publicly about her childhood.

Occasionally Teresa still heard an orphan train rider say, "For goodness sake, don't let anyone know that you rode on an orphan train. Don't let anyone know you're from an orphanage." She once believed that, too; that's how she spent most of her time in Denver, hiding. However, after finding Arthur and OTHSA, and after making dozens of speeches, her ideas changed. She felt secure enough to buy a cream-colored OTHSA jacket with "Orphan Train Rider" printed in large scarlet letters across the back. She wore it proudly.

She had reason to wear it proudly. In her life, she had been part of an enormous relocation of children, the displacement of a half million youngsters. Like every one of them, when Teresa stepped on that orphan train she left behind not only her birth family but also the metropolitan culture into which she had been born. She, like every other orphan train rider, had to deal with displacement whether she liked it or not.

Teresa was one of the rare riders who lived into the twenty-first century. As of 2010, fewer than one hundred orphan train riders still lived. Soon all their tongues will be stilled, but Teresa's story remains to speak for them. It represents those half-million riders who, no doubt, fought equally fascinating battles of their own. It flashes like a beacon for the tens of millions of orphan train descendants who wonder just how it was for their own ancestor.

In addition, Teresa's life holds a message for all of us. Like other similar testimonies, such as Anne Frank's diary, her life is a tribute to the resilience and power of the human spirit.

ACKNOWLEDGMENTS

I want to express my gratitude to the many people and organizations that helped me research and write this book. Any mistakes in *Mail-Order Kid,* though, are solely my responsibility.

My thanks to:

Readers of my manuscript, including Carla Barber, Doris Crippen, Margaret Dent, Kira Gale, Paul Gatschet, Kay Golden, Gus Hallin, Sandy Hill, Jack Loscutoff, Michael Meade, Ann Moncayo, Mildred Rosell, Steve Trout, Grace Witt, and Kate Yarrow.

Members of LineWrights, a writing group in Hays, Kansas, and the Omaha NightWriters Fiction Collective for their support.

Don Coldsmith and Greg Tobin, The Tallgrass Writing Workshop, Emporia, Kansas.

The Orphan Train Heritage Society of America, particularly Mary Ellen Johnson, Founder.

Research helpers at the National Orphan Train Complex in Concordia, Kansas; at the Nebraska Historical Society in Lincoln; at the Ellis County Historical Society, Hays Public Library and Fort Hays State University's Forsyth Library, all in Hays; and Lorena Smith, Phelps County Historical Society, Holdrege, Nebraska.

Others who assisted my research, including Dwight Ganzel, Robert Hodge, Eloise Thomsen, Jane Tinkler, and Arthur Weinstein.

The Phelps County Historical Society, Holdrege, Nebraska, for its early sponsorship of my orphan train presentations.

The Nebraska Humanities Council and particularly Mollie Fisher for supporting my orphan train programs.

The New York Foundling and the Children's Aid Society, New York.

Barbara Franzen, South Central Counseling, Hastings, Nebraska.

Leona Pfeifer, German professor, Fort Hays State University, for her help with language.

Sandra Wendel, editor and owner of Write On, Inc.

Lisa Pelto, Ellie Pelto, Erin Pankowski and Gary James Withrow at Concierge Marketing, Inc.

And to the 352 orphan train riders whose stories I read.

(Courtesy of David Loyd)

ABOUT THE AUTHOR

G reat Plains writer Marilyn June Coffey has written three books, 600 poems, and dozens of articles and stories. A trained journalist (B.A., University of Nebraska, 1959) and creative writer (M.F.A., Brooklyn College, 1981), she has produced work that includes a popular memoir, a record-setting novel, and a prize-winning poem.

Her poem, "Pricksong," reviewed in the *Los Angeles Times Book Review* and *Newsweek,* won a national Pushcart Prize.

Coffey's novel *Marcella* made literary history. It was the first novel written in English to use female autoeroticism as a main theme. Gloria Steinem called it "an important part of the truth telling by and for women." Quartet in London published it in paperback; *Pol* in Australia and *Ms.* excerpted it, and Danish newspapers serialized it.

In 1989, Coffey's memoir, *Great Plains Patchwork,* appeared. *The New York Times* called it entertaining and insightful. *Atlantic Monthly* featured a chapter as its cover story. *Natural*

History bought two chapters, *American Heritage* one. Harper & Row, McGraw-Hill, Macmillan, and Harcourt Brace Jovanovich printed excerpts.

Known as a prose stylist, Coffey received a Master Alumnus award for distinction in the field of writing from the University of Nebraska in 1977. Since 1987, the UNL Archives has collected forty boxes of Coffey's papers in its Mari Sandoz room.

In 1991, Coffey investigated the orphan train movement, developing three programs for the Nebraska Humanities Council. One became the second most popular of the 232 programs underwritten by NHC and spurred her to write *Mail-Order Kid*.

Now retired, Coffey taught writing at Boston University, Pratt Institute in Brooklyn, and Fort Hays State University in Kansas for thirty-four years, twice earning tenure. She became an interpretive reader/performer, appearing on local radio stations, statewide TV, and before more than 130 groups in twelve states, from Maine to Texas.

Coffey is an Admiral in the Great Navy of Nebraska, the state's highest honor. However, the honorary title is given tongue in cheek, since Admirals in landlocked Nebraska claim jurisdiction over little but tadpoles. Governor J. James Exon appointed Coffey, a Nebraska native, an Admiral in 1977 for her writing achievements.

Resources
and References

Find information
on orphan train riders

For tips on researching an orphan train rider, see Mary Ellen Johnson's *Waifs, Foundlings, and Half-Orphans,* published by Heritage Books and available for purchase at major booksellers.

As of June 5, 2010, the Children's Aid Society's archives (from 1853–1930) are stored at the New York Historical Society, 170 Central Park West, New York, NY 10024-5194. Phone: (212) 873-3400. Web site: https://www.nyhistory.org.

Following the lead of the Children's Aid Society, many other social services that were part of the orphan train movement are arranging to donate their orphan train documents, too. Soon the New York Historical Society will become one of the nation's largest repositories of information about the orphan trains.

The Orphan Train Heritage Society of America, Inc., since 1986 in Arkansas, has relocated to Kansas. It is now part of the

National Orphan Train Complex, P.O. Box 322, Concordia, KS 66901. Phone/Fax: (785) 243-4471. Web site: www. orphantraindepot.com.

The New York Foundling is located at 590 Avenue of the Americas, New York, NY 10011. Phone: (212) 633-9300. Web site: http://www.nyfoundling.org.

IMPORTANT SOURCES

Adams Co. [NE] Historical Society. "How the Little Orphans Lived." *Historical News,* 14, no. 1 (1981).

——. "The Little Orphans." *Historical News.* 13, no. 12 (1980).

——. "The Orphan Trains." *Historical News.* 13, no. 11 (1980).

Birkby, Evelyn. "The Children's Train." *Kitchen-Klatter Magazine* (April 1979) 11, 19.

Brace, Charles Loring. *The Dangerous Classes of New York,* 3rd edition. New York: Wynkoop & Hallenbeck, 1880.

Brophy, A. Blake. *Foundlings on the Frontier: Racial and Religious Conflict in Arizona Territory, 1904–1905.* Tucson: University of Arizona Press, 1972.

Endorf, Charlotte M. *Plains Bound: Fragile Cargo, Revealing Orphan Train Reality.* Denver: Outskirts Press, 2005.

Fry, Annette Riley. "The Children's Migration." *American Heritage,* 26, no. 1 (1974) 4–10, 79–81.

Hodge, Robert A. *Kansas Orphan Train Riders—These We Know.* Emporia, Kan.: Robert A. Hodge, 1996.

Holt, Marilyn Irvin. *The Orphan Trains: Placing Out in America.* Lincoln: University of Nebraska Press, 1992.

Jackson, Donald Dale. "It Took Trains to Put Street Kids on the Right Track Out of the Slums," *Smithsonian* (August 1986) 95–103.

Johnson, Mary Ellen, ed. *Crossroads*. Vol. 1–20. Orphan Train Heritage
    Society of America.

——, comp. *Orphan Train Riders: Their Own Stories*. Vol. 1–4. Baltimore:
    Gateway, 1993, 1994, 1995, 1997.

——, comp. *Orphan Train Riders: Their Own Stories*. Vol. 5. Wever, Ia.:
    Quixote, 1999.

——, comp. *Orphan Train Riders: Their Own Stories*. Vol. 6. Concordia,
    Kan.: Orphan Train Heritage Society of America, 2007.

Langsam, Miriam Z. *Children West: A History of the Placing-Out System
    of the New York Children's Aid Society, 1853–1890*. Madison: State
    Historical Society of Wisconsin, 1964.

Magnuson, James, and Dorothea G. Petrie. *Orphan Train*. New York: Dial
    Press, 1978.

Milner, Anita Cheek. "Orphan Trains." *The Genealogical Helper,* 35, no. 6
    (1981) 7–9.

O'Connor, Stephen. *Orphan Trains: The Story of Charles Loring Brace and
    the Children He Saved and Failed*. Boston: Houghton Mifflin, 2001.

Patrick, Michael, Evelyn Sheets, and Evelyn Trickel. *We Are a Part of
    History: The Story of the Orphan Trains*. Virginia Beach, Va.: Donning,
    1990.

Riley, Tom. *Orphan Train Riders: Entrance Records from the American
    Female Guardian Society's Home for the Friendless in New York,* Vol. 2.
    Westminster, Md.: Heritage Books, 2006.

Sherard, Judy. "Last Orphan Train Rider Dies at Age 95." *The Hays Daily
    News* (18 June 2001) A3.

Simpson, Eileen. *Orphans: Real and Imaginary*. New York: Weidenfeld and
    Nicolson, 1987.

Toepfer, Amy Brungardt, and Agnes Dreiling. *Conquering the Wind: An
    Epic Migration from the Rhine to the Volga to the Plains of Kansas*.
    Revised edition. Lincoln, Neb.: American Historical Society of
    Germans from Russia, 1982.

Vogt, Martha Nelson, and Christina Vogt. *Searching for Home: Three Families from the Orphan Trains.* N.p.: Dickinson Bros., 1979.

Walters, George J. *Wir Wollen Deutsche Bleiben: The Story of the Volga Germans.* Kansas City, Mo.: Halcyon, 1982.

Warren, Andrea. *We Rode the Orphan Trains.* Boston: Houghton Mifflin, 2001.

——. *Orphan Train Rider: One Boy's True Story.* Boston: Houghton Mifflin, 1996.

Weinstein, Arthur. *The Breitowichs on Division Street.* Skokie, Ill.: Arthur Weinstein, 1984.

——. *Our Exodus: The History of the Feit, Weinstein, Breitowich, and Fenig Families.* Chicago: Arthur Weinstein, 1978.

Wheeler, Leslie. "The Orphan Trains." *American History Illustrated* (December 1983) 10–23.

Young, Patricia J., and Frances E. Marks. *Tears on Paper: The History and Life Stories of the Orphan Train Riders.* N.p.: 1990.

Made in the USA
San Bernardino, CA
28 April 2014